Cashing In
With Content

Advance praise for *Cashing In With Content* ...

"Content is the life blood of the information economy. *Cashing In With Content* is full of ideas to get your heart pumping"
—Alex Hungate, Chief Marketing Officer, Reuters Group

"Every organization I encounter wants to know, 'How do we harness the magic of the internet?' The case studies and practical advice that suffuse this book can help them answer that question."
—Lee Rainie, Director, Pew Internet & American Life Project

"Content, community, context—debates rage about which is king in a web-driven world. David Scott blows those debates out of the water by demonstrating in real and relevant ways how to use all of them to make cash king. Chock-full of examples and to-do's—this one is a must-read for anyone running a website and an enterprise. Ca-ching!"
—Anthea C. Stratigos, Co-founder & CEO, Outsell, Inc.

"*Cashing In With Content* is an essential read for any marketer who wants to maximize their website's power to convert visitors and retain customers."
—Harry J. Gold, CEO, Overdrive Marketing Communications

"To those of you who may be thinking, 'another book about the web? I already know everything there is to know about the web,' snap out of it. The '90s are over, and so is the idea that the web is all about technology. As this book so astutely illustrates, content—not functionality or transactional capability—is at the value epicenter of the web. Before you embark upon yet another expensive web development project, read this book. You'll save yourself both time and money as a result."
—Mike Jensen, Chief Brand Officer, GMAC Insurance/Personal Lines

"If you want to find and keep customers online, you need to understand the ideas and emulate the examples in this book. David M. Scott makes it clear why content is the once and future king of the internet."
—Craig Danuloff, CEO, The Pre-Commerce Group

"I love the fact that every case study in this book is based on in-depth interviews with top executives at the websites profiled. This isn't theory or opinion—these are real-life marketing lessons."

—Anne Holland, Publisher, Marketing Sherpa

"In the Information Age, is it possible that the best web strategy is one that gives visitors—gasp!—something meaningful to read? Scott says it's not only possible, it's probable and, most importantly, profitable. *Cashing In With Content* is a must-read book that shows you why and how."

—Jonathan Kranz, author, *Writing Copy for Dummies*

"The most successful web marketers, regardless of industry, consistently use content to communicate their value proposition to customers in order to get the sale. In this practical book, David Scott provides research, illustrations, and examples that demonstrate the enormous power of content as a web marketing tool. *Cashing In With Content* is compelling in its coverage and its clarity—if you have a web presence, you need to read it."

—Steven Goldstein, CEO, Alacra, Inc.

"Uniquely and convincingly makes the case that content is the essence of successful digital marketing."

—Marty Bell, Founder/CEO, Prescients LLC

"*Cashing In With Content* is a highly insightful and useful view into the ever-widening galaxy of companies using content online to build profitable relationships. Rich in valuable case studies that can help any institution use today's best practices to get bottom-line results."

—John Blossom, President, Shore Communications, Inc.

"Not enough profit from your website? Read *Cashing In With Content* and grab your share of the growing e-commerce pie!"

—Peter Cohan, author, *Net Profit* and *Value Leadership*

Cashing In
With Content

HOW INNOVATIVE MARKETERS USE DIGITAL
INFORMATION TO TURN BROWSERS INTO BUYERS

David Meerman Scott

Information Today, Inc.
Medford, New Jersey

Cashing In With Content

Copyright © 2005 by David Meerman Scott

Library of Congress Cataloging-in-Publication Data

Scott, David Meerman.
    Cashing in with content : how innovative marketers use digital information to turn browsers in buyers / David Meerman Scott.
        p. cm.
    Includes index.
    ISBN: 0-910965-71-4
    1. Electronic commerce. 2. Electronic commerce--Management. 3. World Wide Web. 4. Internet.   I. Title
    HF5548.32.S295 2005
    658.8'72--dc22

                                                                2005012786

Printed and bound in the United States of America.

President and CEO: Thomas H. Hogan, Sr.
Editor-in-Chief and Publisher: John B. Bryans
Project Editor: Michelle Manafy
Managing Editor: Amy M. Holmes
VP Graphics and Production: M. Heide Dengler
Book Designer: Kara Mia Jalkowski
Copyeditor: Pat Hadley-Miller
Proofreader: Mary Ainsworth
Indexer: Sharon Hughes

Cover design by Doug Eymer

For Allison

young marketer extraordinaire

CONTENTS

Acknowledgments xvii

Foreword by Michelle Manafy xix

Introduction
Content: The Missing Ingredient 1

    Selecting Content-Smart Sites 2

    Asked and Answered—Marketing on the Web 4

    The Web Isn't TV 5

    Branding Is for Cattle 6

    The New Publishers 7

    Getting the Most Out of this Book 9

PART 1: E-Commerce

Chapter One
Crutchfield: A Friend in the Electronics Business 13

    Turning Complexity into Opportunity 15

    A Little Friendly Advice 15

    Car Stereo for Everyone 17

    Creating Content That Sells 19

    Customer Feedback 20

    Cashing In 21

Chapter Two
Alloy: Generation Y Marks the Spot 23

    Like, Keep It Fresh 24

    Quizzes, Guys, and Style 26

I Wanna Go to the Mall.com 27

Cool? Click. Buy. 28

Cashing In 29

Chapter Three
Design Within Reach: Form Follows Function 31

Going Against the Grain 33

Please Take a Seat 34

Newsletter of Note 35

Cashing In 37

Chapter Four
mediabistro.com: Pitching Content to the Media 39

Online Community for the Media 41

Media Community 43

Media Content to Sell Media Services 46

Cashing In 47

Chapter Five
Esurance: Content Replaces Agents 49

Great Content as a Marketing Tool 50

Driving Traffic to Auto Insurance Content 51

Content Drives Transactions 54

Ensuring Compelling Content 56

Cashing In 58

Chapter Six
Aerosmith: Content for Extreme Fans 59

Not the Same Old Song and Dance 60

Walk This Way 63

Roadies, Managers, and the Chef 65

A Band and its Fanatic Fans 66

Aerosmith, the Brand 67

Cashing In 67

Chapter Seven
The Wall Street Journal Online: Free Content Sells Subscriptions 69

Selling Subscriptions with Free Content 72

Not Your Father's Newspaper 75

Cashing In 77

PART 2: Business-to-Business
Chapter Eight
Alcoa: Content Drives Large Deals 81

It All Starts with Dirt 83

Bright, Shiny Content 84

The Good Guys 86

Crafting the Content 87

Cashing In 88

Chapter Nine
Weyerhaeuser: Managing Trees with Internet Content 89

Seeing the Forest for the Trees 90

Content with Priorities 92

Excellent Corporate Neighbors 93

Growing (Content) Like a Tree 95

Cashing In 95

Chapter Ten
ebuild: Everything for the Professional Builder, Including the Kitchen Sink 97

Building ebuild One Room at a Time 98

My Bucket Is Your Taxonomy 100

Tagging Content Makes It Useful 101

Cashing In 102

Chapter Eleven
ServiceWare: Level the Playing Field with Content . . . 105

Are You a Call Center or a Help Desk? 107

Hard Data and Useful Information 109

If You Have Great Content, Get It Out There 110

Cashing In 111

Chapter Twelve
Colliers: Commercial Real Estate for the World 113

Content from Warsaw to Sydney 117

Real Content from All Over 117

Cashing In 120

Chapter Thirteen
Booz Allen: Career Content 123

The Right Fit for You? 124

We Want You to Work Here 126

Please Complete Your Profile 127

Career Content Creation 129

Cashing In 130

Chapter Fourteen
UPS Investor Relations: Delivering Stock 131

Airplanes and Those Funny Brown Trucks 134

Environmentally Friendly 136

On-Time Delivery 138

Cashing In 138

PART 3: Nonprofit, Education, Healthcare, and Politics

Chapter Fifteen
CARE USA: Content Fights Global Poverty 141

Content to Drive Donations 143

Comprehensive Content in a Soundbite World 145

Get Involved with Content 146

Cashing In 149

Chapter Sixteen
Tourism Toronto: Hit the Site and Hit the Town 153

Individuals, Groups, and Conventions 155

Content to Book Trips 156

Recovering from SARS 157

Content Voyage 159

Interactivity and Small Bits of Content 160

Cashing In 160

Chapter Seventeen
Kenyon College: A Literary Tradition on the Web 163

The Right Way to Rebuild a Web Site 166

A Site That Speaks to All Constituents 166

Literary Content 167

Cashing In 169

Chapter Eighteen
Sharp HealthCare: Putting Patients in Control with Content 173

I Need to Know Fast 175

Viral Healthcare Content 176

Healthy Demographics 179

Creating Compelling Healthcare Content 180

Cashing In 181

Chapter Nineteen
Dermik Laboratories: More than
Skin-Deep Content 183

Aggregating the Best of Available Content 185

Maintain Integrity 188

Drive Interest in the Category 189

The Right Stuff 191

Cashing In 191

Chapter Twenty
Dean for America: Internet Presidential Politics—
The New Grassroots 193

Introducing the Presidential Blog 196

Making Readers Feel They Have a Stake 197

Meetup with Other Supporters 200

Internet Content: The New Grassroots 201

Cashing In 202

PART 4: Putting Content to Work

Chapter Twenty-One
Best Practices from Innovative Web Marketers 207

Marketing with Web Content 208

Best Practice #1: When launching a new site, start with
a comprehensive needs analysis 209

Best Practice #2: Speak with one voice to create a
consistent site personality 210

Best Practice #3: Dedicate editorial resources to create
consistent and informed content 213

Best Practice #4: Encourage browsing by using appropriate
self-select paths 215

Best Practice #5: A separate URL or blog facilitates
providing targeted content 217

Best Practice #6: Push content to users to pull them
back to your site 219

Best Practice #7: Don't forget images—original photos
are powerful content 221

Best Practice #8: Consider making proprietary content
freely available 223

Best Practice #9: If you serve a global market, use
global content 225

Best Practice #10: Include interactive content and
opportunities for user-feedback 227

Best Practice #11: Use content to trigger viral marketing 229

Best Practice #12: Link content directly to the sales cycle 231

Practices Make Perfect 233

Chapter Twenty-Two

Lessons Learned 235

You're a Publisher Now, So Think Like One 235

Make Content the Focus of Your Site 236

Focus on Your Customer's Problems 238

A Web Site Is More Art than Science 239

Content Drives Action 240

A Special Note to Executives 240

What Content Means to Marketers 241

About the Author 243

Index 245

ACKNOWLEDGMENTS

Few worthwhile projects are possible without the valuable advice, help, ideas, and support of colleagues, friends, and family. The many months of research and writing that culminated in this book would never have been possible without the terrific contributions of my virtual team.

I'm amazed at how passionately people speak about their favorite (and not so favorite) Web sites and I learned a great deal from those often heated discussions—thank you! Many more people offered help and suggestions on the project than can possibly be listed here. Some of the more valuable input came from Rafat Ali, Marty Bell, Nick Copley, David Curle, Michael Donovan, Doug Eymer, Michael Fix, Steve Goldstein, Ronald Gruner, John R. Harris, Dianna Huff, Russ Iuliano, Maryglenn McCombs, Emily Pilk, Larry Schwartz, Alan Scott, Eric Wholley, and Lisa Wright. Special thanks to the crew at Grub Street Writers, to Phil Fougere who came up with the wonderful title of the book, and to Bradley Smith for some great design ideas.

I'm grateful to John Bryans of Information Today, Inc. John has been an enthusiastic supporter from the start of the process and his valuable insights made the book much better than it otherwise would have been.

Michelle Manafy, my dedicated, funny, smart, and talented editor guided the project from the first (very) rough outline through to the final polished manuscript. Her strong convictions and solid understanding of both content and marketing as well as her wise editorial suggestions and unending cleanup of my writing tics made the book more than I had ever hoped. Thank you Michelle!

Thank you to my wife Yukari for patience and support. Yukari, who is also a writer (four books and hundreds of magazine articles all in the Japanese language), knows what it takes to bang out nearly a hundred thousand words under deadline and her encouragement made the process easier.

Finally, to the thousands of marketers who build sites that take full advantage of the opportunities the Web provides by leveraging the value of content: Keep up the good work!

David Meerman Scott
Boston, Massachusetts

When Words Collide

In journalism school, amid learning the basics of publishing and honing my reporting and writing skills, I came to think of marketing as "the dark side." It was largely unspoken yet tacitly understood that no real journalist would even consider crossing over—that would prove that he or she was driven by (shudder) financial incentives. However, what they didn't teach us in J-school (nor, as I've since learned, in B-school) is that marketing and journalism typically enjoy a precarious symbiosis. These fields demand similar skills and attributes of practitioners—the ability to communicate, to write effectively, to think creatively—yet are often at odds given the marketer's need to promote a single point of view and the journalist's goal of providing a balanced perspective.

The Web has altered the way we create, deliver, and consume information in a multitude of ways, and neither the journalist's nor the marketer's role has gone unscathed. More than ever, professionals working in these fields are pressed to produce in real time and to communicate directly with the public. For journalists, this has been seen as the natural (though sometimes ungainly) evolution of the medium, but the transformation of the marketer's role has been less clear, if equally misunderstood by the general public. In the past, press releases were filtered by editors before being reported as news to readers, but today's marketing professional is often directly responsible for what the world learns about any type of organization through its public face—its Web site.

In their early iterations, Web sites often fell into the domain of IT, with marketing departments offering varying degrees of content support, but these days the Web is recognized as the front lines of marketing. An individual's first impression of an organization may well come from a visit to its site, and marketers have taken a leading role in making that impression a good one.

Unfortunately, many of them forget the rule that "form follows function," focusing on creating pretty-faced sites rather than offering the kind of useful information that encourages consumers to linger, to return, and—most importantly—to do business with the organization.

You might say I have a serious relationship with content. The magazine I edit—*EContent*—focuses exclusively on strategies and solutions that help organizations create, manage, and deploy content in order to support larger business objectives. When David Scott first proposed writing a marketing column for the magazine a few years ago, I met the idea with suspicion: Should I, nay, *could I* bring a marketer into the fold? But as David told me then (and as his columns and articles for *EContent* have since illustrated), marketing is an area of the digital content arena that is often misunderstood and poorly executed, with serious implications for organizations. Through his work as a marketing executive for leading digital content companies such as Knight-Ridder and NewsEdge Corporation, David has learned how marketers help lead their organizations' digital content strategies; on a monthly basis in *EContent,* he eloquently communicates his knowledge of content and marketing. Now—thankfully—he has created *Cashing In With Content* to offer an even broader and deeper view.

The 20 organizations profiled in the book—which range from nonprofits, to corporations, to rock bands—are leaders in content-centric Web marketing. David persuaded them to share their experiences and strategies, and then adds his own analysis of how they use content in order to help marketers in virtually any industry understand how they can, too. He explains that the very best sites provide content that surprises the reader or exceeds their expectations, but doesn't stop there: He shows how content can (and does) bring visitors back to a site while serving to develop an enduring relationship.

Digital delivery poses new hurdles at every turn but, at the same time, it provides novel ways to enlighten and entertain, to reach people with more immediacy—even intimacy—than ever before. Content may not have been at the forefront of marketers' work in the past, but it is today and the trend will continue. Over the past 15 years, David Scott has both practiced and preached powerful tactics for marketing with content. In *Cashing In With Content*, he shares successful strategies and offers a wealth of insights and advice that will help you use content to achieve *your* marketing objectives.

Michelle Manafy
Editor, *EContent* Magazine & *Intranets*

Content: The Missing Ingredient

The Web has fueled a new era of information delivery and thousands of organizations have harnessed its power to cash in. There's no doubt: Online content has propelled many an upstart organization (such as Amazon and Dell) to fame and profitability and solidified the position of top-tier established brands (such as Microsoft and the *New York Times*). Marketers working at companies with innovative Web sites know that, first and foremost, site visitors want access to information, not just fancy graphics and advertising hype. The organizations these savvy marketers represent—educational institutions, non-profits, and companies of all kinds and sizes—are emerging as leaders because of an unrelenting focus on the Web as a place for *Cashing In With Content*.

It's simple really. But most organizations forget that the reason people use the Web is to gather, read, interact with, and use content. It might seem evident that certain organizations have content to sell—publishers being the most obvious example—but companies and organizations of all types have available information that can be leveraged in a variety of ways. By putting that content to work, a Web site visitor may actually come to view the organization behind the site as a trusted resource, rather than just a place to spend spare time or dollars. The innovative marketers interviewed for this book understand this and build sites that take full advantage of the opportunities the Web provides by leveraging the value of content.

You might ask: "Content? What's content and what's it got to do with me?" Specifically, content is whatever data, photographs, stories, specifications, or information people desire that a site provides. Content could be, for example, a book review, the latest specs on a set of snow tires, or 10 steps to a healthy heart. Perhaps content is a list of every song the Grateful Dead ever played at New York's Madison Square Garden or it could be the number of people in

California who speak Cambodian as a first language. A company might possess a great deal of information about a promising new technology. Some individuals could track a political candidate's issues platform and how she compares to the other candidates. Others might provide readers with lively and informative stories and photos about each of the sports teams, service organizations, and clubs offered by a favorite school. But no matter what form it takes, corporations, government agencies, educational institutions, nonprofits, and individuals all possess compelling content that could be valuable to someone right now. And, through effective content delivery, organizations can deliver a powerful marketing message at the same time.

Selecting Content-Smart Sites

In order to discover the Web sites profiled in the 20 illustrative case studies that appear in the book, I cast a wide net for candidates. The initial process included asking friends and colleagues to send me to their favorite sites. I looked at the sites of marketing and advertising agencies (the so-called "Web marketing experts") and hit featured client sites. In social situations—cocktail parties, at my daughter's school events, or on a plane—I'd turn the conversation to Web sites and quiz people about their favorites. Whenever I saw a new URL, I would click through and take a peek and, over the course of a year, I checked out about a thousand sites.

While researching, I came across many examples of marketers using Web content in interesting and compelling ways. I learned how content tells a story; I found out how content drives people to make decisions—by anticipating what visitors need and why. I also discovered how content turns browsers into buyers (or subscribers, contributors, employees, or students) and what gets site visitors to return again and again. If a site was particularly interesting and innovative, I reached out to its marketing team for possible inclusion in the book. I wanted to profile as many varied sites as I could, so my goal was to find fascinating examples from the worlds of e-commerce, business-to-business, nonprofit, education, healthcare, music, and politics. I also wanted to find examples of innovative smaller sites from less well-known organizations. Sure, sites from organizations like UPS and the *Wall Street Journal* are profiled, but so are tiny Kenyon College and ServiceWare. The common ground is that all of these organizations cash in with content. I talked to marketers at a wide variety of organizations that use content to create profitable action on their Web sites. It was important for me to profile sites from older established companies with extensive offline businesses as well as much newer companies formed exclusively to exploit the Internet. Profiles range from 100-year-old *Fortune* 500 companies, such as Weyerhaeuser, to e-commerce start-ups, like Esurance. While I profile traditional e-commerce sites, I also look at the sites' of organizations that cash in through other methods: Booz Allen uses its site to attract and retain the best employees at a lower cost than traditional methods, while Dermik Laboratories uses its Skin Health Solutions site exclusively to build awareness—cashing in occurs offline.

The content found on the sites profiled here varies tremendously: photos of Aerosmith lounging backstage are vastly different from the aluminum casting specifications Alcoa provides to jet engine manufacturers. Notes from the campaign trail found in Howard Dean's Blog for America couldn't be more different than the detailed floor plans of an office tower in Melbourne, Australia (on the Colliers International site), or Booz Allen's descriptions of what it would be like to work at its company. While the content differs widely on the 20 sites discussed, the ability to cash in for success remains constant.

I was fortunate to have interviewed dozens of successful Web marketers to learn how they use content to cash in. I thank them for their participation (and apologize to those not included in the book). The case examples offered in these pages are told in the marketers' own words so we can learn from their personal experience.

I'd be the first to admit that my selection process and criteria weren't scientific, but neither is successful marketing—which is as much art and intuition as business process. I'm sure there are many worthy sites that have not been included in the book. However, I'm confident that each of the 20 sites profiled here vividly illustrates how to cash in with content.

It's also worth noting that dozens of innovative marketers declined to speak to me and their stories remain untold. The fact is that the effective use of Web content is a competitive advantage and marketers at some organizations felt they would be exposing trade secrets by telling their stories. I reached out to marketers working for major computer manufacturers, a large online bookseller, business-to-business technology companies, pharmaceutical firms, consumer packaged goods companies, and nonprofit organizations who, for their own reasons, didn't want their sites to be profiled. Clearly, the marketing people in these companies reveal the power of content as much by their decision not to participate as others did by the choice to tell their tales.

For each marketer who understands that effective Web sites are built around content, there are many more that just don't get it. While I was researching, only a small percentage of the Web sites I reviewed were considered for inclusion in the book. For the most part, sites simply lack a content strategy and for that and other reasons, fail to help companies accomplish business objectives. Sure, the site may look pretty and may even win awards; the graphics might be cool, displaying the latest technology at its flashy best. But these superficial sites fail, at least in part, because they don't offer the visitors anything worthwhile to read (yes, read). Further, they miss the chance to better leverage the rich content opportunities the Web provides—opportunities to download, view, or interact with content.

Asked and Answered—Marketing on the Web

Looking at less successful sites, I uncovered commonplace marketing tactics that are not as effective as focusing on content. I found that marketers at most organizations focus on two ineffectual ways to market on the Web: what we might call *answer marketing* and *ad marketing*, while at the same time they don't focus on the most effective form of Web marketing: *content marketing*. Many organizations create sites or build online marketing programs that either mimic a search engine (answer marketing) or adopt a slick advertising style (ad marketing). Sites that focus on simply providing answers to questions or deploying slick graphical images may serve the needs of some people, but without effective content—organized in the way people think and browse—these sites do little to advance the objectives of the organizations behind them.

Surprisingly, many people visit a site expecting to be told what to do next. These readers want to be pointed to the right place to learn more. Just as with a leisurely read of the Sunday newspaper, where they aren't necessarily looking for anything in particular, people often visit sites with little more than a vague idea about what they want. Most sites aren't built for these readers. When content is optimized for searching alone, a whole category of Web browsers is left out.

At the broadest level, there are exactly two ways to use and deploy content on the Web. Most organizations put too much effort into one way: *Answer my question*, while not spending enough energy on the other: *Tell me something*. Too often the content that's deployed on sites helps visitors with only half of their needs. To avoid this pitfall, it is better to conceive of site navigational design in a way that provides valuable information visitors might not think to request in addition to answering any questions they may have. To illustrate this concept, consider one of the Web's best known sites, Google (www.google.com), which in its purest form exists only to answer questions. With a site or content product organized only around answering questions, users must already know what they want before proceeding. But people also need services or sites to tell them something. Contrast Google with another famous site, Drudge Report (www.drudgereport.com). Drudge Report doesn't exist to answer questions; rather, it tells visitors things they didn't think to ask. While it does provide search functionality (far down the home page), Drudge Report provides content that's meant to be browsed.

Many sites of all types are built to act like a search engine, but in most cases this a mistake. Those who design their sites to be navigated primarily through search functionality apparently believe that the average visitor is looking to answer a specific question, or to satisfy a clearly defined need (for instance, they want a price quote or the latest product specs). This form of online marketing—"answer marketing"—is only effective if visitors know just what they're after; since many do not, such visitors represent lost prospects.

For example, many bank and brokerage firm Web sites organize around simply searching for rates such as mortgage loans, certificates of deposit, or stock prices. But visitors may just be browsing for investment ideas. If none are readily apparent, they click away never to return. These sites miss out on a major audience: people who do their own research and take time to consider options before committing to a decision. Sites that only focus on fulfilling free quotes for mortgage rates lose the opportunity to educate and enlighten potential customers—and develop relationships along the way.

While people use the Web for much more than searching, too many Web marketers haven't actually thought about the differences and what these distinctions mean for the content on their sites. Web browsers typically have hundreds of subjects of interest to them: work-related issues, industry data, family, hobbies, music, art, travel, kids, health, and much more. People can't possibly do a search on each and every relevant topic. People like serendipity, so their online lives are organized in a manner that allows them to stumble across interesting and useful content. Bookmarked sites, e-mail newsletters, and blogs tell us what we want to know and many things we didn't think to ask. Smart marketers know that the most effective Web strategies anticipate needs and provide content to meet those needs, even before people know to ask.

The Web Isn't TV

Another common mistake organizations make is designing sites that feature slick, TV-influenced, one-way broadcast messages that feel like advertising. This type of online marketing (ad marketing) is the least effective of all.

Visitors who actually want to learn something aren't satisfied and sales are lost. For example, most automaker sites are organized with the assumption that the site visitor is ready to buy a car immediately. These sites employ slick TV-style ad marketing with Flash Video introductions and pop-ups offering discounts or low financing. Often automaker sites try to hook visitors into the dealer network before they're actually ready to buy. While there certainly are people who visit an automaker's site to find a dealer, learn about financing, and even buy right away, the large number of visitors who are simply browsing aren't satisfied by these sites and quickly leave. Automaker sites that don't provide detailed vehicle information, for example, miss out on a major audience: people who shop and compare, considering a purchase over many months before making a commitment. Sites that are too busy advertising lose not only the opportunity to educate and enlighten potential customers, but also the chance to build relationships with them that may pay off in the long run.

Perhaps the reason so many sites adopt an advertising model on the Web is because decision makers entrust their organization's valuable Web site to an advertising agency. In the auto business, hundreds of millions of dollars are spent on television and print advertising, with a Web site representing a small part of the marketing budget. With these numbers, advertising agencies are focused on grabbing attention in print and TV advertising models, not in a content-marketing Web model. But guess what? When a visitor gets to a Web site, there's no need to grab their attention; you already have it. So, on the Web, the challenge has shifted from grabbing attention to informing and educating visitors through content. However, since most advertising people don't understand this, they create ineffective sites. Remember, people aren't looking for TV commercials on the Web, they are looking for content.

Branding Is for Cattle

Another common mistake marketers make online is focusing on aesthetics over information. Imagine if the people who publish newspapers and magazines only cared about how the publication looked. What kind of magazines would we have if no one was in charge of the content, yet dozens of people worried about cover color palates and graphic placement? What kind of publishing world would it be if Pulitzer Prizes were only given for design, usability, and functionality but not the actual content? Yet this is exactly the current state of the Web. Companies build sites based on design, rather than content. In short, many sites are built around the wrong assumptions and the organizations behind them suffer as a result.

Branding, as an advertising and marketing term, has as its origins the visual mark burned into a cow's butt. Branding was one of the most over-hyped concepts forced on Web marketers by the media and advertising agencies in the dot-com era. The result was that countless Web marketers got their knickers in a twist about the outward manifestation of an organization's brand—including logos, image ads, and tchotchkes—all at the expense of content.

Even today, when marketers consider "the brand," they think visually, rather than about Web site content. Yes, the visual aspects of branding are certainly important to Web marketers, but what's really at stake—in fact what branding's really about—is a focus on the customer. As each customer builds an emotional response to a company, that emotion becomes the brand-image for that person. Fortunately, some great Web marketers understand that the provision of quality Web content, together with useful layout and reliable customer support, does more to build brand than pretty logos, cool design, and hip color choices.

Many of my interviewees recalled going against the suggestions of self-proclaimed "Web marketing experts" when planning a site launch. In many cases, people from marketing and advertising agencies and Web design firms tried to convince them to focus on the sizzle instead of the steak. The advice was to pay more attention to colors and graphics than to the information content; typically marketers were told to include attention-grabbing images or Flash Video introductions on their home pages. Fortunately nearly everyone I interviewed rejected this well-meaning but flawed advice. The innovative marketers whose cases are profiled here knew instinctively that providing excellent content would yield successful sites. These marketers have learned to think like successful publishers: It is important to make a book or magazine readable, and attractive, but not at the expense of providing something worth reading.

The New Publishers

Back in the days of print domination, there were basically two choices an author had to getting content published: Go with a traditional book or periodical publisher or do it yourself. We've come a long way. The Web has turned all kinds of companies, nonprofits, and even rock bands and political campaigns into just-in-time and just-right publishers. Organizations—the new publishers—churn out boatloads of content to the benefit of many constituents. Until recently, nobody ever thought of these organizations as publishers; a newspaper, magazine, university, or book company was a publisher. But that's all changing. Self-publishing Web-style is mainstream and organizations large and small are doing the publishing.

All types of firms are now publishers in every sense of the word. For example, the corporate sites of many software companies now include reams of detailed information on viruses, worms, and other pests that affect the products sold and supported. For these companies, frontline technical support is actually Web-based content. Because the papers were published by a trusted source and given the company's stamp of approval, the authors' works are read by millions, just as if the material had appeared in a major computer magazine or technology book.

As a new form of grassroots politics has emerged on the Web, campaign sites have become a significant publishing forum; academic papers go straight to university sites, often bypassing peer-reviewed print journals or university presses; pharmaceutical companies publish detailed information about medical concerns and products on well-organized sites for health care professionals and the general public alike.

Every organization possesses particular expertise that has value in the new e-marketplace of ideas. The Web has made it easy for smart organizations to publish that expertise in the form of Web content, allowing companies, institutions, and nonprofits to function much like traditional publishers and broadcasters. Organizations gain credibility and loyalty with customers, employees, the media, investors, and suppliers through the content supplied on their Web sites.

On the Web, content takes many forms and includes such offerings as product information, Webcasts, photos, how-to guides, white papers, and more. Savvy organizations have started to look at when and how customers and prospects will turn to each type of content and develop a process to publish accordingly, producing content for each stage of the consideration cycle.

Organizations everywhere are taking the role of the new publishers. In today's world a publishers' brand name is still critically important but it's not just McGraw-Hill, Oxford University Press, or the *New York Times* anymore. The new publishers are nonprofits like AARP and the NRA, companies like Pfizer and Nike, politicians, rock bands, and upstart e-commerce companies. As organizations of all types begin to behave like publishers, many are adapting to the rigors of the publishing business and learning the editorial process. At the same time, new rules are emerging as *digital* publishing continues to mature.

In an increasingly competitive marketplace, all organizations are searching for the elusive key to success. Well, look no further for the key: Content will unlock success in almost any product category—even in highly competitive industries where small players are ordinarily eclipsed by larger competitors.

Getting the Most Out of this Book

Cashing In With Content explores how successful organizations publish content on the Web and organize it to get the readers of that content to do something: buy, subscribe, apply, join, or contribute. These Web sites use content in effective, unusual, and innovative ways and succeed in bringing in the numbers. This isn't a new concept: For years, successful Web site marketers at Dell Computer, for example, have convinced people to buy computers online by providing useful content about computers. Executives at Amazon.com have built a billion dollar business selling books and other consumer goods by organizing offerings like a content site. Many businesses were launched or expanded on the Web and have been successful for years. But because the vast majority of "Web marketing experts" and how-to books devote their attention exclusively to Web technology, graphics, organization, and branding, the content aspect has been under-appreciated and misunderstood—until now. With the innovative marketers behind successful sites telling their stories here, content finally emerges in its rightful place at the forefront of a plan for success.

While every chapter offers insights that will aid any type of organization, to make it easy to quickly choose individual profiles to read, the book is divided into sections based on the types of organizations profiled. The sections are Part 1: E-commerce, Part 2: Business-to-Business, and Part 3: Nonprofit, Education, Healthcare, and Politics. Although the profiles are organized in sections by sector, these are not rigid descriptions of each site's category. In fact, many of the sites profiled were appropriate for more than one category. For example, Design Within Reach is in the e-commerce category, but many of its sales are business-to-business. Alcoa is in the business-to-business category, but employs e-commerce components on its site. The profiles can be read in any order based on your interest. Because the ways that companies can profit from a successful content strategy transcend given industries, these strategies and practices can provide valuable ideas for a variety of different organizations.

The last section of the book, Part 4: Putting Content to Work, pulls together top techniques employed by the savvy Web marketers featured in the profile chapters. In Chapter 21 are a dozen best practices taken directly from the research I conducted over many months, organized thematically to help you, the reader, put these lessons to work in your own organization.

I was a little surprised by the amount of strategic overlap among the variety of firms I profiled, which is apparent in the best practices. For example, nearly every marketer described a focus on editorial consistency and the need to have all content speak with "one voice" to create a distinct site personality. Some interesting best practices emerged in regard to the use of humor and photographic images. I consistently heard from marketers a disdain for flashy movies and other heavy graphical elements on their sites: "Clean and fast" is a common preference.

In the pages that follow, you will encounter 20 organizations that have built and then reaped the rewards of content-based Web sites. One constant among these informative case studies is a focus on using content to drive action. Content does more than just sell itself, a product, or an idea—it sells an organization by branding it as an expert or a trusted friend. The marketers interviewed here understand this. They use content as a tool to turn browsers into buyers. In presenting these stories and the best practices that result from them, it is my hope that you too will use Web content to make your own organization more successful.

PART 1

E-Commerce

CHAPTER ONE

Crutchfield

A Friend in the Electronics Business

➤ **Organization**
Crutchfield Corporation
www.crutchfield.com, www.crutchfieldadvisor.com

➤ **Interviewed**
Lawrence Becker, Vice President, E-Commerce

What's For Sale

Crutchfield sells millions of electronic devices to aficionados and beginners alike.

What's So Interesting

Crutchfield stands out in the crowded consumer electronics marketplace by focusing on providing superior service; a major service component is the provision of excellent content. While many e-commerce sites (think Best Buy or Amazon.com) can sell you a car stereo system, Crutchfield.com walks you through the entire process—from choosing the right system for your make, model, and year of car to installing it yourself. Started 30 years ago as a print "magalog," Crutchfield has successfully extended its high-quality educational content model to the Internet. With the Crutchfield.com e-commerce site and its educational companion site, CrutchfieldAdvisor.com, content successfully drives commerce.

Why You Should Care

Crutchfield has built one of the most successful consumer electronics stores online by providing more informative content than its competition. In particular, useful content is written for novices and audiophiles alike, so everyone is empowered to make the right selection. The company employs a team of editorial professionals who write about the products they love. By continually optimizing the site around content tailored to buyer behavior, Crutchfield takes the sometimes daunting task of purchasing a gizmo or gadget online and makes it fun for consumers. E-commerce sites in virtually any category can learn from the tried-and-tested Crutchfield approach.

Crutchfield Corporation began 30 years ago when Bill Crutchfield founded the company in his basement with a $1,000 investment. Initially, he focused on car stereo equipment, selling through a catalog he wrote himself. But the initial catalog was a failure, producing hardly any sales. In a tradition that continues to this day, Bill wanted to find out why people weren't buying, so he conducted some basic market research by contacting customers and asking them what they thought of his catalog. He quickly learned a valuable lesson: The public was confused about car stereo equipment and intimidated by its installation. The result was the launch in 1975 of a "magalog"—a cross between a magazine and a catalog—for car stereos. As soon as Bill provided customers with not only catalog information but also articles he wrote (for example, "How I Evaluate and Install Quality Car Stereo"), he created a business selling consumer electronics.

Soon Bill was running a rapidly expanding company. He hired staff, moved out of his basement to a much larger space, and diversified his product line beyond car stereos. Today the company distributes about 30 million

Crutchfield.com extends the company's print "magalog" to the Web, delivering high-quality content to help consumers choose and purchase electronics.

Crutchfield magalogs each year. Crutchfield launched its Web site in 1995 with the same strategy as its magalog: To provide high-quality content that helps consumers choose and purchase electronic equipment.

The Crutchfield site sells what Lawrence Becker, Vice President of E-Commerce for Crutchfield Corporation, calls "information-rich products"—those things that need to be explained, described, and specified to help consumers make intelligent purchases. Crutchfield even seeks to enhance the customer experience with content addressing something as seemingly self-explanatory as instructions. Becker says that the often complex products sold by Crutchfield are assembled by Crutchfield staff just as a customer would be required to do. The Crutchfield team follows the directions and uses the products to see how they work, and then they write content that helps consumers understand what they will get and what to expect if they buy.

Turning Complexity into Opportunity

Many of Crutchfield's customers are electronics enthusiasts who are looking for specific products; Crutchfield.com delivers distinct content for this type of consumer. These customers can sort by brand, price, top sellers, new products, or specials within individual product sections on Crutchfield.com. Thus, if you're already knowledgeable and know you want a flat panel HDTV in a certain price range, you can easily comparison shop online.

Clicking on a product leads to an individual product specification page. From there, users can drill down through a series of tabs on the essential information page to more detailed pages, photos, or features and specs. In addition, details about what's included in the package and recommended accessories are listed on other tabs. Because the information is written by Crutchfield people and organized around the Crutchfield product and feature taxonomy, users are guaranteed consistently valuable content that allows them to compare products across multiple brands and price ranges.

A Little Friendly Advice

Professionals at Crutchfield also recognize that visitors come to the site at various stages of a purchase decision with a wide range of product understanding. While some customers are highly knowledgeable enthusiasts who jump right to the product pages, many others know next to nothing about a particular product category. Crutchfield has developed compelling content for both audiences (and anyone in between).

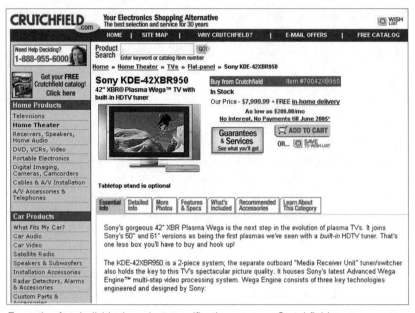

Example of an individual product specification page on Crutchfield.com.

If you're considering an electronics purchase, but are a little confused or intimidated, Crutchfield.com has content for you. Say you're in the market for a new TV. On most e-commerce sites, it can be a daunting experience to be confronted with a dizzying array of choices: flat-panel, HDTV, tube-style, front- or rear-projection… and the list goes on. Specialists at Crutchfield recognize the problem of consumer confusion (that can lead to shopping-cart abandonment) in providing the necessary value-added content to make informed decisions. At Crutchfield.com, you can read about each category of TV; you can study a primer on how to choose the right set for you, and potentially confusing terms can be clicked on so the term is defined in a pop-up glossary window. "Content on the Crutchfield.com site builds confidence in the customer's ability to understand, use, and enjoy products," Becker says.

To underscore its unique position among retailers and to supply even more helpful information to those in the early stages of the buying process, Crutchfield Corporation launched CrutchfieldAdvisor.com as a companion site to Crutchfield.com. "Crutchfield Advisor is a complete Audio/Video content resource. It's the equivalent of a trusted friend who knows a great deal about electronics," says Becker. An added benefit of Crutchfield Advisor as a

The Crutchfield Advisor site provides the details you need to make an informed purchase decision.

separate site is that it provides an alternative "front door" to the consumer electronics shopper who is in research mode and not yet ready to go to the store.

Car Stereo for Everyone

Although there are two separate sites, visitors can seamlessly click back and forth from Crutchfield.com and CrutchfieldAdvisor.com. Depending on their point in the purchase process, they may choose to link from the product descriptions on Crutchfield.com through to the "How-to-buy" information on Crutchfield Advisor and back again without even knowing they've moved to a companion site and back. "Audiences experience the two sites holistically," Becker says. "We try to reach people who are in all stages of the consideration process with appropriate content. Crutchfield.com is designed for those who are further down the shopping path, while the Crutchfield Advisor site is designed for those who are earlier in the process and simply looking for helpful information about electronics."

By creating layers of information and anticipating the needs of people at various stages of the consideration process, Crutchfield sells to enthusiasts and novices alike. For example, with car stereos (the product category Bill Crutchfield launched his business with in the mid-1970s), its customers cover a wide range that includes the highly knowledgeable urban street rod outfitter looking for a particular sub-woofer to boom, as well as the suburban mom who enjoys soothing adult contemporary as she transports the tykes in her minivan. Crutchfield optimizes content to reach both audiences. "Much of what determines how you're going to enjoy a new unit in your car starts with installing it in the car," says Becker. Although this may sound obvious, most other e-commerce retailers just proffer the goods and let you deal with the research and decision-making process on your own. Instead, Crutchfield Advisor walks you through a process to identify your exact make, model, and year of car and then presents only the product options and shopping comparison tools appropriate for your vehicle.

The professionals at Crutchfield understand that when many people investigate a piece of electronic equipment in an unfamiliar category, it's so confusing that they abandon the process in frustration—without a sale being made. "Content helps build confidence and anticipates questions," says Becker. As

Enter the make, model, and age of your car to find the right products.

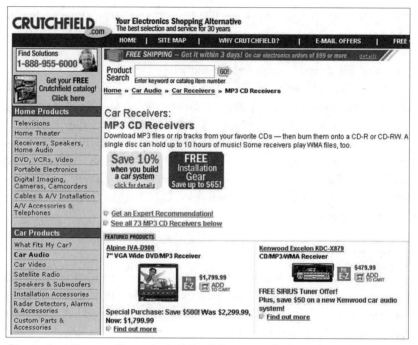

Choose from the specific products that will fit your particular make and model car.

the content is built and organized around the various stages of the consideration process, Becker helps his prospects go from confusion to delight. "Content is there to create excitement," he says. "Ultimately, we have fun stuff to sell."

Creating Content That Sells

Content for both Crutchfield sites is written in-house by two teams of writers, each with a managing editor and a Web editor. One team focuses on car electronics and the other on home electronics. Each writer within a team maintains content on a specific product category, creating and updating all of the information. What sets the content creation apart from many other sites is the level of interest for the products the writers possess. "The people who work here have a passion and an enthusiasm for the products we sell and that comes across in the content we write," says Becker. "We're gear heads and we love the equipment. We particularly enjoy bringing the products home to test them. Many of us have equipment like four-channel amplifiers, component speakers, and 12-inch sub-woofers... in our cars."

Although Crutchfield employs people who have studied writing, Becker is proud of the diverse background of the editorial staff. "For some reason, we've attracted a lot of musicians," he says. "Crutchfield Corporation is conducive for providing a career path for creative people." Many of Crutchfield's writers are also veterans of the sales department, which allows them to enhance their copy with an understanding of customers' needs. Because it's written by enthusiastic, creative people who love electronics, content on the Crutchfield site is lively and effective. The enthusiasm of the writers comes through in the content, which in turn helps Crutchfield to sell and to make happy repeat customers.

Customer Feedback

With a staff of editorial professionals and a strategy to provide content to people at each stage in the shopping process, one might think Crutchfield has everything down to an exact science. However, Becker knows that the way people buy electronic products is constantly changing and he wants Crutchfield to continue to be the best place for getting product information. In order to remain current with his online customers, Becker constantly tests, asks questions, and gathers feedback—a tradition begun by Bill Crutchfield when he launched his print magalog business 30 years earlier. "Information-rich products are sold with great content," Becker says. "How do I, as the writer, cull out what would be most important to the audience? How can I anticipate questions? We do this with many types of feedback. We always review customer comments to learn about how people use the sites."

Crutchfield uses multiple methods to gather input, comments, and suggestions from customers. As direct customer response mechanisms, each page has a "rate this page" link to give a quick "thumbs up" or "thumbs down" as well as opportunities for more detailed written customer comments. Crutchfield also links to the BizRate.com service where consumers can rate their overall experience across multiple parameters. Other ways Crutchfield gathers marketing research include reviewing competitive sites and usability testing of their own site. These tests are performed in a lab environment to determine how people navigate the site. Additionally, live, multiversion testing is conducted on the site to help understand which presentations customers find most appealing. By performing studies and gathering feedback,

Crutchfield is able to develop better content. Helping customers better understand the products ultimately helps Crutchfield.com sell more.

With so much feedback and testing, Becker and his team sometimes have difficulties sorting out what's important. "Certainly there are prototypes we've tested online or in user testing that didn't work out," he says. "There's a finite amount of space between any set of ears, so a challenge can be adding too much content without effective layering. Customer experience is important to us, so we may prune or reformat content to help improve the experience."

$$$$$$$$$$$$$$$$ Cashing In $$$$$$$$$$$$$$$$$$$

Crutchfield.com and CrutchfieldAdvisor.com are potent e-commerce sites because they were built from the start as content sites. Drawing on Bill Crutchfield's success with his print magalogs, well-written content sits front and center on the sites. By any measure, Crutchfield.com is a great success. The site generates well over 100,000 visitors per day and consistently wins awards and accolades such as the Circle of Excellence from BizRate.com and Best Site for Electronics from Time Magazine Online. But to cash in, Becker and the Crutchfield team of editorial professionals work on a basic principle that content sells. "Content simplifies the process of choosing a product," Becker says.

As successful as Crutchfield is, Becker says many people think of them as a specialty site for electronics enthusiasts more than a place for the novice consumer to learn and buy. In the past several years, broad e-commerce sites such as Amazon.com have demonstrated average consumers will buy products online in huge numbers. Amazon, being one of the most information-rich consumer shopping sites, has demonstrated that an incredible number of people will shop online—enthusiasts and novices alike. Where Crutchfield had focused more on the educated consumer who wanted to choose the right product, Amazon has proven that virtually anyone will buy online. Therefore, Becker believes there is a larger market for the content-driven e-commerce model for products. "The challenges for Crutchfield are how to better exploit the nonenthusiast group," Becker says. "How can the top-layer content draw even more people into the process?"

The essence of the usability testing going on at Crutchfield's labs today is in many ways exactly like Bill's basement approach. These tried-and-true techniques could help Becker and the Crutchfield develop the content required to sell electronics to a new group of people and possibly turn them into enthusiasts, too. "For example, digital cameras transcend the enthusiast group," Becker says. "How do we reach potential first-time digital camera buyers? That's what we're working on now and that will make us more successful." Just like that first Crutchfield magalog, products purchased by reading the right content delight consumers. And that's the ultimate goal for Becker who says, "We define success as exceptionally satisfied customers."

CHAPTER TWO

Alloy

Generation Y Marks the Spot

➤ **Organization**
Alloy
www.alloy.com

➤ **Interviewed**
Susan Kaplow, Vice President of Interactive and Print Media

What's For Sale

Alloy.com sells clothing and other merchandise directly to Generation Y girls and sponsorship opportunities to those who want to reach them.

What's So Interesting

With a target market of over 10 million girls in the United States between the ages of 12 and 17, Alloy has found a distinct editorial voice and has become one of the most popular sites for this dynamic demographic. Employing a team of in-house editors, content is written to drive traffic, build buzz, and sell hip merchandise.

Why You Should Care

Alloy's parent company reports sales in the hundreds of millions of dollars annually, much of it from the Alloy.com site. The site makes its money through sales of merchandise (particularly fashion) and sponsorships (movie advertisements are big). The Alloy.com site features quizzes, fashion, entertainment, and other content of importance to teenage girls. Highly interactive, the site includes dozens of chat rooms, message boards, polls, surveys, and other ways for girls to connect.

A lloy.com enjoys a huge number of unique visitors per month for any site: 1.7 million. Yet Alloy not only reaches this impressive figure, it targets a very specific market, teenage girls, who are quite possibly the most fashion- and trend-obsessed demographic there is. Teenage girls move on to the next big thing before adults even know what the last big thing was. They tend to be both experimental and concerned about the latest fashion. So the marketers at Alloy are certainly doing something right if they can continually attract mall rats to their site in record numbers and get them to buy their jeans and t-shirts online instead.

Alloy.com sports the look and feel of a teenage fashion magazine but accessorizes with the Web's interactivity, while maintaining a content-centric approach. Featuring such things as quizzes, polls, chat rooms, and message boards, Alloy.com is a place where girls meet, learn, explore and, of course, shop. Everything on the site is designed to not only attract and hold visitor interest but also to generate buzz and viral marketing. Teenage girls talk up the latest and greatest and Alloy.com is in the thick of their conversations.

Generation Y is the fastest growing demographic group in the United States. According to U.S. Census data, it's expected to grow 14.7 percent faster than the overall U.S. population in the next few years. Thus, this group controls tremendous disposable income and also has significant influence over overall household expenditure decisions. According to Alloy Inc., 40 percent of teenage girls have regular income from part-time jobs and the majority of those who don't work have an allowance. Teenagers have cash and they spend 90 percent of it, directly buying over $100 billion worth of stuff a year.

First and foremost Alloy.com is a content site, but the company is also extremely successful in its mission of collecting revenue from its audience by directly selling the products teenage girls want. And as site traffic has grown, Alloy has also become a successful media company, selling advertising and sponsorship opportunities to other organizations that want to reach teenagers directly.

Like, Keep It Fresh

Susan Kaplow, Vice President of Interactive and Print Media for Alloy Inc., is the individual charged with keeping the content on Alloy.com fresh and hip. "We're in constant communication with our users online," Kaplow says. "The teenagers communicate with us via e-mail, through the chat rooms, and other ways, so we're constantly up to date with the lexicon and what's important to our users."

One look at Alloy.com and you know it's a content site. With gossip, entertainment, movies, and more sitting front and center, you actually might not guess that Alloy sells hundreds of millions of dollars in merchandise. And that's just the reason that Alloy succeeds: To the millions of girls who visit, Alloy is a hip content site that happens to sell some cool clothes and other stuff. But Alloy Inc. is in the business of selling products and has figured out that content is one heck of a delivery vehicle.

Alloy employs a dialect that's perfect for its target audience. But the short sentences, extensive use of slang, and hip references might be a little difficult for those who remember when Ronald Reagan was President. Kaplow describes how they keep up with it all, "We have young editors who are marketing experts and who've worked for teen magazines. I worked for *Seventeen Magazine* as the Music Editor. Because we're constantly in touch with the audience directly, we're Pop-culturally aware."

The top level navigation of Alloy.com is organized into bite-size sections that reflect teen interests: shop, today, quizzes, connect, real life, entertainment, style, guys, and win prizes. Alloy organizes the site in the same way that

Alloy.com attracts teenage girls with hip content, makes it viral, and sells later.

the target audience thinks and interacts, rather than what is for sale—and the strategy works. Alloy's success in keeping the target audience interested and coming back for more (and yes, selling them something) can be directly attributed to how content is organized.

Quizzes, Guys, and Style

Right from the Alloy.com homepage, there's tons of stuff for girls to do. With catchy writing, fun graphics, photos, and bright colors, Alloy draws you in. There are dozens and dozens of links from the homepage alone such as:

- Win Prizes: We wanna hook you up with Pink!

- Gossip: Hilary Duff and Lindsay Lohan duke it out!

- Quizzes: Which *Friends* character are you?

Keeping the site fresh and up-to-date is a full-time job. Actually, according to Alloy's Kaplow, it's several full-time jobs. "All the content is created in-house," she says. "I have five editors working with me."

As mentioned, at Alloy.com the merchandise for sale is not focal; instead the free content is. Sure the site sells clothes and other trendy items, but the

Which *Friends* character are you? Take the quiz now!

Alloy.com recipe for success is to draw the teenager in first and sell later. Kaplow explains how it works, "Our main objective is to engage the user. We want to reach the girl who wants to buy a pair of jeans, but we also want her to come back to Alloy.com even if she doesn't buy a pair of jeans. We like to think of ourselves as like the mall and the food court online and we want the girls to hang out and come back often."

I Wanna Go to the Mall.com

Just like a gang of girls getting together to hang at the mall, Alloy.com organizes around meeting places. The Alloy message boards, for example, are active with ongoing discussions from sports and working out ("How do I do crunches?") to boys ("Pleez help, I need a B'day gift for my BF!!!!" Reply: "Take a cute pic of u w/ ur friends and put it in a nice frame") and much more. (Side note to parents of teenagers: You can get some great insights into how your kids think on the Alloy message boards!)

The viral marketing aspect of the content has also been critical to the Alloy success, according to Kaplow. "We built this company from 10 users to 10

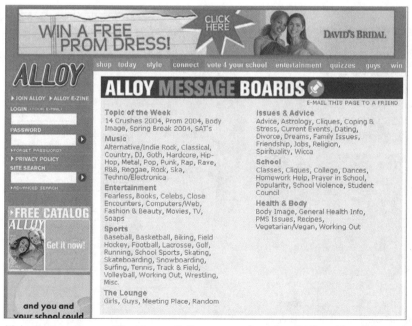

Make it interactive, as Alloy does with its message boards, and the girls will come back for more.

million users very quickly through viral marketing," she says. "Everything is about viral. We want to have a site that people tell their friends about, that's a topic of discussion where teenagers hang out." That also means advertising and sponsorship to drive traffic to Alloy.com from other online and print media properties. Kaplow adds, "We hit teenagers wherever they are. We want to make sure that they know about us."

Cool? Click. Buy.

Alloy makes some effective content moves to drive girls to the shopping section. For example, if you click on the "Style" link and then go to "Looks We Love," you'll find editorial content and photos about, say, some hip jacket that the stars are wearing this season. But guess what? There's also a link to purchase the jacket.

While built-in links drive girls from editorial content to shopping, Kaplow stresses that Alloy is careful about not going the other way by adding editorial to the shopping areas. "There are shopping tidbits on the content page, but when you are in the shopping area, it is a pure shopping environment," she says.

Looks We Love (and by the way we'll sell them to you, too).

A pure shopping experience—with no editorial and few ads.

Once you actually enter the Alloy.com shop, the navigation follows similar thinking to the main site—organized in the way teenage girls think. You can shop by item, by brand, or by style. Alloy.com does a terrific job facilitating shopping for the girl who knows what she wants as well as the casual browser who's just poking around. Just like the mall, at Alloy.com you can quickly get what you want or you can just browse. And like a bricks-and-mortar store, once you're inside, you aren't overwhelmed by advertising. Kaplow says, "In the shopping section, the advertising is less intense than the rest of the site to keep it pure."

$$$$$$$$$$$$$$$$$ Cashing In $$$$$$$$$$$$$$$$$$

Alloy.com's parent company, publicly held Alloy Inc., generates over $100 million in sales each quarter. Besides the Alloy.com site, Alloy, Inc. also operates a related print catalog business and several other sites. While Alloy doesn't break out the revenue directly attributed to the Alloy.com Web site, it contributes a significant percentage to the parent company's revenue. Alloy.com cashes in with two major revenue sources: advertising/sponsorship and merchandise sales. Kaplow describes why the site is chock-full of ads, "We attract the kinds of blue-chip advertisers who want to reach the target demographic that we can deliver."

There are a lot of ads on the Alloy site, but unlike other sites where ads may be untargeted and ultra-annoying, ads work as an integral part of Alloy because they are appropriate to the teenage demographic. In many ways, the ads have their own charm and often fuel a viral effect of their own. Movies consistently command prime Alloy.com real estate. "When you're in an editorial section, the online experience includes advertising," Kaplow says. "Our advertising is often Hollywood driven. When you're on the home page, which is our #1 window on the world, you see significant advertising."

With such a command of the teenage girl demographic through its content approach to sales, competition is popping up everywhere. Kaplow put it into perspective: "We think of all youth media as competition. But we've grown so much online and we own the lion's share of the market. We own 32 million girls in our database and we're the leaders online for this demographic. So we need to pay attention to all kinds of competition. The real competition for us is anyone who gets ad revenue instead of us."

With her focused role on the site's content, in many ways Kaplow bears the key responsibility for Alloy.com's success. She was around from the early days in the late 1990s and has seen traffic reach an astonishing 10 million users. But how does Kaplow measure Alloy's ongoing success? "Financials certainly: We need to make our numbers," she says. Alloy is a public company so everyone sees how things are going each and every quarter. But then she adds, "Growing the community and growing the traffic. We want to create an environment that teenagers want to belong to."

CHAPTER THREE

Design Within Reach

Form Follows Function

➤ **Organization**
Design Within Reach
www.dwr.com

➤ **Interviewed**
Rob Forbes, Founder

What's For Sale

Design Within Reach provides easy access to well-designed furniture traditionally found only in designer showrooms.

What's So Interesting

For many people, great design has been inaccessible, either because it is difficult to find or because it is marketed with pretension. Those not "in the know" about good design tend to feel left out. Design Within Reach provides terrific information on design for the professional and amateur alike. With a site design that makes it easy to poke around by specific designers, by rooms within a home and office, or by furniture type, this design site has an excellent design all its own.

Why You Should Care

Design Within Reach makes use of photographs and product specifications as well as including useful comparisons within each category. Shopping by price, features, design type, designer, or other criteria is made simple. When you look at a particular item, the site suggests others that work with it and features photographs of the items in home and office environments. Biographies of many of the designers are made available on the site and a well-crafted weekly e-mail newsletter puts design into perspective. With sales consistently climbing (up 49 percent to $120.6 million in fiscal year 2005), the company completed a successful public stock offering in July 2004, raising more than $30 million.

S ay you're furnishing your home or office and you'd like to include some interesting, modern, well-designed furniture and accessories. You want to show off your individuality and flair. Where do you go? A quick trip to the local mall ends in frustration because the seating, tables, and lighting all look the same and the style is often shoddy or you find nothing but bad reproduction Americana. If you have access to a major city and can shop at specialty furniture stores, you may find an interesting piece or two, but not everything you need is in one place. Worse, the design emporium staff—slender and chic—may treat you with disdain if you don't recognize names like Enrico Franzolini and Rodolfo Dordoni (not to mention the steep prices that accompany fashionable showroom addresses). To provide a more user-friendly environment, Design Within Reach launched a site catering to all of those who love good design or want to get to know it better.

"Our goal is simply to accelerate the way that design gets to the public," says Design Within Reach founder Rob Forbes. His philosophy with DWR.com is to deliver great products to a broader group of people and to elevate the public's interest in décor and design.

DWR capitalizes on a combination of excellent content and a clean site design appropriate for the products.

The DWR site brings together furniture, rugs, lighting, and accessories from classic designers like Ray and Charles Eames, Mies van der Rohe, George Nelson, Marcel Breuer, and many others. Also featured are many young or less well-known (yet significant) designers, allowing customers the opportunity to compare them to the icons of modern design. Importantly, a great deal of information is provided about each of the designers as well as the products. "We market products from designers to design-savvy clients and we honor the values of the design community," says Forbes, who started his career as a professional designer. This formula resulted in a great success story. Initially launching the company with the Web site and a print catalog, in just a few years, DWR has grown into a major retailer moving substantial volume. Leveraging the success of its online properties, the company now also operates 36 retail "DWR Design Studio" outlets in cities including San Francisco, New York, and Portland.

Going Against the Grain

When Forbes started DWR in 1999, he received a great deal of advice about how to design his Web site. Fortunately, he rejected what the so-called experts said and followed his instincts instead. "When we launched, I think it was worst period in history for graphic design," Forbes says. "At that time, everyone said that Web sites were all about a look; people focused too much on things like color and flash. For us it was different: It was form and function coming together in a Web site. Our site is really fast, has no distractions, and has really great content."

Content on the DWR site is organized to serve distinct visitor types, which is certainly a major reason for the site's success. The professional designer, the retail shopper, and the merely curious will each instinctively know where to go and what to click because the site makes use of multiple paths to organize the same content. You can click by genre (such as seating, tables, and lighting), by room (including workspace and bedroom), or by any one of dozens of featured designers. Once you've clicked through one of the paths, the products can be further organized by other criteria (such as price).

At the individual product level, each item has its own spec sheet, which, importantly, is also available in a convenient printer-friendly format. Because many people take some time in considering a significant purchase such as a sofa or desk, the print version of the content aids in the offline thought process. Most products feature close-up and wide-angle photographs of the item in a home or office environment so you can see the item in context.

Another nice touch is the "We also suggest" feature, which displays additional products that may work well with the selected items in the same room.

Producing a Web site for a company focused on great design has its distinct aesthetic challenges because, not surprisingly, people also expect the site to have great design. Yes, DWR is an attractive and usable site, but not just because of graphics and elegant use of white space. Forbes explains the challenge he faced when starting out, "People are confused about what the Web is. They confuse the look as being what's important but we focused on the content and the performance. We think of our clients as wanting good information—quickly." The site has certainly achieved this goal: It is informative, fast, and clean. And by focusing on delivering good content quickly, the site has attracted a huge following of fans, many spending thousands of dollars a year on DWR products.

Please Take a Seat

Where others might merely assume the products speak for (and sell) themselves, DWR leverages the power of content. Although a design-related site, DWR resisted the temptation to focus on graphic design and images over content and usability. DWR.com is a good-looking site, whose aesthetics exist to serve and highlight content that illuminates the products that are for sale. The site enhances visitors' experiences by giving them more than just a sales pitch or pretty pictures.

Let's say you're interested in a new office chair. A quick click or two and you're viewing some well-organized content that helps you choose the right chair for your room and your bum. The introduction to the section reads, "Finding the right task chair is a little like the story of Goldilocks and the Three Bears—it's hard to find the one that fits both your body and your daily activities. To make it a little easier for you, we've organized our selection of task chairs for ready comparison." Clicking through to any of the chairs provides detailed product specifications.

It's this additional information provided in the right context that helps to satisfy the shopper and move merchandise. Sure, standard specs are there, including height, weight, color options, and the like. But there's much more content on each piece. "We have information like the designer biographies, materials the products are made out of, and more," Forbes adds.

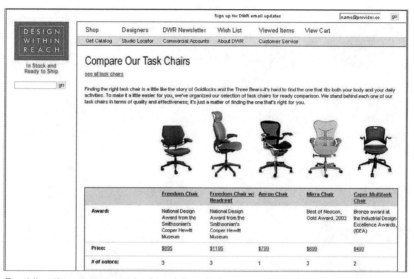

| | Sign up for DWR email updates | | | | name@provider.co | go |

| DESIGN WITHIN REACH | Shop | Designers | DWR Newsletter | Wish List | Viewed Items | View Cart |
| | Get Catalog | Studio Locator | Commercial Accounts | About DWR | Customer Service | |

In Stock and Ready to Ship

Compare Our Task Chairs

see all task chairs

Finding the right task chair is a little like the story of Goldilocks and the Three Bears-it's hard to find the one that fits both your body and your daily activities. To make it a little easier for you, we've organized our selection of task chairs for ready comparison. We stand behind each one of our task chairs in terms of quality and effectiveness; it's just a matter of finding the one that's right for you.

	Freedom Chair	Freedom Chair w/ Headrest	Aeron Chair	Mirra Chair	Caper Multitask Chair
Award:	National Design Award from the Smithsonian's Cooper Hewitt Museum	National Design Award from the Smithsonian's Cooper Hewitt Museum		Best of Neocon, Gold Award, 2003	Bronze award at the Industrial Design Excellence Awards, (IDEA)
Price:	$895	$1195	$799	$899	$499
# of colors:	3	3	1	3	2

Providing the content required to pick a chair: comparisons by price, awards won, colors, designer, and more.

Newsletter of Note

But DWR's content approach doesn't just sit on its site; the company also pushes content out to interested visitors. Forbes writes an e-mail newsletter called Design Notes that goes out weekly to more than 250,000 opt-in subscribers. "The e-mail newsletter expands the reach of design and the form of design," Forbes says. "The newsletter gives readers a window on the world of design that's broader than just the things we sell. For example, in one issue, we talk about the use of arches in design. It's mostly a way of getting people to think about design in different ways. For example, when I travel, I'll think about the design of the restaurant and all the things around me and that's what I write about." The idea of providing design-based content delivered weekly is compelling primarily because it isn't sales or product related, but rather demonstrates Forbes' (and by extension DWR's) commitment to providing information about design. The newsletter is aimed at people who are interested in modern design and written in a way that encourages pass-along value (including "send to a friend" links), so it has a viral marketing effect. The bottom line is that when subscribers need a new piece they think of Design Within Reach first, which is kept front of mind via the interesting and informative e-mail newsletters that arrive in their in-boxes weekly.

DESIGN WITHIN REACH

January 5, 2004

Design Notes

Exclusive Products

Modern Design

In Stock and Ready to Ship

| Home | Products | Get Catalog | Search | Subscribe | Send to a Friend |

Champagne Chair Redux: High-Wire Acts, Classy Glass and French Fashion

"I drink champagne when I win, to celebrate ... and I drink champagne when I lose, to console myself."

—Napoleon Bonaparte

Back After 30 Years: Eames® RAR Rocker

Rick Dean's "number 1", Yukiko Okada's "POP" and "The DaVidRo Chair" by David S. Rose

We have developed a special holiday tradition at DWR: The annual jurying of our Champagne Chair Contest. The event takes place in late December in our offices, where hundreds of chairs arrive in small boxes, some with stories, some without labels, some with extraordinary packaging, some two weeks late. The chairs spur a lot of comments and buzz around the office, creating an atmosphere that is a little like the maternity ward in a hospital, with staff coming by to view the chairs and to make comments on the new arrivals.

We have been getting requests for rockers since we started DWR. Over the years, we've found that, for various reasons, finding a comfortable, practical, lightly scaled modern rocking chair is not easy. We are therefore lucky to be able to reintroduce the classic Eames RAR Rocker from

The company has made forays into publishing with a book and its weekly Design Notes e-mail newsletter.

Forbes personally writes much of the content on the site and in the e-mail newsletter. Even though he is top manager in a large and successful company (with millions in sales and showrooms across the country), Forbes doesn't delegate the content creation tasks. His personal involvement demonstrates Forbes' opinion of the value that content plays in his success. "Web sites that stand out are those that have character and personality," he says. "It's all about information that makes you think—stimulating and entertaining. I always think about what people want when they are online for just a moment. What's interesting? I try to show and tell something interesting."

$$$$$$$$$$$$$$$$$$$$$$Cashing In$$$$$$$$$$$$$$$$$$$$$

The Design Notes e-mail newsletter was conceived and written to build the DWR business. Weekly newsletter content, which includes interesting articles about design from all over the world, gets readers to regularly think about good design and to view DWR as expert in these subjects. Pausing for a moment to reflect on fascinating design all around us helps transform the merely curious into buyers. When you're aware of good design, you want it in your home and office. "We look at our business really broadly," says Forbes. "We're selling modern design. People access us because of design rather than furniture." But of course, it's selling furniture that pays the bills and fuels the rapid expansion of Design Within Reach both on- and offline.

Forbes understands instinctively what's needed on his site and within the newsletter, but he also makes certain to look at what his customers are doing on the DWR site. He personally reviews feedback the site and the newsletter receive. "Our clients are helping us write the rules by how they interact with the site and the newsletter," Forbes says.

The Design Within Reach site is successful by nearly every measure: steady increases in site traffic, millions of dollars annually in furniture and accessory sales, and publishing an e-mail newsletter for more than a quarter of a million enthusiastic subscribers. Building on the success of the site and newsletter, the company has expanded offline, too, opening showrooms all over the United States and even moving into traditional content publishing with an exclusive book about George Nelson, one of the most important designers and thinkers of the 20th century. DWR has republished Nelson's influential classic book, *How to See*, which originally came out in 1977.

Net sales for the company have grown consistently. For example, revenue for the fiscal year 2005 was $120.6 million, an increase of 49 percent over the $81.1 million recorded in fiscal 2004. With such impressive figures, Design Within Reach successfully completed its initial public stock offering in July 2004, raising approximately $31.8 million in net proceeds through the sale of 3 million shares of common stock. Indeed, Design Within Reach cashed in with content.

So what does Forbes say about his achievements? "I define success by having the Web site as a seamless extension of us," he says. "It goes unnoticed as a rational aspect of the business." Then with a pause he adds, "Oh, and success is also no nasty feedback."

CHAPTER FOUR

mediabistro.com

Pitching Content to the Media

➤ **Organization**
mediabistro.com
www.mediabistro.com

➤ **Interviewed**
Laurel Touby, CEO & Cyberhostess

What's For Sale

mediabistro.com is a career and community site featuring job opportunities, courses, and networking events for media professionals such as editors, writers, and producers in magazines, television, radio, newspapers, book publishing, online media, and other creative industries.

What's So Interesting

In a few short years, mediabistro.com has developed into a profitable online community of 270,000 users (and growing) for media people. Offering an intriguing combination of job postings for full-time and freelance work, courses to hone skills, and opportunities to network online and off, mediabistro.com is the go-to site for novice or experienced writers, editors, and other creative types.

Why You Should Care

The mediabistro.com business was built from the ground up with content as the sole driver of growth. The company spends no money at all on marketing, instead focusing on supplying the content that media people want in a dynamic virtual community. The mediabistro.com model shows that an entire business can be started and grown to profitability based on content as the hook.

W riting for a living is a solitary pursuit. No matter whether you're a freelancer doing newspaper articles from home or a magazine staffer scribbling away in an office, it is just you and the keyboard day in and day out. Whether on staff or working from home offices, it can be difficult for media people to find opportunities to share successes, network with colleagues, bounce ideas around, or to complain about those hard-headed editors who just don't understand. To address the needs of writers in this isolated and frustrating world, Laurel Touby developed mediabistro.com to provide opportunities for media professionals to meet and network.

As a former journalist, Touby—founder, CEO, and Cyberhostess of mediabistro.com—knew what her target market required. She began her career at *Working Woman* magazine and moved on to *BusinessWeek* as a staff editor. In 1993 Touby began working from home, editing and writing a column on workplace issues for *Glamour.* As she lamented the lack of face time and water cooler talk her role entailed, the spark that led to mediabistro.com was lit. Initially the company's focus was on hosting cocktail parties in New York City for media professionals where they could talk shop after work in a relaxed and friendly setting. "The company started as an offline community organization. I helped people develop personal relationships with one another," Touby says. The networking parties grew quickly through word of mouth and Touby know she had identified a market that needed to be served.

Organizing parties and networking events was just the beginning. "My users forced me to the Web because that's where they get their information," Touby says. As she drew up plans for the site, Touby knew that content was to be the most important component. She launched the mediabistro.com Web site in 1997. "In my training as an editor, my first concern was that the Web content was valuable to the user. The core foundation of the business is high-quality content."

Years later and with an online community forged, the live cocktail parties continue, and have expanded beyond the New York City beginnings. Events in cities across the U.S. give members valuable face time on a regular basis. But now that the community is organized on the Web, content is the primary business driver that allows mediabistro.com to cash in. Touby has grown the business quickly: She employs 15 people at mediabistro.com plus more than 30 part-time instructors who teach courses around the country. Two of the full-time people plus a part-time editor are devoted to creating content for the mediabistro.com Web site. Nearly 20 percent of the human resources at mediabistro.com are devoted to Web content creation, a much larger percentage than most companies, showing the importance Touby places on content to drive her business forward.

Online Community for the Media

"We think of ourselves as a weird hybrid," says Touby, "a mix between Monster.com, a B2B magazine, the Learning Annex, and a membership club for the media. We're both a professional association and a membership community. We're a B2B magazine, because we have a cool niche thing—and a learning organization, because we also do classes." Copious free content serves as the draw that gets media people interested and keeps them coming back—and eventually paying—for more.

When Touby launched the site, her initial focus was creating the content that would serve as the core of a destination that media people would want to come to again and again. "Much was free in the beginning," she says. "I find you have to build traffic and usefulness first and then start to charge. Because of low barriers to entry, it's easy to start." In the early days, much of the content was career-oriented, with job postings a major draw. In the late 1990s, with the dot-com boom fueling the need for writers and editors who wanted

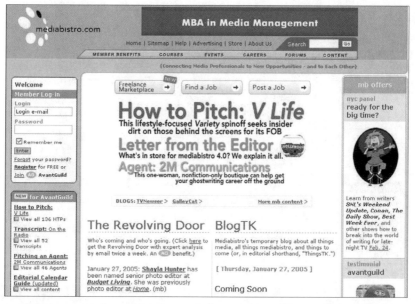

mediabistro.com is the online community for members of the media to network, find work, and gain valuable skills.

to find fame and fortune at online start-ups, the job board on mediabistro.com became the hot place for new media jobs in writing, editing, and other creative areas like photography and graphic design. The goodwill and large traffic Touby had developed with the free content on mediabistro.com allowed her to shift her focus to building revenue. "We started to charge for the job listings because employers were used to paying for them elsewhere," Touby says.

According to Touby, job listings continue to be the biggest moneymaker for the company. Employers pay $199 to post one job on the site for 30 days. Packages are available for multiple job postings. For example, it costs an employer $6,950 to purchase a pack of 50 listings, which also guarantees access to the 270,000 registered users of mediabistro.com. An important sales point for employers is the quality of the potential applicant pool. Unlike general job search sites that don't specialize in a particular industry, mediabistro.com delivers savvy candidates who are well qualified and care about improving their careers. Scanning the job board reveals some 20 to 30 new jobs posted each day, so candidates are likely to find opportunities that interest them, which keeps traffic high.

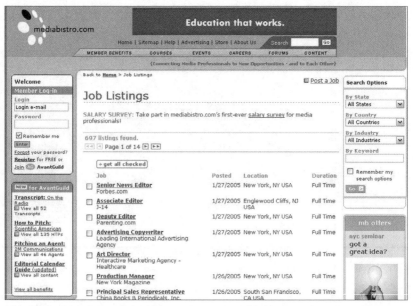

Hundreds of job listings for media professionals help pay the bills at mediabistro.com.

Media Community

While the networking cocktail parties have always successfully brought in large numbers of media people, the parties have never been a mediabistro.com revenue-earner (each person pays for his or her own drinks, but it is free to attend). Touby expanded the model by developing new face-to-face events and making some of them paid. "It's critical for online services to have offline interaction with members," Touby says. "Anything that can bring people together is hugely valuable and builds brand loyalty. We have parties in many cities to build goodwill, but we started doing paid events as well as the free parties." Many events are two to three hours in an evening and cost around $50 to attend and all are marketed on the Web site. Some of the events offered include:

- Pitching for Dollars: How to Write Irresistible Proposals

- Designers and Illustrators, Resell Your Work!

- Copy Editors: Take This Job...and Keep It!

- Scoring a Job in Tough Times: Creating a Killer Resume

- Financial Sanity for Freelancers

- An Introduction to Business Journalism

- Cookbook Writing 101

- Teen Beat: Write that Young Adult Novel!

As the evening paid events became successful, Touby also added a series of longer courses. The mediabistro.com signature class—Boot Camp for Journalists—is held in major cities around the U.S. at a cost of $499 per student. Boot Camp has put hundreds of students through a rigorous eight-week program in which they learn to produce a perfect pitch letter, complete eight saleable assignments, and determine potential prospects for their work. The course description for Boot Camp for Journalists begins with a compelling piece of content:

Let's face it: If you knew you'd still be writing about eraser manufacturing for Pencil News Monthly, covering city council meetings for the Boondock Weekly, or trying to track down a former child star to write a "catching up with" for the Irrelevant Gossip Daily, you would have gone into a lucrative career. You became a journalist because you feel passionate about the truth; there are stories you insist need to be told. And doing a story on the adverse effects of size-8 knitting needles on a yarn-based Afghan doesn't qualify.

Touby has developed a winning model of content that drives an online community of media professionals. Although these professionals are willing to pay for additional valuable services, Touby continually adds to the mix of free offerings. Free content on the site includes a wide variety of career, networking, and job information for the media. A series of feature articles written by mediabistro.com staff focuses on interesting and often funny aspects of the business. A recent feature article description was: *On Interviewing: Part of being a great journalist is conducting a great interview, and some powerhouse reporters told us their secrets for getting subjects to talk.* Interviews with important editors or media personalities are also available to anybody, for example: *So What Do You Do, Helen Gurley Brown? The legendary editrix on her storied career, the state of women's magazines, and the reissue of her best-selling book, Sex and the Office.* Other content includes How to Pitch

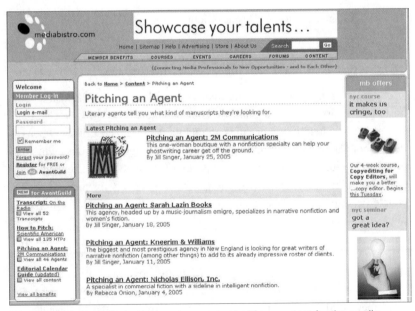

Pitching an Agent is included among a vast set of free content for the media community.

Guides, which tell reporters the best ways to approach editors with story ideas, and include a section on Pitching an Agent. Bringing the roots of the company back full circle to the content on the site, there's an extensive collection of mediabistro.com Party Photos available—linking the offline community with the on.

The great thing about Web content as a marketing tool is that it allows experimentation, but not everything has been successful according to Touby. "We added personals, but that's been tough," she says. However, she is quick to try new things on mediabistro.com. "The more things you add, the easier it is to have orphans. We throw a lot of things at the wall to see what sticks." She says that they give new ideas time to catch on, but rethink those that don't draw sufficient interest.

A popular offering that has been available for several years is the mediabistro.com Daily News Feed, a roundup of news about the media business in the form of a daily e-mail newsletter. With an audience of 65,000 people, Touby uses the newsletter to cross-sell other content. "I don't mind giving people free information to show them what else we have," Touby says. "The newsletter has the 'job of the day,' which shows people that we have job postings on the site

TVnewser.com is the first in a series of target-specific content sites for the media community.

and we also have ads for our courses. All the free content is one step away from people paying money. It's like Jupiter's atmosphere—things swirling around and helping to sell and promote everything else."

The company has started experimenting with specialized media content targeted to specific audiences. According to Touby, growth opportunities come from appealing to each of the specifically identified target markets (magazines, television, radio, newspapers, book publishing, online media, advertising, PR, and graphic design). "The challenge with one homepage is reaching each target market," says Touby. "So we're looking to launch a series of sister sites. One of the first is TVnewser.com—while the TV people may come to mediabistro.com, they'll end up at the sister site. We're hoping that this site eventually pays for itself through job listings and cross selling." The free TVnewser.com is off to a great start—it has 200,000 users and is growing fast.

Touby has some specific advice for those who use content to draw people in. "Don't be wedded to one URL," she says. "You can successfully build subbrands that draw from the best of the original main site. The lesson is: Don't be afraid to break down users into groups." Touby has taken the unusual approach of building the new mediabistro.com sister sites as blogs rather than straight Web sites. "Blogs are easy and cheap to launch," she says. "You can hire someone to blog and create constantly updating content. It's genius."

Media Content to Sell Media Services

As mediabistro.com continued to add registered users, Touby says her next natural progression was to add a membership program. "We have commonalities with our members who all have similar psychographics and demographics," she says. "A lot are freelancers, well educated." The membership program called AvantGuild, which costs $49 per year, includes additional content not found on the free site, such as transcripts of some of the offline events and a full library of How to Pitch Guides. Touby says the entire site is now organized around providing free content that will entice people to step over the line to become members. "For example many people come to the site for career information," she says. "We provide upgraded content, which we lead them to with baby steps. We have, for example a resume revamp service, which is paid. With the free bulletin board discussions, we can help to show them about the classes and other paid information. Because we're considered an expert about media jobs, we build goodwill. We take the expertise we've developed and honed and the relationships we've built around building paid services for our members. We're not just a job board, we're a career destination. People can learn stuff they can't learn anywhere else."

Leveraging the value of a tight group of like-minded people, mediabistro.com has ventured into partnerships that offer members benefits with select companies including discounts and added value. Many of the partners focus on services ideal for the media such as a free e-mail address (*you*@AvantGuild.com), which is perfect for applying for jobs when you don't want responses sent to your current employer's system. Other services are discounts on tax preparation services for freelancers as well as health and dental insurance. AvantGuild members also enjoy discounts on mediabistro.com courses and events. But Touby won't stop there. "Now we have 270,000 people on the site, so we look to do partnerships with organizations that want to reach those people," she says. For example, AvantGuild members enjoy discounts on theatre tickets, rental cars, and more through the partner program.

$$$$$$$$$$$$$$$$ Cashing In $$$$$$$$$$$$$$$$

"This was all driven by free content," Touby says of her successful, profitable, and growing business that generates 4.5 million page views per month. "We don't spend a penny on marketing; every bit of content on the site is a vehicle to bring customers into the sales funnel."

Parties continue to be important for mediabistro.com and party photos are core content on the site, helping to cross-promote other services.

Touby has built what could be described as the perfect pure-play content marketing company and all marketers can learn from her content marketing examples and successes. "We provide content which is valuable and that allows us to do target marketing to a very fine point," she says. "All our marketing is about cross promotion—everything references other things. This is the core of how I peruse every aspect of the business. There's no better way to reach people."

Taking a look at any page on the mediabistro.com Web site, the TVnewser.com sister site, or the e-mail newsletter reveals many cross promotional offers and links. But none of them seem intrusive. "We focus on what's important for our customers, not what's important for the company," Touby says. "We're an egoless company rather than an egocentric company. The egocentric one puts out what the company thinks is best rather than what the customer wants."

Touby insists that everything that goes onto mediabistro.com must be of the right tone. In every aspect of marketing and content, in the way the company conducts parties and the way the classes are run, each follows the mediabistro.com tone. "It's not just the words and grammar, but also the color scheme and design," Touby says. "Our tone is friendly, but not too friendly. We're kind of cool and hip, but not too cool and hip. It's for media insiders, but is open to beginners. I want to appeal to mid-level people who are improving their careers and who want to be smarter."

Touby's title of Cyberhostess perfectly describes her role in the company she founded on networking parties. Like a whirlwind in the middle of a budding content-driven empire serving the media community, she not only supports 270,000 registered users, her employees and part-time instructors, and hundreds of employers looking for job candidates, she also attends many of the parties in person. Of course, mediabistro.com is a for-profit business and now that the profits are coming in, she can breathe easier than the early days. "We have investors, so we manage for net income," Touby says. "In the end, success comes from keeping costs down by generating as much user-generated content as possible. But income also comes from providing a quality product to our many members. I can only do this online due to the power of the Web. The Web offers a great business model for cost control."

Even though she's built a successful site, Touby knows that her ongoing success will come from continually adding new content to appeal to her target market. "Nobody knows how to do this well yet," she says. "There's no such thing as the perfect Web site. We're all putting our seeds out as Web gardeners and we're waiting to see how it grows."

CHAPTER FIVE

Esurance

Content Replaces Agents

➤ **Organization**
Esurance
www.esurance.com

➤ **Interviewed**
Kristin Brewe, Director of Corporate Communications

What's For Sale

Esurance sells automobile insurance online, competing against larger insurance companies with vast armies of agents.

What's So Interesting

As an online-only auto insurance company, Esurance has carved out a successful niche in a tough space. Nobody likes to buy auto insurance. Knowing that, Esurance created an online experience designed to make the process as quick and painless as possible. And because they only sell online, the site's content must serve the role of the traditional neighborhood insurance agent: providing information, answering questions, working up quotes, and writing policies.

Why You Should Care

In the past decade, thousands of companies were started with the intention of moving traditional businesses onto the Web. Because the majority of these dot-com companies focused on the wrong things—logos, fancy branding, and the like—most failed. Esurance thrives because it realized early on that the content on its Web site needed to replace the traditional form of selling insurance through agent networks. And the process needed to be fast—because people hate to buy insurance—so everything on the site is written to make insuring your car as quick and easy as possible. Esurance offers a terrific example of useful, simple, and easy to understand content to drive e-commerce.

A ccording to most state laws, every automobile must be insured. But automobile insurance is expensive, often frustrating to acquire, and all and all a rather mysterious commodity. Bottom line: People hate buying it. The traditional way to purchase insurance is through a neighborhood agent you find via word-of-mouth. Once insured, people usually stay with the policy until they're hit with a price increase, which prompts an angst-riddled search for a cheaper alternative. A referral like, "John's brother-in-law is an insurance agent," serves as the way most people buy insurance.

Esurance, a subsidiary of White Mountains Insurance Group, set out to do things differently. As an online-only automobile insurance company, Esurance relies on content to sell insurance rather than a personal visit or phone call to somebody's relative. With online auto insurance content serving the role of virtual agent, Esurance is, "Building an auto insurance empire one word at a time," according to Kristin Brewe, Director of Corporate Communications.

"People don't like auto insurance," Brewe says. "It's like a conspiracy: People don't want it, but the state says they have to get it." According to Brewe, everything on the Esurance site is optimized for speed. "The goal of the site is to get people in and out of the transaction or information search as quickly as possible," she says. "In 15 minutes someone can apply for insurance, get insured, and print out their card. They're pleased with how fast they can do the transaction."

As an online-only insurance company, Esurance can't rely on the strong offline brands and advertising leveraged by their competitors. "We focus our marketing efforts online," Brewe says. "State Farm, Geico, and Progressive are online, but they started with the agent model. We also compete with insurance aggregators who present our quotes to customers, but we'd rather have them come to us directly." The content on the Esurance site makes all the difference to those who are shopping. "We make it easy to step through the process," adds Brewe. "We want to demystify the business of getting insurance. We use content to provide the same kind of information that a personal agent would."

Great Content as a Marketing Tool

"We're not trying to reach people who'd rather transact with their local agent," Brewe adds. "Those people are looking for something else. What's great about competition is that everyone can find a way to transact that they're comfortable with. For those who already pay bills online, surf the Web to find the best deal for a hard-to-find book, and print out their own e-ticket receipts for plane trips, Esurance is a natural fit."

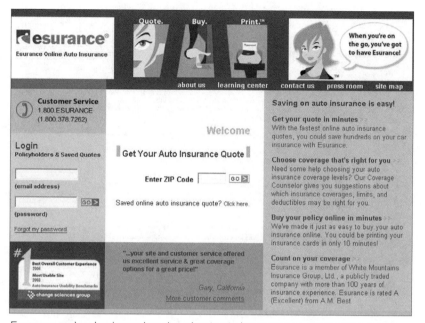

Esurance makes buying or learning about auto insurance as quick and painless as possible.

Brewe and her team of four people create all of the site's content in-house. "We want to offer consumers reliable, factual information," she says. "One of our fundamental beliefs as a company is that people—when given accurate information written in plain English—can best decide what's right for them." Because automobile insurance is regulated at the state level, creating accurate and informative content for the Esurance site becomes particularly demanding. "Customers continually let us know that they never understood auto insurance before visiting our site," Brewe says. "As far as I know, no competitor gets as detailed as we do in explaining coverage, especially in terms of coverage differences between states. For example, information provided to a Pennsylvania customer differs from that provided to a visitor from Colorado." Esurance operates in 17 states, including the large markets of California, New York, Texas, Florida, and Ohio.

Driving Traffic to Auto Insurance Content

Much of the new business at Esurance comes through search engines—people who do their own insurance research online. Because of its focus on

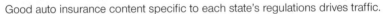

esurance™
A member of the White Mountains Insurance Group

Get Your Auto Insurance Quote
Enter ZIP Code
GO

home   about us   learning center   site map

Main >>

Esurance Features & Benefits >>

Benefits for California
Policyholders >>

Easy California
Car Insurance >>

Save on your California
Auto Insurance Rates >>

Insurance Tips for
California Drivers >>

Understand Your California Insurance Coverage

California living can be expensive— high rent and real estate prices, skyrocketing electric bills, the cost of filling up your car... it seems the list of things that cost you more grows by the minute. California insurance coverage can be expensive too, unless you know how to make the most of your insurance dollar.

It pays to understand insurance no matter what kind of coverage you're in the market for. Along with great rates on auto insurance, Esurance offers features to help you manage your policy and understand more about insurance in general. The Esurance Coverage Counselor explains California insurance coverage requirements to you, and makes it easy for you to know which coverages, limits, or deductibles are right for you.

The amount of auto insurance you need as a California driver depends on a variety of factors. When you choose your coverage limits and deductibles, consider the various risks that you, your passengers, and your auto are likely to face. You also need to consider the assets you own, which your coverage helps protect.

Below are explanations of some of the coverages you'll need to consider as a California driver when you buy your insurance.

- **Bodily injury and property damage**

  Bodily injury and property damage are the only mandatory coverages in California. Keep in mind that if you select limits that are too low, you could be putting yourself at risk financially. For example, if either you or a driver covered by your policy cause a serious injury or accident where damages exceed your limits, you'll be held responsible for the amount above your limits.

Good auto insurance content specific to each state's regulations drives traffic.

creating compelling content optimized for search engines, new traffic to Esurance is steady. "Content helps the search engines find us," Brewe says. "When someone types in information about some auto insurance issue, they find us through search." Esurance makes a large library of insurance-related articles available to visitors and customers alike. "We provide a service to educate consumers," Brewe says. "Because of the ways we advertise online and because of the fact that many Americans now use the Internet to find information, a lot of different people find us. Search turns words into a commodity," she adds.

Brewe cites a number of interesting examples of targeted searches people use to reach the site and how they developed content to optimize those searches. For example, every year hundreds of thousands of collisions with deer and other larger animals occur on U.S. roads. According to Brewe, many people conduct Internet searches for information on the insurance ramifications of their encounter. An article on the Esurance site called *Don't Take a Ride on the Wild Side* discusses auto-deer collisions and what it means for your insurance. When an insurance shopper searches for information on this

Information must be good (or better) than the neighborhood agent.

topic, Esurance's targeted article appears at the top of the results in many popular search engines. Those who don't yet do business with Esurance or aren't currently shopping for insurance will find these articles helpful and may remember them when it comes time to renew their policy. "Driving safety information helps to show we care about consumers," says Brewe. "We educate with helpful information."

Consumer education is a major goal for the site. Brewe and her team write compelling content about many aspects of automobile ownership to make the complex more understandable, all with the goal of helping to sell more auto insurance policies. "We also try to alert people to driving safety, from techniques to equipment," says Brewe. "In short, we strive to offer any consumer a one-stop shop for information on anything that relates to auto insurance, automobiles, and the expenses associated with owning one." For a commodity as boring as auto insurance, Brewe tries to spice things up with some humor. For example, *Got Gas? How to Save Money at the Pump* educates consumers about fuel conservation. And ideas for content can come from customers as well. "We learned from the fact that customers asked about cell phones so we wrote a section on cell phones called *Don't Dial and Drive*," Brewe adds. "Our content explains and expresses who we are. Especially in our driving safety pieces, we try to inject a bit of personality into the information we provide, to educate and make you smile. These are not mutually exclusive goals."

Content Drives Transactions

Of course, all of the content on the Esurance site is designed to get people to purchase auto insurance and a particularly interesting set of useful tools helps make the process quick and painless. Tools might not strike some companies as content, but in fact, interactivity is one of the things that sets Web content apart from its terrestrial counterparts. Companies have vast amounts of information and expertise amassed and can design tools that present this content to consumers in engaging and useful ways.

The Esurance site features an interactive Coverage Counselor tool, into which people enter information about their automobiles, driving habits, and other details. The Coverage Counselor then provides information about which insurance coverage, limits, and deductibles would be right for their particular situation. According to Brewe, many consumers find the Coverage Counselor very useful as they plan coverage. "Our Coverage Counselor is designed to give recommendations," Brewe says. "We tell folks that, if they have an auto club membership, there's no need to buy towing coverage from us. We also help people realize the costs and benefits associated with having more or less coverage." Esurance supplies the Coverage Counselor tool to partner Web sites to help drive interested people back to Esurance. According to Brewe, this form of syndicated content is valuable to users. "People get useful recommendations that they can then use when they get a quote from us," she says.

The interactive Auto Insurance Quote tool is the most important part of the site because it's where the actual purchase transaction starts. For that reason it occupies the prime real estate of the site's home page. According to Brewe, 70 percent of consumers decide on auto insurance based on price alone. "We capture interest when they are renewing," she says. "We can sell at a lower cost because we have automated so much, such as printing the proof of insurance card online."

Brewe and the Esurance team devote considerable resources to make the interactive tools user-friendly. "People want a more convenient auto insurance experience, especially those who prefer to transact online," Brewe says.

esurance
Insurance. Only Better.

| home | about us | learning center | contact us |

Planning Tools   24/7 | Customer Service & Claims Handling | Call 1-800-926-6012

Use our auto insurance Coverage Counselor planning tool to get suggestions about which insurance coverages, limits, or deductibles may be right for you. Just answer the following questions and we'll provide you with some suggestions for your auto insurance plan.

▶ **Information about you and your household**

1. What's your marital status?	Select ▾
2. Do you have children who live at home with you?	Select ▾
3. If you have children who live at home, how many are licensed to drive?	
4. If you have children, how many of your children are 18 or older?	
5. Do you own or rent your home?	○ Own ○ Rent
6. If you own your home, what is its approximate value?	Select ▾

The Coverage Counselor helps consumers choose the best insurance for them.

"Content on pages in our quote and purchase processes get people through our Web site." A major consideration is speed. "We want to provide the fastest auto insurance quotes on the Web to insurance shoppers," says Brewe. "We want to turn those 'quoters' into policyholders, making our online purchase experience as quick and painless as possible," she says. Most customers can fill out the online forms, get a quote, and make a purchase complete—with printable insurance cards—in less time than it takes to drive to an insurance agency.

The extent to which Brewe and her team focus on content details is remarkable. "We even write the error messages to help ensure that people have all the information they need to buy a policy," she says. "These words in particular are a huge driver of business. You can find that one improperly written error message causes bailouts on a certain page to increase ten-fold. Without proper instructions about what information to enter, or what to do next, a customer would get lost, leave our site, and never become a policy-holder." Brewe feels strongly that it's necessary to carefully think out each and every word on the site. Nothing can be left to chance. "E-commerce companies that leave something as important as instructions, error messages, and the like to nonwriters must not mind losing tons of sales," she insists.

Ensuring Compelling Content

"Our content is written to attract and explain," says Brewe. The Esurance corporate communications team serves as the company's internal creative services agency and writes all of the content themselves. "We're a very small shop," says Brewe. The team includes four people: Brewe, an editor, a producer who publishes content, and a graphic designer. "I still write a lot of what appears," Brewe says. "My editor and I have written every word since the company started. I'm really proud of the fact that this small, very efficient team is able to do what some 40-person-strong shops couldn't pull off. Every word and picture about Esurance—internal communications, online and offline advertising, Web content, and design—is done by us."

According to Brewe, much of the content starts with research. "We consult internal resources by interviewing associates in claims or insurance operations or external resources by reviewing census data or FBI crime statistics," she says. "We analyze underwriting guidelines to get details about specific states' auto products and discounts, then we fact-check. If in doubt, we'll fact-check again."

Content goes through a rigorous editorial process to ensure accuracy and a good, consistent writing style; then it gets posted on the Esurance site. "We do our content updates in special weekly releases solely designed to keep all the content fresh," Brewe says. "As a content creation process, it's very methodical, in part because of the technical nature of the subject matter. However, the process also involves a high degree of craftsmanship."

The Esurance site takes a utilitarian commodity like auto insurance and strives to make it educate, inform, and hold a reader's interest. "The role of words on Esurance is very cut and dry—they explain the promise that a customer is buying," Brewe says. For example, "If you hit your neighbor's house while driving, property damage coverage will cover that expense. Obviously, the words on our site also help someone follow instructions to get to the next step, and hopefully, buy a policy." But the rather dry, technical nature of the commodity can be made interesting according to Brewe. "We try to soften with humor, by using conversational speech—abandoning formal writing conventions by using contractions, employing idiomatic expressions—and by using customer comments when we talk about Esurance. Reminding our customers that humans are behind and involved with Esurance is vital."

Brewe clearly knows how to write both useful and interesting content that holds a reader's attention, but knows that she can't go off the deep end either. "Of course, we are an insurance company, so we can't be as funky as we would be if we were writing for a lipstick company," she says. "Ultimately, no one wants an insurance company to come off like the class clown. One of the ways we convey the requisite gravity is quality writing. We break convention only when it shows an underlying humanity or makes it easier to read something online." The bottom line, according to Brewe, is to know your audience. "People deserve to be exposed to the quality of a well-constructed phrase, even when that phrase is about something as potentially boring as auto insurance," she says.

The Esurance site also makes use of customer comments. "We get unsolicited e-mails from customers every day," Brewe says. The content team obtains permission from the writers to use the comments and then posts them on a special section of the site. "We let the customers know that they're starring on our Web site," Brewe says. "They forward it around to their family and friends. This is a really nice, low-key, authentic way to market Esurance, and it actually says a lot about our company in terms of our responsiveness

esurance
Insurance. Only Better.

About Us

Our customers talk about Esurance car insurance...

Would you describe your car insurance as cool, first-rate, or pleasant? Esurance customers do!

Unlike a lot of insurance companies, we don't spend money on fancy focus groups or funny mascots. We think that one of the best ways for folks to learn more about our company is from our visitors and policyholders. People like you.

So don't take our word for it. Every day, we get phone calls, emails, and letters from our customers about how happy they are with their Esurance Experience. Here's what they have to say about us.

Even car insurance companies like being cool, "pieces of cake" & a pleasure...
Though that's a mouthful (pardon the pun) these are some of our favorite customer comments. Glenn from Colorado Springs, Colorado wrote, "Painless and smooth... I am a computer professional and this site is done well... no... it is COOL! Thanks for the experience of a site well done." (That one made our day. Who doesn't want to be cool?)

Chris, from Sunnyvale, California, let us know that "Getting a quote from Esurance was a piece of cake." Bet you've never said that when you shopped for car insurance on other Web sites.

And Robert, from Laguna Niguel, California, thought our Web site was actually a pleasure! He told us, "I have been trying to make some comparisons over the last several days. I have tried several sites and found yours to be one of the very few that is truly user friendly. It actually does everything it says it will. Thanks so much for the great site and the opportunity to conduct this in the comfort of my own home. You have done an excellent job and it was a pleasure to use." (That's why we're here, but it's nice to have our customers notice!)

Customers send their comments and Esurance turns their comments into site content.

to customer feedback and how much we value it. Word-of-mouth comments like 'Hey, I finally understand my stupid insurance policy. Check out Esurance,' said to a friend, is extraordinarily important to our business."

Brewe is keenly aware that the site and its content is the only customer-facing entity to sell the Esurance product. Without the site there would be no company. "A Web site, in order to be truly valuable to consumers, has to perform the way consumers expect," she says. "For an online company, fulfilling on these functional and information-seeking requirements is essential. Because we are an online auto insurance company, we cannot view our Web site as an interactive brochure. It has to do more, and it has to work. If we failed to attract and engage our visitors and customers, we would not be in business."

Cashing In

Brewe and her team have created the content required to make Esurance a success. "In 1999 we were incorporated," she says. "We launched in 2000 and had no customers then. We've grown to 120,000 policyholders today." A major component for continued growth in insurance or any renewal business is customer retention. "We price as low as possible, retain customers, and grow quickly," Brewe says. "It's easier for us than with big traditional companies because we're all automated." As Esurance retains its existing customers and adds new ones, the financial aspects of the business become more and more important according to Brewe. With the content that Brewe and her team created as the driver, Esurance has grown written premiums from under $5 million in 2000 to $200 million in 2004 (up 70 percent from 2003). "In insurance, you can't just grow, grow, grow without thinking of things like loss ratios and insurance fraud," she says. "As a writer for an insurance company, you have to be particularly cautious about whom you're attracting, what you're promising to folks, and how all that might impact the bottom line—not just at the end of 2004, but in 2008," she says.

Being responsible for all of the content on a successful auto insurance Web site, Brewe has many things to look back on with pride. "I define success as participating in building a business from the first word on up," Brewe says. "It's strange to reflect on the fact that my editor and I—two women—wrote all the words you now see for a multi-million dollar company. Not many people can say they do something they love and get to help build a company, creating jobs for hundreds of people around the country."

CHAPTER SIX

Aerosmith

Content for Extreme Fans

> ➤ **Organization**
> Aerosmith
> www.aerosmith.com, www.aeroforceone.com

> ➤ **Interviewed**
> Michael Lundgren, General Manager of the
> Aerosmith Online Fan Community

What's For Sale

With more than 100 million albums sold worldwide over 30 years, Aerosmith owes much of its ongoing success to a loyal fan base. At the Aero Force One site, fans have access to exclusive content, merchandise, and opportunities to meet the band in person.

What's So Interesting

Fans make the band. Aerosmith is keenly aware of the importance of its most loyal supporters and provides a separate Web site devoted expressly to them. With content not found anywhere else, those who choose to become members of the Aero Force One fan club are treated as part of a unique family.

Why You Should Care

Aerosmith has perfected the art of locating and courting its most loyal and profitable customers and treating them to special experiences not available to the average listener. When you're in the Aero Force One club, you have access to the best tickets and the ability to download exclusive photos, audio, and video clips. Best of all, membership perks include opportunities to get backstage and meet the band members. Aerosmith uses its general site as a portal to allow fans the opportunity to join at the premium membership level. Anyone who relies on customer or fan loyalty can learn from Aerosmith's tremendous success.

A erosmith has been rocking for more than 30 years. Throughout the band's journey, it has cultivated an incredibly loyal fan base, many of whom have stuck with them through good times as well as periods of waning popularity and even breakup. Aerosmith endures year after year as one of the most exciting forces in American rock music. The band—Steven Tyler (vocals), Joe Perry (guitar), Brad Whitford (guitar), Tom Hamilton (bass), and Joey Kramer (drums)—has transcended generation gaps and spearheaded some of the most important trends in pop music: from groundbreaking early '70s heavy metal to the invention of the power-ballad to the first fusion of rock and hip-hop.

Unlike many bands, Aerosmith directly controls its various Web sites and official fan club, using them as vehicles to build and maintain loyalty with its most rabid followers. Fans choosing to participate at the premium level are rewarded with unique and exciting opportunities to get closer to their idols through Web content, visits backstage, and the ultimate fan experience: opportunities to meet band members.

Most bands couldn't be bothered with something as mundane as a Web site. The typical "official" band site lacks depth and only offers superficial content dished up by an overworked publicist. Most band sites are constructed as little more than an afterthought, thrown together by the record label to promote the latest album and tour.

At the other end of the spectrum, sites serving true fans often spring forth from the fans themselves. An individual might put up some photos and essays on a new band as a labor of love and all of a sudden that site becomes the *de facto* hub for every interested fan. These many and varied "unofficial" sites sport interesting and exciting content but with a lack of band or record label involvement, they have an outsider feel and can sometimes actually work counter to the bands' wants and needs.

Not the Same Old Song and Dance

Enter Aerosmith (stage left). This band controls its own sites and, as a result, has created an unusual hybrid that contains the best elements of official and unofficial band sites. Visitors to the main Aerosmith.com site find a well-designed homepage with a solid set of functional free content. For those who want a bit of information, such as tour dates, this basic site suffices, but Aerosmith.com is just the beginning. The band went much further by creating a separate site for its most extreme fans. Aeroforceone.com is where the real action happens in the form of original content about and—even cooler—*by*

Aerosmith. Michael Lundgren, General Manager of the Aerosmith Online Fan Community, explains the reasoning behind the two sites, "The goal of the band is to provide its self-selected and most ardent fans a direct connection to the band."

Links to the fan site appear prominently on the main Aerosmith site and anyone can easily click through to Aero Force One. Aero Force One doesn't rely on overt promotion or the mystery-factor to get people involved, rather it functions on the assumption that if you're a fan, you'll find your way from the main site. The main site and Aero Force One share some basic design elements, but the extreme fan site has a more extreme design and, of course, features much more extensive content; expanded content includes exclusive reports from the road, video, news, photos, and interviews with the band. A typical report might include details about the band's visit to a radio station for a promotional interview prior to a concert or might tell about a visit to a favorite Mexican restaurant. These reports of real band experiences allow fans to bond with their idols. "We provide much more content than the record label

The Aerosmith main site has basic content for those who want to learn about the band.

sites," adds Lundgren. "Because Aero Force One is band-operated, the band has more creative license over the content and its presentation than with a record label site."

Aero Force One includes a wide variety of free content to satisfy fans and keep them coming back for more and maybe to upgrade to a fee-based membership. Unlike many rock band sites that stagnate, new content is regularly posted to Aero Force One. "Content is continually updated and tweaked, even between album releases and tours," says Lundgren. "Our model is based on providing the brand identity and connection for those people who self-select Aerosmith as one of their favorite bands. Our job is to provide Aerosmith content—video, news, fan reviews, fan art, fan photos, plus features—from the artists themselves."

Once fans find their way to the Aero Force One site, they have an option of joining the Aero Force One fan club at $29.95 per year for the Gold Level or $59.95 for the Platinum Level, which includes additional offline content, such as photos and DVDs, mailed to the member's home. With membership, fans are able to access richer site content, purchase unique merchandise, and get

Aero Force One includes exclusive content for the rabid fan.

the first crack at the best tickets for shows. "Part of the mission of Web site content is to recruit members," says Lundgren. "For example, there are 12 photos on the public site but if you want to see the full 600 photos, you need to become a member. We also provide a newsletter for members-only and we want people to opt in. We have very high open and click-through rates on our newsletters." The newsletters are written by Lundgren's staff and provide an e-mail push of the content found on the site. For example, when the band played the pregame show in the 2004 Super Bowl, a special newsletter delivered the news into fan inboxes with links to photos and reports on the site.

The Aero Force One newsletter serves as subscription-based marketing and, as with any subscription business model, the key to success is retention, so the Aerosmith fan site relies on members renewing year after year. The fan club uses a number of tools and techniques to reward the most loyal fans with special deals just for them. "Seniority is important," adds Lundgren. "For each year you are in the club, you grow in seniority. Some people have been in the club for 20 years, well before we went online." One of the biggest seniority perks is ticket selection. A 10-year member will receive seats in front of a five-year member. With a few years seniority, members sit in the first 20 or so rows at concerts.

Walk This Way

Of course, rock and roll always comes back to the music—in particular, live music. Aerosmith has been touring on and off for 30 years but in the years since its induction into the Rock and Roll Hall of Fame in 2001, the band has been a touring machine, with stops at the Super Bowl, Soccer's World Cup, the American Music Awards, Dick Clark's New Years Eve show, and other signature events. "In the past few years, Aerosmith tours have been among the most successful," says Lundgren. With millions of tickets sold, Lundgren wanted to create a way for the most loyal fans to have even more: The Velvet Rope Experience.

Because brokers, venues, and promoters control tickets for most concerts, the only way to sit up front at most shows is to pay big bucks to one of these ticket sellers. Aerosmith is at the leading edge of major acts that have taken control of premium ticketing—offering them to Aero Force One members. "I invented the fans experience program," says Lundgren. The ultimate way to enjoy an Aerosmith concert, the Velvet Rope Experience, is only available to Aero Force One members and can be booked at Aeroforceone.com. "Aerosmith provides the experience and we give fans a way to avoid the risk

Backstage! Only for Aero Force One members.

of scalping a ticket. The seats are in the first five rows, they get a backstage tour, they go through the dressing rooms, they hear the sound checks, and often they meet the band members themselves. They stand on the stage before the show and scream into the microphone," he continues. "It's all very real. It's the total experience as if they were relatives of the tour manager. There are a fixed number of participants at each show, usually around 50 people maximum. There's a lot of value for people."

For $595 per person, per show (plus the requisite annual membership fee), fans get a laminated backstage pass and ultimate bragging rights. With Aerosmith playing as many as 100 dates per year, this program generates more than goodwill; it makes serious money. Fifty people per show at $600 per person over the course of a year's touring yields some 3 million extra dollars in revenue per year for the band. But the experience for the fan can be incalculable. "Aerosmith, particularly Steven Tyler, is very approachable," adds Lundgren. "They are hip across time. For many people who go on the experience, they meet their heroes in person. We have people who break down in tears." And of course, the viral marketing aspect is huge; 5,000 people who've been backstage each year tell all their friends. And Aeroforceone.com features a section where fans can post photos taken with the band along with gushing reviews of their backstage experience, further fueling the viral flame.

Roadies, Managers, and the Chef

"Aero Force One provides a voyeuristic experience of the band for fans," says Lundgren. "Some content is provided directly by the band, by roadies, by the band's personal chef, and tour manager." The chef doubling as a writer for the band fan site might seem a little odd. But the extent of club members' interest in anything personal about their heroes is insatiable, so the chef's musings provide a tantalizing taste of the insider info fans crave.

"Content is generated by us, by the band, by the Aerosmith 'family,' by the fans, and via press releases," says Lundgren. Tom Hamilton (Aerosmith's bass player) likes to write for the site and the band gives exclusive interviews for the site and for the newsletter. There are also "John B Road Reports" that are written by an assistant tour manager for the band. Additional content is fan-generated, including extensive material contributed directly by fans for the site. "We

Thursday the guys blew the roof off of the old Forum. The band has played here many times. A lot of guys from other bands were in attendance such as Billy Duffy from the Cult, Bruce Kulick from KISS, some Skid Row guys and up and coming rocker John Mayer. Joe again joined KISS for "Strutter." It's scary because he looked way to comfortable in those 7 inch leather heels.

After the show Steven, Tom and Joey headed over to Russ Irwin's house in the hills for an after show bash. Tommy Thayer from KISS was there along with Paul McCartney side man Brian Ray and jewelry designer Loree Rodkin.

After a well deserved day off on Friday the guys put a fork in the tour of the Summer/Fall. I remember someone telling me last April that the word on the street was that these two mega bands with mega egos won't make it past 3 shows before sparks would fly and we ain't talking pyro here. Well, 60 some odd shows later and it looked like they could go on for 60 more.

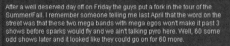

After the Fresno show both bands jumped on their jets and headed home. KISS with Russ Irwin along for the ride took the 45 minute flight back to Los Angeles while the rest of us flew 5 hours back east to cooler climates.

After Christmas some of the guys took a little time off. Steven and family went to the Bahamas while Tom and Joey will head to Florida. Joe spent a very cold windy afternoon rooting the New England Patriots on in their last regular season home game against The Buffalo Bills on Dec. 27th. Joe hung out in the Parking lot with all 4 of his sons and BBQ'd every kind of meat you could think of before the game. Who said these guys were vegetarians?

Hopefully the Patriots will still be playing when the guys head off to Houston later this month.

Exclusive content for fans—reports from the tour from roadies and even the band's personal chef.

run contests, such as a Super Bowl contest, and we use that as a way to get people to opt-in to our mailing lists," says Lundgren. To enter many of the contests, fans must submit content to the site—like pictures of their Aerosmith tattoos.

A Band and its Fanatic Fans

"The Web site is the gathering place for fans," continues Lundgren. "This is the inside track. You'll feel closer to the band than those who just bought the CD or went to the show." And fans can also express their devotion by contributing content to the site including sharing photos, writing reviews of concerts, or creating original artwork for display.

"Fan-to-fan reviews are one of the best ways to communicate because they are credible," says Lundgren. "The community of Aerosmith fanatics is a real exciting animal that's kind of wild, edgy, and fun to be around. It's a real kick," he continues. "The band has survived the test of time because of its fans. One of the best ways to generate content is through the fans—they are the real deal."

Lundgren and his team review and select fan material that's appropriate for the site. He explains the process: "Fan content goes to specific e-mail links

Fan generated content—online gallery with portraits of band members.

and we pick the most interesting ones to post. We also run contests to help generate fan content." As with any large community of diverse people with shared interests, there are stories of all kinds. "We get letters from fanatics and from those who were touched or inspired in some way," says Lundgren. "We've gotten letters from people who are terminally ill who use Aerosmith as an inspiration." Other opportunities for fans to participate, like message board discussions and blogs, are also available to members of the community.

Aerosmith, the Brand

When the band is on the road or when a big event or major appearance is pending, the urgency to keep the site updated increases dramatically. "The tempo of adding content is real fast," says Lundgren. "I'll get something in the afternoon that needs to go out and we turn it around very quickly."

At the same time, because of the band's commitment to its Web sites, the process for adding new content can be complex. Lundgren says, "We have a high level of content approvals and a set process. For many parts of the site, we need to get band approval so the cycle can become long sometimes." The attention to detail pays off, asserts Lundgren. "The bands that have paid attention to the brand, like Aerosmith, have done very well over time."

$$\$\$\$\$\$\$\$\$\$\$\$\$\$\$\$\$ \text{ Cashing In } \$\$\$\$\$\$\$\$\$\$\$\$\$\$\$\$$$

Besides the millions of dollars that come in from Aeroforceone.com for exclusive fan items including membership, merchandise, and the Velvet Rope Experience, Lundgren also measures success through paid membership levels. "We've been growing 50 percnet to 100 percent yearly since I've been working with the band. We look to continue that growth going forward but we have a ways to go. We're in continuous improvement mode all the time. We look at how many people click links, open rates on the newsletters, and so on."

It might seem to casual observers that a rock band fan site would be easy to build and maintain; you just put up exclusive content—like photos, essays, and interviews—and you're done. But there's a world of difference between a rock site and an extreme fan site. Lundgren clearly thinks content needs to be much deeper. He worries about Aerosmith as a brand and the site's role in the band's ongoing success. "It's important to maintain the pedestal that fans have put the rock star on," he says. "The members of Aerosmith are immanently cool. The mystique is important. The role of our editorial function is to guard and maintain who Aerosmith is; it's part of our job."

Lundgren must balance fans' demand for exclusive content about their rock star idols with the possibility that the site might reveal too much and deflate the myth. The band's rock star status must be maintained at all costs. So how do you know where to draw the line? Easy, according to Lundgren, "Content is like a woman's dress, it needs to be long enough to cover the subject but short enough to keep it interesting."

CHAPTER SEVEN

The Wall Street Journal Online

Free Content Sells Subscriptions

➤ **Organization**
The Wall Street Journal Online
www.wsj.com

➤ **Interviewed**
L. Gordon Crovitz, Senior Vice President, Dow Jones &
Company, and President, Electronic Publishing

What's For Sale

The Wall Street Journal Online may well be the most successful paid subscription
news site on the Web. Published by Dow Jones & Company, the Online Journal provides in-depth business news and financial information, with insight and analysis,
along with breaking business and technology news from around the world—24 hours
a day, seven days a week.

What's So Interesting

With more than 712,000 subscribers worldwide paying $79 per year ($39 a year for
the *Wall Street Journal* print subscribers), the Online Journal cashes in despite the fact
that the vast majority of newspaper sites are free. As the debate about free content has
raged, more than half of the early subscribers who signed up in 1996 happily remain
Online Journal subscribers today. The Online Journal also extends the Wall Street
Journal brand to new users.

Why You Should Care

The Wall Street Journal Online Network includes a number of free content sites to
attract and interest potential subscribers to the Online Journal. With content-specific free
sites such as CareerJournal.com, OpinionJournal.com, StartupJournal.com, RealEstate
Journal.com, and CollegeJournal.com, the network serves as an ideal tool to gain the
interest of those who are the target demographic of the Online Journal, but who haven't
yet signed up for a subscription. Any current or wannabe subscription-based content site
can learn from the Online Journal's techniques, but even a site that simply wants to drive
more traffic across sites should pay attention to the Journal's techniques.

T he Wall Street Journal Online at WSJ.com, arguably the largest paid subscription site online, is a true Web content success story. While the vast majority of online newspaper sites provide all content for free (and make money exclusively by selling advertising and site sponsorships), the Online Journal has always focused on selling subscriptions as well as generating ad revenue, just like its print counterpart.

At the same time, the Wall Street Journal Online Network includes sites intended to give browsers a tantalizing free sample of the Online Journal's premium content. The network of free sites employs clever interest-based marketing techniques to build communities and to establish long-term relationships with users. The Online Journal provides an ideal case study for Web marketers, particularly those with current subscription models or perhaps wanting to convert free sites to subscriptions. By providing the right amounts of free content and organizing it intelligently, the Online Journal drives subscription revenue.

In the early days of the Internet and through the dot-com boom of the late 1990s, the Web world gave away free content and made money selling advertisements. Thousands of new companies were born of venture capital money to exploit this "new economy" business model, while pundits and consumers alike scoffed at "old economy dinosaurs" that insisted on sticking to what were seen at the time as quaint old-fashioned ways of making money. Business managers at the *Wall Street Journal* never bought the "new economy" hype. "We knew professionals would pay for content because many organizations were already paying millions a year for content in other forms," says L. Gordon Crovitz, Senior Vice President of Dow Jones & Company and President of Electronic Publishing. "High-value content retains high value in whatever medium." Crovitz describes the Journal's thinking as it prepared to launch its online version, "In the mid 1990s, when we looked for an electronic way to deliver the content of the *Wall Street Journal*, we went at it with the assumption that we would charge for the high-value content. It's a combination of the expectation of the brand and because, for business and financial news, it may be easier to justify the expense." While the rest of the world insisted that content would always be free on the Internet, Crovitz and his team resisted. "We've never understood why publishers give away content in one medium and charge in others," he says.

With over 712,000 paid subscribers, the Online Journal has been successful enough that, if it were ranked as a print newspaper, it would enjoy the seventh largest circulation in the United States—ahead of such papers as the

Chicago Tribune and the *New York Post*. And at $79 per year ($39 a year for the *Wall Street Journal* print subscribers), the Online Journal commands a substantial revenue stream. "We're pleased, but it's just a start," says Crovitz. He's gunning for the Online Journal to reach circulation numbers lofty enough to put it ahead of such print newspapers as the *Washington Post,* number five at over 700,000, and the *Los Angeles Times*, ranked fourth at nearly one million. Then only print editions of the *New York Times, USA Today,* and the *Wall Street Journal* itself would have larger circulations.

How did the Online Journal grow its impressive subscriber base? While high-quality content certainly attracts a fair number, all of those paid Web-content subscribers had to come from somewhere—and that's where free content comes into the equation. "We have a public page with the Online Journal," says Crovitz. "People go to the WSJ.com home page and they can look at headlines much like they would see the print paper at a newsstand." But Crovitz and his team know that just a peek at the front page isn't enough to draw in subscribers. "There is also some content that is free to give people a taste of the Journal for those who aren't print subscribers," he says.

As on a newsstand, you can look at the front page of the Online Journal for free.

As a newswire and newspaper publisher, Dow Jones has no problem creating compelling content for its free and subscriptions sites in the Online Journal Network. Choosing from more than 1 million items a day at its disposal, the Online Journal adds more than 1,000 news stories and other articles to the site per day. The Online Journal is published by a dedicated news staff of more than 60 editors and reporters who draw on the Dow Jones network of nearly 1,700 news staff—one of the largest networks of business and financial journalists in the world. While the problem isn't content creation, deciding what content is free and what should be subscription-only is a challenge. The idea is to give potential subscribers an enticing sampling of what's inside. "Our experience is that many subscribers originally subscribed to read about a particular topic or a story," Crovitz says. "For many people, a particular story or trend leads them to subscribe then they continue to use the site after they've read articles." The key to cashing in at the right moment, of course, is to give people the ideal item for free so they're compelled to want the full subscription.

Since anyone can read the headlines and article-openers on the Online Journal's home page, lots of nonsubscribers hit the site regularly for a peek at front page news. Therefore, the company uses specific strategies to convert this type of visitor to paid subscriptions. "There are marketing techniques we use for visitors who come to the page with great regularity," Crovitz says. "They will get unique messages based on the frequency of visits to the free site." For example, offers of a two-week trial subscription or discounts on the first several months' subscription might appear.

Selling Subscriptions with Free Content

The Online Journal Network of service-oriented sites serves as a huge referral service for the Online Journal. Content-specific free sites—including CareerJournal.com, OpinionJournal.com, StartupJournal.com, RealEstate Journal.com, and CollegeJournal.com—serve as ideal tools to gain the interest of those who are the target demographic of the Online Journal. The sites leverage the power of building communities of like-minded people by providing specific information on a particular subject. This interest-based targeting is what many other types of sites do in the B2B and B2C space, particularly sites focused on e-commerce, which segment users into a defined category so they can be reached more effectively. While the Online Journal Network sites are free, they are advertising and sponsorship supported. This provides an additional revenue source for the Online Journal at little additional content-creation cost because the Journal can leverage its massive content repository by breaking out and offering content that will appeal to these specific groups. About 70 percent of Online Journal revenue comes from subscriptions and the remaining 30 percent from advertising and sponsorships. As a marketing and promotional tool, the Online Journal Network delivers information to huge numbers of people. In a press release dated January 27, 2005, the company reported more than 6 million average monthly unique visitors and over 83 million average monthly page views to the Journal Network.

"CareerJournal.com is the largest site for higher end jobs," says Crovitz. "There is free content, but much of the value of the site is other services such as posting resumes and learning which companies might have jobs open" (some of which bear a fee). CareerJournal.com targets senior executives at the Director, Vice President, and higher levels. The market includes many professionals who don't mind charging services onto a credit card if they think they can advance their careers. The CareerJournal.com site includes a vast amount of free content, including job hunting and career advice, salary information, resume services, ads from companies that are hiring, and other interactive content.

Individuals in the thick of job search mode often spend hours on the CareerJournal.com site for weeks or even months at a time. During this very stressful period in life, the hope is that they come to rely on CareerJournal.com

The Online Journal Network of free, service-focused sites such as CareerJournal.com funnel potential subscribers to the Online Journal.

for valuable information throughout the long and sometimes daunting process. Undoubtedly, they would also remember if the content found on CareerJournal.com led to a lucrative job offer and might be inclined to subscribe to the Online Journal when up and running in a new position. Or, given the Journal's expertise in this aspect of information, they might give the remainder of the sites' content a for-fee run to see if it similarly impacts other aspects of their career. "Subscriptions from the network of sites are important channels," says Crovitz. Thus, the Online Journal relies on its free content to help develop long-term relationships that will eventually pay off.

Another member of the Online Journal Network of free sites is OpinionJournal.com and its popular Best of the Web Today column, which provides free summaries of editorial page content from the *Wall Street Journal* and links to the Online Journal. "Best of the Web Today was started a few years ago with modest expectations," Crovitz says. "But the amount of traffic is remarkable. It is tremendously popular, with hundreds of thousands of people subscribed to the free daily Best of the Web Today e-mail. We use it to

Best of the Web Today on OpinionJournal.com not only helps sell subscriptions to the Online Journal, it also has its own Political Diary subscription at $3.95 per month.

introduce people to the editorial page and the unusual content of the *Wall Street Journal*. We want users of Opinion Journal to become subscribers of Online Journal," says Crovitz. "There's a set of people for whom the editorial page is important."

The OpinionJournal.com site has also served as a bit of an experimental area, according to Crovitz. "We launched Political Diary, which is $3.95 per month, as our first subscription service from OpinionJournal.com," he says. A political Diary subscription includes a daily e-mail with summaries and links to detailed content and it provides a low-cost introduction to the network's content, which may eventually lead a subscriber to subscribe to the Online Journal as well.

Not Your Father's Newspaper

When the Online Journal first launched, management thought that the primary readers would be those who take the print newspaper. While there are many thousands of people who subscribe to both the print and online versions, 60 percent of Online Journal subscribers are not print subscribers. "It was a surprise that there are so many who don't take the print version," says Crovitz. "We look at these people as new subscribers to the *Wall Street Journal* franchise. The Online Journal has brought in new subscribers who are demographically similar to print subscribers but are about a decade younger," Crovitz adds. The Online Journal has lowered the average age of overall *Wall Street Journal* readers and increased the lifetime value of a loyal subscriber to the Journal franchise. "But online subscribers are different," Crovitz says. "They like to get their news online vs. the serendipity of a print paper."

Interestingly, the lower average age of the Online Journal subscriber has helped to solve an issue the print publication struggled with, according to Crovitz. "One issue we faced for many years, decades really," he says, "is we know that when people graduate from university they tend not to subscribe to The Wall Street Journal newspaper. Our research showed that in their early career, people are focused on their job function and their industry and they don't have time for the full print publication." Using the power of interest-based targeting made simple on the Web, the Online Journal was set up perfectly to appeal to the younger demographic, says Crovitz. "Having recognized that," he says, "we can use the Online Journal to reach out to the people who value the content." The company produces industry editions of Online Journal that couldn't be offered in print. Pricing for the service and the content found in the industry editions of the Online Journal are the same as the base service. They key difference is the editorial organization and the content of the industry-specific daily e-mails.

"The first was Health Industry Edition," says Crovitz. "These are marketed through trade organizations and industry groups." The Health Industry Edition offers analysis, breaking news, and commentary from top health industry journalists. "The Health Industry Edition is marketed to those who would use a vertical trade publication," Crovitz says. "Subscribers get news from the Online Journal edited with your industry in mind and it includes online-only content not found in print."

The Media & Marketing Edition, launched in 2003, is designed for professionals in the advertising, marketing, entertainment, and media industries. Subscribers to this and other industry editions also get access to the full content of the Online Journal. "Many thousands of subscribers have come on," says Crovitz. "And just as we've hoped, many younger people have subscribed including people even younger than Online Journal. In a way, it's using content to drive subscriptions by delivering the content in the context of how people want it. The Online Journal provides usefulness and a customer

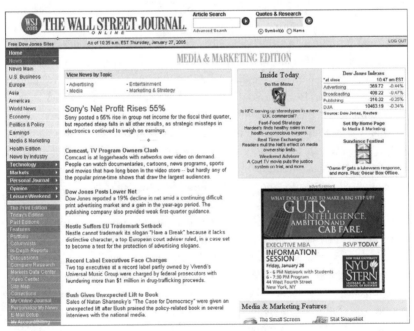

Industry editions, such as the Media & Marketing Edition, help to attract a younger demographic.

experience to access just the news that they need when they want it," adds Crovitz. "Of course, it is economical to create industry editions online when we wouldn't be able to do it in print."

$$$$$$$$$$$$$$$$$ **Cashing In** $$$$$$$$$$$$$$$$$

The Online Journal certainly proves that people will pay for content on the Internet that they'd pay for offline as well. But it is the thoughtful ways that Crovitz and his team organize the content—both free and subscription-based—that allows them to cash in to an extent that many traditional publishers (not to mention other types of businesses) only dream about "The issue for Dow Jones is not 'do we have a problem with content'," says Crovitz. "We publish a million pages of content a day in our online properties. The issue is 'how we deliver the content in the way that subscribers find more useful.' If you have significant content, it's more important to deliver that content in context, in an efficient way, so readers don't suffer from information overload."

It's difficult to get a precise handle on the revenue to the *Wall Street Journal* franchise that generates from the Online Journal Network. A good proxy is to look at the Dow Jones consumer electronic publishing, which reports somewhere around $20 million in revenue per quarter. Besides significant revenue from subscriptions, advertising accounts for 30 percent of the total revenue. Although the Online Journal charges a subscription fee, like a print newspaper, total revenue figures include subscription, advertising, and sponsorship.

So what about all those publishers that sell print subscriptions but give away valuable content online for free? Speaking from success, Crovitz offers his view: "Publishers must have more faith in their content's value," he says. "The Internet made many publishers get off on the wrong foot with free content. Many more publishers will pursue subscription models over time I think. All publishers need to figure it out."

PART 2

Business-to-Business

CHAPTER EIGHT

Alcoa

Content Drives Large Deals

➤ **Organization**
Alcoa
www.alcoa.com

➤ **Interviewed**
Kevin Lowery, Director of Corporate Communications

What's For Sale

The Alcoa corporate Web site provides extensive content—with all roads leading directly to the ability to conduct transactions online, a rarity for a B2B site, especially one with this level of product and client diversity.

What's So Interesting

As a large multinational company involved in all things aluminum, Alcoa's materials are used worldwide in products large and small, from aircrafts to beverage cans. While Alcoa brands consumer products (such as Reynolds Wrap aluminum foil), the company relies on its Web site to help promote and sell its B2B products.

Why You Should Care

Alcoa's content helps the company sell and the results are measurable. This successful approach is uncommon among B2B sites selling high-priced items, particularly for Alcoa's fellow Fortune 500 companies, whose sites are often little more than online brochures. B2B firms that want to facilitate online transactions can learn form Alcoa's success.

S ay you're responsible for product development at a computer manufacturer and you want to go to market with a hip new model. Your design
team looks at all aspects of the market and hits on what it sees as a key product differentiator: using something other than the standard beige box that
every manufacturer uses. Maybe some sleek brushed aluminum would make
the new computer stand out? The marketers at Alcoa want to make it simple
for your team to choose aluminum and they have the mettle to use content to
sell it to you. The Alcoa site provides a variety of useful content, above and
beyond detailed specifications, that is targeted at those responsible for designing and building thousands of diverse products in markets all over the world.

The Alcoa site gives appropriate entry points and links to facilitate browsing or
quickly locate specific content.

Alcoa is all things aluminum. The company is a leader at all stages of the aluminum production cycle (technology, mining, refining, smelting, fabricating, and recycling) and it sells materials for use in products from the very large (airplanes) to the very small (electrical conductors), serving customers all over the world. As a product component, aluminum challenges Alcoa's marketers and salespeople to be creative and one of the ways they excel is with Web site content.

It All Starts with Dirt

Alcoa's home page does an excellent job of welcoming both the person who knows exactly what they want (for example, to find information in French about Alcoa's businesses in Belgium) as well as a potential customer who wants to browse within categories (say, aerospace components). It's noteworthy that the Alcoa home page organizes content in several ways by using tabs across the top as well as pull down menus and "headlines." It features information about the company's environmental activities and provides a convenient place to learn about aluminum manufacturing from the ground up

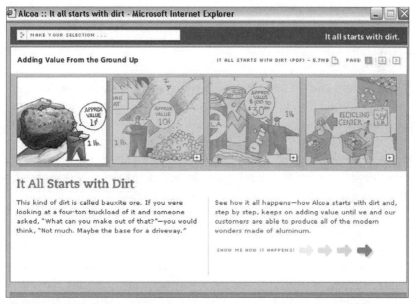

Content on the Alcoa site ranges from the very basic to extremely complex and detailed.

(check out 'It All Starts with Dirt' under 'About Alcoa') in addition to product information.

Kevin Lowery, Director of Corporate Communications, helms the global Alcoa Web site. "Alcoa.com is our face to the outside world," he says. "We provide the information you require." But Alcoa is different from many large corporate sites because its extensive content is organized to drive browsers to places where they can interact with the company. Lowery explains the dual goals of the corporate site: "One is to facilitate the transfer of information on the company, our businesses, our products, our management, and what we are doing in our communities for our various stakeholders," he says. "Second is to facilitate transactions. We have a Buy Now and a Request for Proposal section for our products and we also provide ways to get more information on our products. Our goal is to facilitate the conversion to our Alcoa Direct mechanism that allows our customers and suppliers to track shipments, place orders, and do hard commerce in a secure area."

It's incredible that a company with as complex a product offering as Alcoa provides a mechanism for both existing and potential customers to transact business with them over the Web. It almost sounds like a too-good-to-be-true dotcom business plan from the late 1990s. "Many of our products are custom-made and the specifications are unique to individual customers," Lowery says. "We use the Web site to facilitate that dialog. We can then get you into the Alcoa Direct secure environment for both buying and selling directly with Alcoa."

Bright, Shiny Content

The Alcoa site includes detailed product information in over 100 categories. It's easy to get to the content if you know exactly what you're looking for; importantly, the content is also simple to browse if you come to the site not knowing your precise needs. Lowery sums up the importance of content for Alcoa when he says, "Look and feel can be wonderful, but if you don't have good content, nobody is coming back. All successful Web sites have good content."

A few quick clicks reveal that Alcoa makes more detailed product information available on their public site than many other B2B companies feel comfortable doing. Sure, the vast majority of organizations put some teaser content on the site and then at some point, you will be required to fill out a form requesting information, or to speak to a salesperson for more. Not Alcoa. The company confidently makes available the sorts of detailed information that other companies would not for fear of disclosing corporate secrets. "I find

ALCOA   Worldwide

Markets >   contact us > country sites > customer login >

About Alcoa >   Community >   Environment >   News >   Invest >   Careers >   Products/Services >   --search-- > go

Products and Services

Home : Car & Light Trucks : Brazing Sheet : Brazing Sheet : 4045 Clad Alloy Specification - English

Contact Information

Dave Starling
Alcoa Foil Products
248.455.5710
→ Email

4045 Clad Alloy Specification - English

Automotive Header / Stiffener Material Limits (lower forming components)

Alloys:	C204, C344, C363	
Skin -Top Side:	C190	
Core:	C817	
Composition:	Skin - Top Side:	C190 (Parent: AA4045)

Si	Fe	Cu	Mn	Mg	Zn	Be	Ti	Oth-Ea	Oth-Tot	Al
9.0 to 11.0	0.5 max	0.2 max	0.05 max	0.05 max	0.10 max	.0005 (a)	0.05 max	0.05 max	0.15 max	Rem

(a) No primary Be shall be added and use of metal, scrap or otherwise, containing Be in excess of 0.0005 is not permitted.

	Core:	C817 (Parent: AA3003)

Si	Fe	Cu	Mn	Mg	Zn	Be	Ti	Oth-Ea	Oth-Tot	Al

Detailed product information that others might consider proprietary is available on the public site.

that 90 percent of what is claimed as proprietary really isn't," Lowery says. "I say let's put it on the site and not worry about the content being proprietary."

The Alcoa approach effectively drives visitors to the point of sale. As you drill down into the specific content about one of the products, you get increasingly detailed information. At each point, there are links to move into the secure area to conduct a transaction online or to submit a request for proposal, as well as links to contact information to reach an Alcoa representative. The Alcoa site also features tools for its customers to find the best products suited to their specific needs.

Lowery continuously looks for new ways to improve: "Even though our content is good, it can get even better," he says. "Why can't we put a tool in place to help a builder buy aluminum siding? For example, I'd like to have a content tool on the Alcoa site that takes data such as the size of home and determines how much aluminum siding is needed. We need content tools to facilitate the use of the product," he says.

As a corporate site, Alcoa.com must also meet the needs of a wide variety of visitors from all over the world, not just existing and potential customers. Investors, the media, educators, and others interested in learning about the

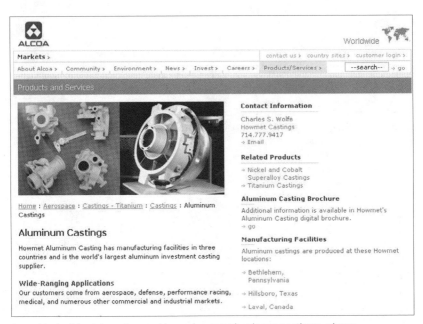

I want to build a jet engine and I need some aluminum castings, please.

company, the market, and the process of aluminum manufacturing are served with content appropriate to them. "There are various sets of people who come to the site and we need to speak to all of them," Lowery says. "Customers look for product information; in a tough economy, many people look for jobs, and some customers who we already work with come looking for how else we can help them because they want to limit the number of suppliers they work with."

The Good Guys

As part of its corporate communications role, Lowery makes certain that Alcoa's commitment to the environment is described on the site, but he also understands how good corporate citizenship can help win customers. "The values of the company include a commitment to sustainability," he says. "We want people to understand our commitment to the environment and the achievements of our environmental record. We take it seriously—there are very few companies who make public statements about their environmental record. We think customers want to work with companies that have good environmental records. Who wants to work with scoundrels? This is a big part of the reputation of the company."

Real-time content shows Alcoa's concern for its workers, communities, and the environment.

A particularly interesting way Alcoa delivers the message that the company is one of the good guys is through real-time content. Front and center in the environment section is real-time safety data on such things as its workplace injury record, which is updated throughout the day. The data is presented in easy-to-understand snippets, such as, "38.4 percent of Alcoa's 479 locations worldwide had zero recordable injuries compared to 42.4 percent one year prior." Lowery says, "We go forward and use the Web site as a prime content delivery tool for real-time safety data. No other company has this."

Crafting the Content

"The vast majority of the site content is created in-house," Lowery says, although some of the design work is done externally. "From the editorial perspective there are two full-time people. There are also a lot of people working on the technical side of the site."

Alcoa.com features content from over 100 product lines and also includes a network of nearly 100 country-specific sections in multiple languages. With so many different permutations of content appearing in one vast network on the Alcoa site, content management is critically important for the site's success. Lowery explains how it's done: "We have a Web content management system that is run centrally and then we hand the CMS tools off to the field people to add their content. Hundreds of updates come in from the field per day." Lowery understands the importance of having content contributed from multiple product lines and countries; he also believes it's most critical to make certain that both the internal and external content that appears on Alcoa.com is consistently strong and appropriate to the values of the company. That's where his team's central editing role comes into play. "We have a review process to make certain the content is appropriate," he says. "We think about how a posting of the content affects our other businesses."

The Alcoa site features a robust backend architecture designed to support much more traffic than the site typically gets. Interestingly, because Alcoa is the first Dow Jones Industrial Average component company to report earnings, the Alcoa site experiences a huge spike each quarter and Lowery uses that day as a test of his systems. "Every economist in the world goes to the site on the day we announce earnings," he says. "The traffic increases 50-fold that day."

$$$$$$$$$$$$$$$$$$$ Cashing In $$$$$$$$$$$$$$$$$$$

The well-organized and detailed content on the Alcoa site is designed to facilitate commerce and Lowery is constantly monitoring his success. "We measure revenue," he says. "For example, now we supply the aluminum for Apple's new Macintosh computer. And they found us from our Alcoa Web site. That's a whole new customer for us. If we didn't have good Web site content, we wouldn't have Apple as a customer today." While Alcoa doesn't break out online revenue in the company financial statements, it is safe to say that online revenue is quickly growing into an important line item, a rarity for a Fortune 500 manufacturing company with more than a hundred years of history.

CHAPTER NINE

Weyerhaeuser

Managing Trees with Internet Content

➤ **Organization**
Weyerhaeuser
www.weyerhaeuser.com

➤ **Interviewed**
Jason Plute, Senior Communications Manager, Internet

What's For Sale

Weyerhaeuser is an international forest products company with sales of
$22.7 billion in 2004, but what's really for sale on its site is the company's
commitment to the environment and managing the sustainable resources
under its care.

What's So Interesting

Weyerhaeuser is a business that relies heavily on natural resources to create its products. The company uses its Web site as a primary vehicle to communicate its environmental record and values to the communities it serves. As
a company that makes a profit from timber and other natural resources,
Weyerhaeuser must show the world that it is a good corporate citizen and that
the company treats our fragile environment with care.

Why You Should Care

Weyerhaeuser's site is a perfect model for any organization that maintains
a corporate message balancing act. With extensive use of highly valuable and
interactive content, the Weyerhaeuser site provides information that individuals need to make up their own minds about the environmental issues facing us
all. The company has won many corporate reputation awards based on its
environmental policies; its policies are all publicly available on the site.

W eyerhaeuser's diverse businesses touch nearly every aspect of the forest products industry, from growing and harvesting trees to producing pulp, paper, packaging, and building products. The company is the world's largest producer of softwood and hardwood lumber, the second-largest producer of containerboard and Kraft paper used in packaging, and among the top United States exporters of any product.

As a massive forest-products company heavily reliant on natural resources, Weyerhaeuser has a particularly interesting challenge in telling its story. The corporate site must show its good citizenship and, as a for-profit enterprise, it must also serve its paying customers and investors. While products and services are focal on the homepage, also front and center are Weyerhaeuser's citizenship values, which guide the company to "communicate openly with the public." The Weyerhaeuser site excels at making the environmental record and values of the company freely available to the varied groups of people who are interested: environmentalists, teachers, shareholders, and the media. And by association, the content surrounding the company's environmental policies and initiatives help it sell product.

Jason Plute, Senior Communications Manager, Internet, oversees Weyerhaeuser's content, encompassing a vast site containing more than 6,000 pages. "We appeal to a large audience from customers, to our own employees, Wall Street, and certainly to the communities in which we operate, as well as educators and policy makers," he says. "The goal is to offer each audience the information they need. We do that in an interactive way and one that offers cross-marketing—when you look at one set of content on the site you will be exposed to content from other parts of the site. For example, within public relations, if you hit the philanthropy section, you might also be exposed to the environment section."

Plute clearly understands the difficult role he has in communicating to the wide variety of people who visit the Weyerhaeuser site. Content appropriate for selling the many Weyerhaeuser products must share the site with content telling the fascinating 100-year history of the company. Importantly, as a company in a business that is often in the spotlight—the focus of the environmental lobby, the media, and concerned individuals alike—content on the site is a way to stand up, respond, and tell the company's side of the story.

Seeing the Forest for the Trees

Plute organizes the site for his varied constituents, but he also understands that some people want a brief overview, while others are looking for detailed

Weyerhaeuser has a home page with a message: Forest products are a renewable resource and this site tells that story.

information. He explains how the site maximizes the experience for both types of visitors: "I struggle with giving people quick lists and bulleted information but also telling the long history of Weyerhaeuser," he says. "So I find myself in flux as to how to best accomplish both things. In each section, the first-tier page is a quick overview, but navigation allows you to go deeper."

With content that uses the "show, don't tell" approach, Weyerhaeuser demonstrates that the company cares about sustaining forest resources because otherwise it couldn't continue into the future. "An example of content describing our long history is our timeline, an interactive look at more than a hundred years of business," Plute says. "Having the process controls to make it in business for so long is important to our customers, particularly those overseas. We have a fun and interactive way for customers to see what we've done over the years. People, those overseas in particular, are looking for a

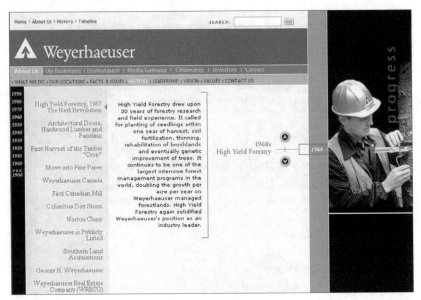

The Weyerhaeuser interactive timeline shows how the company has managed natural resources for over 100 years. An obvious implication is that the company will manage well for the future, too.

company to trust when they buy paper or forest products, so when they send us money, they're certain to get the product delivered as promised."

Content with Priorities

Unlike organizations that bury corporate citizenship and environmental content (if they include it at all), Plute has chosen to place Weyerhaeuser's front and center. "Citizenship is a core value of the company," he says. "And it's a main navigation button on the homepage; we give consumers a direct line to the Ethics and Business Conduct Office so they can share their concerns directly."

With some 40 million acres of timberland under ownership or lease, Weyerhaeuser has an awesome responsibility. Plute describes the Weyerhaeuser position further, "We like to say that we operate 'by license of the public.' Our communities need to be comfortable with the way we operate and that the ways we treat the land, air, and the water are appropriate. You plant a seedling and it takes 45 years for the tree to mature—we need to show we're in it for the long term."

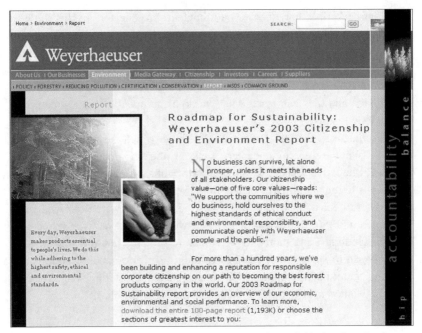

The Weyerhaeuser roadmap for sustainability report is available for download.

In order to deliver this message to its various constituents, Weyerhaeuser makes environmental content available in either bite-sized chunks, for those who just want an overview of one area of interest, or in the form of large reports. Plute adds, "We have a major environmental report on our own performance that's available for download in PDF or HTML. The feedback is that people want to be able to drill down in the PDF and print what they need. By being proactive with our environmental content, for example talking about the renewablilty of the resource, we try to provide good information on the home page to keep people up to speed on our positions. We also react to the current atmosphere and add content accordingly."

Excellent Corporate Neighbors

Plute also uses the site to show that a huge company can also be a good neighbor. For example, there's a section on the site for those who would like to use Weyerhaeuser land for recreation purposes such as camping or hunting. The company has a strong focus on philanthropy and provides details on the site. Plute describes how they've built content for educators so that the next generation of young people can understand Weyerhaeuser's positions, too. "We offer teachers the opportunity online to sign up for summer opportunities with our foresters, so they can learn more about issues and can develop appropriate curriculum," he says. "The curriculum can be built from the real-life examples we provide and they can teach what we do as an open and honest company with a long history."

Weyerhaeuser also targets the public directly with its educational programs. "We have learning centers such as the one featuring Mount St. Helens," Plute says. "There we show the story of the volcano and what it was like for us to replant millions of seedlings. Weyerhaeuser is the largest private landowner affected by Mount St. Helens; 65,000 acres were destroyed when it erupted in 1980. In the learning center, we talk about how we tested soil, planted seedlings, and more." On October 11, 2004, when the volcano suddenly began to spew steam again, heralding a series of small eruptions, the learning center on Weyerhaeuser site became a source of knowledge for people who wanted to check on the details of the big 1980 blast.

Weyerhaeuser is the largest landowner on Mount St. Helens. Learn more about how the company managed the 1980 volcanic disaster there.

Growing (Content) Like a Tree

So where does all this content come from? The short answer is from Plute and his team. "All content is created in-house," he says. "I did all of the writing until about a year ago and that was a lot of work. So now we have a team of people in Corporate Communications who help write. I still manage the site and review all the content before it goes live."

"It's a challenge to keep over 6,000 pages of content interesting," Plute says. "Our content team is dedicated by each major section," he says, describing the flow of information, "So one communicator may take the environment section and that person helps businesses with environmental messaging and also helps the Office of the Environment with their materials. This has been a tremendous help and has made the site better," he says. "Many of these people have been professional communicators for many years; I help make their writing work on the Web. It's working very well. We see it as a big part of our future to communicate with our various audiences."

"I've been with company 17 years, always in communications," Plute says. "Four years ago, I took on this Internet role. At the time there were 30 sites, some product focused, some business focused, and more; these many sites had diluted the Weyerhaeuser brand. So we've created a policy that we all use one look and feel with consistent navigation. Now all the businesses come through the communications department. We're pleased to have businesses contribute copy but we rework it so we speak with one voice and have one corporate face to the user."

$$\$\$\$\$\$\$\$\$\$\$\$\$\$\$\$\$$$ **Cashing In** $$\$\$\$\$\$\$\$\$\$\$\$\$\$\$\$\$$$

Clearly Weyerhaeuser is not some sort of quasi-National Park. It is a for-profit company using natural resources to generate $22.7 billion in revenue, employing 55,000, and serving customers around the world. Of course, the Web site must meet the requirements of customers and prospects, but the company has seen the value of content to meet its fiscal and social responsibilities. Plute describes some of the ways they use content to help sell: "We're the world's largest producer of many forest and paper products," he says. "Along those lines, we try to provide customers with tools and information on the Web other than static content. For example, customers can calculate the linear footage in a certain roll of paper and this part of the public site is available to anyone."

A good example of using content to combine corporate citizenship with a sales opportunity is Weyerhaeuser's services for recycling paper products. According to Plute, "We produce this renewable resource and create paper products but we also have a major recycling business. Another tool is provided

The site includes an interactive tool to calculate how much product you need to purchase.

to calculate how much paper you can recover within your business. By applying methods we've developed since 1974, we can give a good estimate on the amount a company can recover based on known waste streams. Then you can work with us to find a way to sell your surplus."

Plute takes his role as a communicator very seriously. He has the famous NASA photo of the earth at night on the wall of his office and uses it to remember that his audience is global and it's his job to reach people all over the world. And by reaching those people, Plute is an integral part of Weyerhaeuser's role in sustaining the environment (and its business) for future generations. With such a long time horizon, success might seem difficult to measure. But Plute measures by his own yardsticks. "We would define success in one of two ways," he says. "One: by the metrics we gather on the site through statistics. We'll move a document to a particular place to see if it gets read more, for example. Two: in the end if Weyerhaeuser is seen by our stakeholders as the best forest products company in the world, we're successful."

ebuild

Everything for the Professional Builder, Including the Kitchen Sink

➤ **Organization**
ebuild
www.ebuild.com

➤ **Interviewed**
Mitch Rouda, President of Hanley-Wood e-Media

What's For Sale

A targeted advertising and sponsorship vehicle for the hundreds of companies that sell products to professionals in the building trade.

What's So Interesting

ebuild provides a great example of how a targeted online catalog can become the preferred site for an entire demographic group. Building professionals, including contractors, architects, and remodelers, use ebuild to find and compare products quickly. And manufacturers want to reach the targeted audience that relies on ebuild to make purchase decisions every day.

Why You Should Care

The success of ebuild's site is due in large part to the strong editorial aspects of its content organization. Anyone looking to cash in on a content catalog should study the ebuild model. The site was designed from the ground up by people who understand the building trades. Product information fits into the hundreds of categories based on editorial decisions made by experts in the building profession, all designed to make finding the perfect product easy for visitors.

I magine being able to find the perfect product for any building situation with just a few clicks and keystrokes. That's the simple premise Hanley-Wood—the leading B2B media company serving the housing and construction industry—set out with when the company created ebuild. The ebuild site has become the Internet's most comprehensive collection of professional building product information. The content found at the ebuild site provides essential information for those who swing a hammer or wield a wrench for a living. Say you've contracted with a homeowner for a bathroom renovation. As a professional, you need to be aware of thousands of products so you can offer your clients the sorts of fittings and materials they want and need. You're the expert, so it just won't do for you to claim ignorance about, say, a certain sort of faucet the client wants. But there's no way any mere mortal could keep up with the myriad manufacturers, product lines, options, or costs, or have direct relationships with every potential vendor.

Enter ebuild, a place where professional builders can easily locate products matching even the most wacky client request—such as pink marble flooring, green countertops, a shower that sprays from all angles, or a sink with an extra large gooseneck faucet. Need a gooseneck faucet? At ebuild, you can quickly learn that there are 166 gooseneck faucets and then refine by criteria such as price, manufacturer, color, material, or any combination of features. Presto: You are equipped to offer your clients with the exact set of products that meet their needs. You're seen as a font of product knowledge, you've impressed your clients, found what you need to know, and where to get it—and best of all, it only took a few moments online at ebuild.

Building ebuild One Room at a Time

Mitch Rouda, President of Hanley-Wood e-Media, explains how demographics drove the creation of the site: "ebuild is so important because 91 percent of our industry is online and 78 percent is online daily—and these are construction professionals," Rouda says. "When we ask why they go online, the number one answer—95 percent of people—is they are online 'to research products'. When the question is asked differently: What's your preferred way to look for product information? The answer is 'on the Internet' by a margin of three to one." Rouda and his team used this information to create what the building trade needed.

OK, so builders need to know about a truckload of stuff and they want to find out about it on the Internet. How did Rouda and his colleagues at Hanley-Wood take those two simple facts and create a destination site now visited by more than 300,000 buyers per month?

The company began with expertise. Hanley-Wood publishes the leading magazines in the residential and commercial construction industry, including *Builder, Custom Home, Residential Architect, Concrete Construction, Remodeling,* and other similar titles. But unlike hundreds of other publishers, Hanley-Wood didn't design its site solely based on the content it already had, which would have been the easy way out. Instead, it created what the building trade needed.

Hanley-Wood's Rouda says, "The core content of ebuild is our product database, which is unique online content that was created by our e-media group solely for this application. A builder's job is to put together hundreds or thousands of products to create a building and construction is kind of a fashion business—like who has the coolest faucets. What we discovered is that

ebuild reaches professional builders with a proprietary taxonomy of over 250,000 building products.

aggregation of all that product content has tremendous value. Our taxonomy is critical for the 300 buckets of information because each has unique specifications."

My Bucket Is Your Taxonomy

The core of ebuild is the way the site organizes the many different categories of building products. Sometimes called taxonomy by publishers, the "300 buckets of information," as Rouda calls them, allow builders to either browse or search the huge collection of product content by product type.

An easy way to think of taxonomy is like a tree. The trunk of the tree, in the ebuild case, is all building products. (Keep in mind that this is one *huge* tree—ebuild catalogs more than 250,000 unique items.) Going up our ebuild tree, we come to the first set of branches that include 26 "Product Supercategories," such as Appliances, Cabinets, Countertop Materials, and Faucets. Further along the Faucets branch are eight categories including Bar/Hospitality Faucets, Bathtub Faucets, and Lavatory Faucets. At the end of the Lavatory Faucet branch are 2,060 individual products listed. To complete the metaphor, each Lavatory Faucet listed represents one leaf of the building products tree.

Once the taxonomy was created, the editorial experts at ebuild needed to slot the products into the right categories. To make things more difficult than it might seem at first, each product needed to be mapped based on the manufacturers specifications and also by a generic taxonomy that would allow easy comparison over many manufacturers. Rouda explains: "For example, we need to coordinate color both as each manufacturer's propriety color" (say emerald) "and the generic color that can be mapped" (green). It's critical to get this aspect of the editorial process right or the entire site is rendered useless. Without the ability to map products from a myriad of manufacturers into a useful and common classification system, ebuild would have been too haphazard to have succeeded with the busy building trade.

The ebuild site also includes links within each of the categories to appropriate news and articles. What makes this feature particularly useful is that the news and articles are appropriate for the category you're browsing or searching. For example, while browsing the plumbing fixtures category, one could click to an article called: "Standing Tall: Pedestal sinks hold steady with a variety of shapes and sizes." News is sourced from ebuild parent Hanley-Wood's building publications as well as syndicated news from content aggregator Yellowbrix.

Tagging Content Makes It Useful

The organization of multiple content types within ebuild (including product information, manufacturers, news, and articles) works brilliantly. When you're looking for bathroom fixtures, you see appropriate news and articles on, you guessed it, bathroom fixtures. This sounds obvious, but it's no simple accomplishment. The ebuild team members had to assign each one of the myriad products with the appropriate tags so the content would appear within the right categories and then the product tags needed to be coordinated with useful tagging of news stories and articles.

Like most successful sites, ebuild works for those who are searching for a particular item as well as for those who are perusing a category. Sure, a builder can search for a manufacturer or a product type, but she can also browse by category. And no matter which way building professionals hunt for the right product, the site brings content together usefully.

The importance of the editorial function required in creating the classification scheme cannot be underestimated. Mapping over 250,000 products from hundreds of manufacturers into the right supercategories and subcategories is extremely people-intensive and the process cannot be done well without lots

ebuild effectively links news and advertisement to product taxonomies.

of building product domain expertise. ebuild started with the foundation of a strong parent company: Hanley-Wood. Hanley-Wood's expertise in publishing magazines that reached the same target audience coupled with its excellent raw content materials and editorial experts provided a strong foundation for ebuild's growth. But without ebuild's tremendous focus on the intelligent organization of the hundreds of thousands of product permutations, the site would not have been as successful. The people, and their ability to organize ebuild's content, made the difference.

$$$$$$$$$$$$$$$$ Cashing In $$$$$$$$$$$$$$$$

So the ebuild content is the Internet's most comprehensive online resource to help professionals research, compare, and specify building products. Congratulations to ebuild: the site is now an industry standard for product information. But that's just the beginning of the ebuild story. With a content taxonomy built, product information populating it, and thousands of builders visiting the site each day, Hanley-Wood needed to leverage this tremendous asset to make money.

ebuild cashes in on its content investment by selling advertising and sponsorships to building product manufacturers and others who want to reach the highly targeted professional audience that visits the site. Here's another area where the ebuild focus on editorial excellence has paid off. The same content taxonomy driving the ebuild product content also organizes the advertising and sponsorship links, banners, and other site offerings into ebuild product categories.

"According to our most recent eMonitor study, 94 percent of ebuild site visitors specify, purchase, or influence the selection of building products," says Rouda. "You've now created an advertising opportunity that's unbelievable. We reach not only builders, but builders who are looking for faucets."

With 300,000 unique visitors a month, the vast majority being a valuable audience of builders browsing or searching for specific products to buy, ebuild is perfectly positioned to sell advertising and sponsorship programs by product category. And with its well-organized content taxonomy, ebuild offers a slew of different opportunities for those who want to reach builders, including:

- So-called "run of site" banner advertisements shown to all visitors regardless of the category they are viewing

- Banner advertisements shown to visitors of specific categories

- Category-specific or product-specific sponsorship messages

ebuild reaches builders specifically looking for faucets as well as those who might just be browsing for ideas, creating a tremendous advertising vehicle.

- "Good Deals" section within product categories

- Premium listings, including the availability of detailed product specs in a PDF format or product photos beyond the standard listing

So visitors to the plumbing fixtures category would see not only product listings and news articles, but they might also see an appropriately targeted offer of free shipping from a manufacturer or distributor of plumbing fixtures.

Providing visitors with a well targeted mix of content, including advertisements, sponsorships, product information, news, and articles can be an overwhelmingly complex proposition. Site visitors could become confused and frustrated if they can't tell whether they're looking at a paid advertising section, a product listing, or a news article. This is another aspect of content-offering at which ebuild excels. Specific areas are clearly marked with the word "advertisement" so visitors won't be confused. According to Rouda, "We do a good job with trust. We make it clear what is an editorial function and what is paid sponsorship."

It's fascinating to note that for many builders, paid content may sometimes be just as valuable as editorial content. For example, if you're researching gooseneck bathroom faucets for your client and want to save a few dollars, you could click on any one of the "Good Deals" links, such as:

- Premium bath and kitchen fixtures, low prices

- Plumbing Fixtures - Free Shipping

- Save on plumbing fixtures at HomeCenter.com!

The fast growing Hanley-Wood e-Media division—of which ebuild is the core component—now generates $22 million in revenue, representing about 10 percent of the company's overall revenue. Rouda and his team are continually improving ebuild and refining the site by adding new content. Product listings are increasing by the thousands each month and visitor counts are also rising. With a strong focus on editorial content, in particular the brainpower required to create the vast product taxonomy over hundreds of thousands of products, Hanley-Wood's ebuild is a powerful franchise that should allow them to cash in with content for years to come.

CHAPTER ELEVEN

ServiceWare

Level the Playing Field with Content

➤ **Organization**
ServiceWare Technologies
www.serviceware.com

➤ **Interviewed**
Andy McNutt, Director of Marketing

What's For Sale

ServiceWare provides Web-based knowledge management solutions for customer service and support teams.

What's So Interesting

As a small software company providing big-ticket solutions to large organizations, ServiceWare levels the sales playing field with content. ServiceWare's Web site directly contributes to 75 percent of the company's sales by delivering content that moves prospects down the sales consideration cycle and collecting leads along the way. ServiceWare uses Web content, particularly a series of syndicated white papers, to present the company's considerable strengths to its target market.

Why You Should Care

A small company can leverage informative content to demonstrate that it can go head-to-head with the big boys. But this is easier said than done. ServiceWare provides a terrific example of content at work—its entire business model puts the "A great Web site makes you seem bigger" theory into practice. With three-quarters of the company's clients coming directly from Web content marketing and lead generation, ServiceWare makes the theory a reality. Organizations of any size that want to look, act, and earn big can learn from the ServiceWare approach.

S erviceWare provides knowledge-based software for help desks and call centers. The ServiceWare technology uses a patented self-learning system that mimics the way the human mind learns through interaction. Telephone call centers and help desks at large organizations such as EDS, H&R Block, AT&T Wireless, and QUALCOMM make use of the system so operators can very quickly find answers to customer questions and problems. Basically, when a call comes in, a representative logs the problem and then the ServiceWare software helps them to quickly determine if others have experienced similar issues and suggests possible solutions. A decision-tree approach reveals collected customer experiences and raises likely solutions to the top.

The ServiceWare market includes large corporations with extensive help desks as well as financial institutions that maintain call centers. "Our targets are Chief Information Officers, Vice Presidents of Call Center Operations, and Vice Presidents of Customer Care and Support," says Andy McNutt, Director of Marketing for ServiceWare Technologies. "Some companies even have Chief Knowledge Officers and they're also prospects. If you're running a big call center or multiple call centers, we want to talk to you."

According to McNutt, the biggest marketing challenge faced by ServiceWare is the company's relative size. At about $12 million in revenue, ServiceWare is quite small compared to its competitors as well as to the size of its target-market customers. ServiceWare sells big-ticket software—installations run between $250,000 and several million dollars. Being a small, relatively low-profile company, ServiceWare relies on its extensive collection of expertise-demonstrating content—especially its library of white papers—to sell these high-ticket products. "The primary goal of the ServiceWare site is to show that we are a real business," McNutt says. "We're leaders in the field and we've been around for a long time."

According to McNutt, content gets people interested in the company and its products. He's developed content that educates prospects throughout the sales consideration cycle. Besides the challenge of being a small company serving large companies, McNutt also has to deal with a product category that's not very well understood by his target market. Most call centers use Customer Relationship Management (CRM) software and prospects know how that works. But ServiceWare's products work in conjunction with CRM systems. "Someone who has CRM software uses our product integrated into the existing systems," McNutt says. "The CRM system creates the trouble ticket and our system helps to manage the resolutions and suggest fixes for the

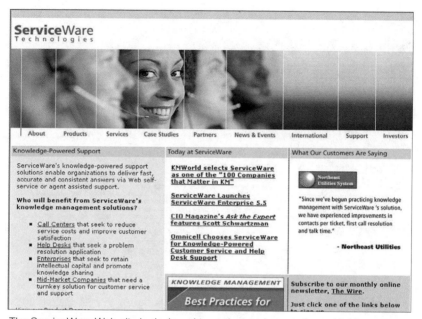

The ServiceWare Web site is designed to project an image of a much bigger company.

problem. When they are integrated, the agent doesn't need to open another application to find the solution."

Are You a Call Center or a Help Desk?

The ServiceWare site makes extensive use of self-select paths to segment and identify its target market right from the home page. This also helps potential customers understand what the company can do to help them solve a variety of problems. When you first log on to the site, you're presented with the question: "Who will benefit from ServiceWare's knowledge management solutions?" Beneath the question, target markets are listed along with links people can choose based on their profile or requirements. "A lot of companies know they need a service like ours, but there is quite a range of products out there related to what we do," McNutt says. "People coming into the site have some idea that they're looking for a product like ours but they don't know *exactly* what we do."

Where ServiceWare content really shines is with its white papers. To make them easy to find, links to free downloads are available throughout the site. In

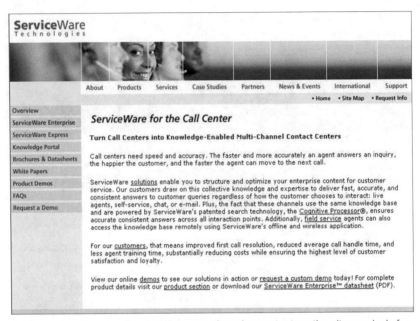

ServiceWare
Technologies

About   Products   Services   Case Studies   Partners   News & Events   International   Support

• Home   • Site Map   • Request Info

Overview
ServiceWare Enterprise
ServiceWare Express
Knowledge Portal
Brochures & Datasheets
White Papers
Product Demos
FAQs
Request a Demo

ServiceWare for the Call Center

Turn Call Centers into Knowledge-Enabled Multi-Channel Contact Centers

Call centers need speed and accuracy. The faster and more accurately an agent answers an inquiry, the happier the customer, and the faster the agent can move to the next call.

ServiceWare solutions enable you to structure and optimize your enterprise content for customer service. Our customers draw on this collective knowledge and expertise to deliver fast, accurate, and consistent answers to customer queries regardless of how the customer chooses to interact: live agents, self-service, chat, or e-mail. Plus, the fact that these channels use the same knowledge base and are powered by ServiceWare's patented search technology, the Cognitive Processor®, ensures accurate consistent answers across all interaction points. Additionally, field service agents can also access the knowledge base remotely using ServiceWare's offline and wireless application.

For our customers, that means improved first call resolution, reduced average call handle time, and less agent training time, substantially reducing costs while ensuring the highest level of customer satisfaction and loyalty.

View our online demos to see our solutions in action or request a custom demo today! For complete product details visit our product section or download our ServiceWare Enterprise™ datasheet (PDF).

If you run a call center, ServiceWare organizes the content on the site precisely for your needs.

addition, ServiceWare employs an electronic advertising program via e-newsletters and syndication on other sites, which allows the white papers to serve as a call to action.

"Our big thing is white papers," says McNutt. "They are a tool where we can help to address our potential customer's problems. We have a lot of experience with business pains and we provide valuable free content to people to help them." To be truly helpful to potential clients, white papers must offer useful information and not a product sales pitch. Fortunately, McNutt finds good fodder for writing in the call center and help desk markets. Titles of papers available at the site include:

- Knowledge Management Best Practices for Service and Support

- The Insider's Guide to Knowledge Management ROI

- Employee Self-Service: Benefits for the Help Desk

- Knowledge Management: The Key to Customer Service Success

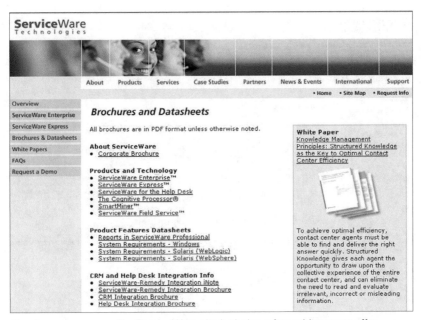

Nearly every page on the ServiceWare site includes a free white paper offer.

"We've got tremendous experience helping people to solve help desk and customer services problems," McNutt says. "We put a catchy title onto the white paper and make certain that they have good content value."

With a large purchase price and a six-to-nine month sales cycle, McNutt leverages potential customers' need-to-know by using white papers to consistently lure new prospects into the sales pipeline. All of ServiceWare's white papers are free but in order to receive them, you must register on the site. Upon registration, you gain access to the entire white paper library and in return, ServiceWare gets a new sales prospect. "We get good leads from the white papers," McNutt says. "We have to put out content that will get people interested. Good content has wide appeal to many different prospects."

Hard Data and Useful Information

At ServiceWare, white paper creation is done in-house and is generally a collaborative effort. "Most of the white papers are started between me and the Director of Public Relations," McNutt says. "We write an outline then we have an in-house knowledge management expert write the paper using a lot of

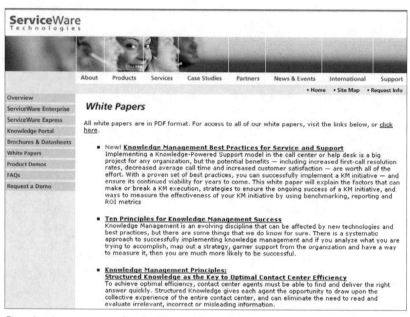

Download one or many ServiceWare white papers.

hard data to make it valuable." Finally, the papers are edited for consistency and published with attention to attractive graphics and design. So as to not confuse potential customers with industry-specific jargon, McNutt adopts generic terms like "problem resolution tools" when writing content for the site.

According to McNutt, ServiceWare publishes a new white paper every three months or so. Constantly coming up with new and interesting topics can be a challenge, so the company is considering creating a series. "We're looking to make white papers for vertical industries to reach more specific audiences," McNutt says. He also looks at data from less-popular white papers when he's planning new titles to add to the library. "One that didn't work well was called 'Structured Knowledge as the key to Optimal Contact Center Efficiency.' It just doesn't roll off the tongue. The appeal wasn't as broad; it just didn't get the click through that we had wanted," McNutt says.

If You Have Great Content, Get It Out There

Besides providing the cornerstone of the ServiceWare Web site, content in the form of white papers also serves as its primary advertising vehicle, again using a demonstration of expertise rather than a sales pitch to generate interest in its products. "We advertise the white papers a lot," McNutt says. "We position our ads as content with headlines like 'Find out what people are doing to implement Knowledge Management and make their call center better'." Most of the advertising is through e-mail newsletters; the white papers serve as a call to action for prospects. When readers see a title that will help them solve a business problem, they act by requesting access; ServiceWare follows up with the promise of further expertise and assistance.

ServiceWare also syndicates its white papers through the BitPipe network, which serves as a conduit between white paper authors like ServiceWare, distribution partners such as vertical market portals, and readers. Syndicating through BitPipe allows McNutt's white papers to reach people beyond the ServiceWare site. BitPipe syndicates white papers from hundreds of companies and maintains a list of top papers downloaded. "On the BitPipe network, ServiceWare's 'Ten Principles for Knowledge Management Success' paper was in the top 10. ranking—above white papers from Microsoft and other big companies. Our papers do very well on BitPipe, even when we don't advertise them."

McNutt also gets requests for his more popular white papers from other Web sites and newsletters. "What happens with good content is that newsletters and other sites pick up the papers and republish them," McNutt says. According to McNutt, the white papers serve as a PR tool as well, generating interest in the company from the media and industry analysts.

Cashing In

McNutt tracks his lead flow from newsletter advertising, but he admits that some metrics are more a gut feel than hard numbers. He says he can count on spending about $10 per lead on his syndication and advertising program using white papers. "If I spend $30,000 on newsletter advertising, I can count on 3,000 leads," he says.

As the primary advertising and lead generation program for ServiceWare, the white paper publishing program needs to show results. Perhaps most impressive is that 75 percent of ServiceWare's closed business in 2003 came from the Web site according to McNutt. "We track closed sales to learn when and how they downloaded the white paper. One quarter of the business was directly attributable to white papers and another quarter came from demo requests," he says. "As a smaller company we can get on a level playing field with much bigger players through content."

CHAPTER TWELVE

Colliers

Commercial Real Estate for the World

➤ **Organization**
Colliers International
www.colliers.com

➤ **Interviewed**
Joshua Fost, Chief Technology Officer

What's For Sale

Colliers is a global real estate services firm providing commercial sales, leasing, and property services from 247 offices in 50 countries.

What's So Interesting

Colliers was among the first commercial real estate companies to recognize the importance of its vast resource of local knowledge in providing value for global customers. Colliers' comprehensive Web site effectively delivers local content delivered to global audiences. Colliers consists of a partnership of commercial property firms in Asia, Canada, the United States, Europe, the Middle East, and Africa. With the goal of providing consistent, superior service in multiple locations, a unified Web presence is vital. But until the current Colliers global site was launched, the firm operated with over 100 different sites and suffered from decidedly muddled results.

Why You Should Care

For global organizations that sell and market locally, creating a one-size-fits-all global Web site can be a nightmare—and even a mistake. Over a lengthy two-year process, Colliers designed its site to be both global and local and accomplished both the unification of the company's Net presence as well as industry-mandated localization. The content is organized to mimic the way customers think and is presented in a clear and concise manner. Global branding is apparent throughout, but headquarters defers decisions on local content to each office. Colliers International can be a model for complex global organizations of all kinds; Colliers knows how to present a consistent message to the market and cash in with local content at the same time.

Colliers International, a partnership of commercial real estate companies, operates in 50 countries. Colliers has a strong focus on being a global organization that provides clients with superior service through its depth of local knowledge and expertise—not an easy feat to pull off. As a global partnership, Colliers International joins together commercial firms in Asia, Canada, the United States, Europe, the Middle East, and Africa to provide consistent service; it employs 8,800 employees in 247 locations. Colliers is among the first commercial real estate companies to recognize the need for (and then develop) a sales and marketing strategy that leverages the power of local knowledge on a global scale.

Commercial real estate at the highest levels requires the Colliers' scale and scope. While most transactions are strictly local (a company needs to rent some office space in its home city) in real estate of this type, uniquely global challenges also exist. Colliers serves many large multinational companies that may be considering strategic moves. For example, a company might want to establish a manufacturing operation in a less expensive European country and would need information on the merits of setting up shop in, say, Belgrade or Warsaw. This hypothetical company needs to understand the commercial and residential real estate markets in the two cities in order to (1) acquire the appropriate industrial space, and (2) provide expatriate housing for the management team that will move to the new country. As a unified global firm, Colliers has long been able to help property managers from multinationals work out the cost-benefit analysis between markets under consideration and, of course, show and close transactions on properties in whichever location the client chooses. Now, with its Web site, Colliers helps anybody do this type of comparison online in just minutes.

While Colliers faced an enormous task in unifying its global enterprise, it was almost as difficult to bring together a slew of diverse Web sites into one offering. The pioneering tradition of global breadth and local depth that Colliers was built on continues with its unique approach to the business of commercial real estate delivered via the Web. "The primary goal of the Colliers site is to unify all of the partner firms," says Joshua Fost, Chief Technology Officer of Colliers International. "Colliers is a partnership of about 50 independently owned and managed companies around the world that are members of the partnership. There had been 100 Web domains before. Most had a common look five years ago but as each firm morphed over time, they diffused. The inconsistent brand and inconsistent navigation caused confusion for end-users."

When he set out to build the site, Fost knew he faced significant challenges because he had to represent the varied requirements of marketers from Collier's offices all over the world. "The site was designed and built in two steps," Fost says. "The first was to make a committee of marketing stakeholders start from a blank piece of paper and organize what the site should be. We had multilingual representation and people from all different-sized Colliers companies as part of the committee." The group Fost organized and led met frequently for more than a year to hash out the different aspects of the site, which concluded with a design prototype.

A major component of the prototype was the implementation of a set of content management features. Fost and the committee knew that marketing people in local offices would be posting content independently from headquarters in cities from Abu Dhabi to Zurich and each needed the ability to control their own contributions. "We knew that we wanted a first-class content management system on the back-end plus e-mail marketing capabilities,

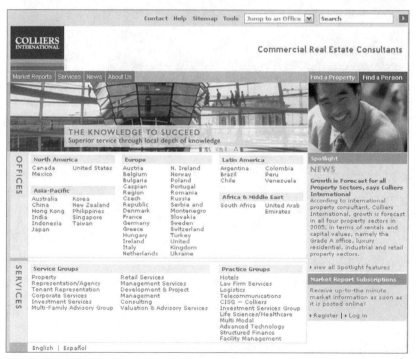

The Colliers Web site provides commercial real estate content from 247 offices with one look and feel.

search, and more," Fost says. Another important design component was the ability to unify the search function across the entire organization.

"The second step was the request for proposal stage," says Fost. After the bids had been analyzed, Colliers chose to work with Molecular, Inc. on development and back-end architecture and PARTNERS+simons for design. "The whole process from the organization of the committee to final launch took more than two years," Fost says. It's fascinating that the design and planning stage took longer than did actual site construction. Many organizations rush through the planning stages and begin to build before they know how the end result should look, work, and *read.*

Each local Colliers office supplies appropriate content and manages its own sections to display a selection of services offered.

Content from Warsaw to Sydney

"Our audience is both existing and potential clients," Fost says. "We provide content for potential clients organized by two fundamental axes: services and location. So if you want to know about Colliers in Los Angeles, we'll provide market reports on particular markets about, say, rent rates." The entire global site works with the same organizational structure so no matter what country or market you're researching, information is always based on location and the type of real estate service. Services range from leasing and sales to property management and advice.

Fost and his team also developed a large collection of e-mail newsletters focused on specific locations and services. With the very long lead times involved in a commercial real estate decision, providing content to people's e-mail inbox on a regular basis is smart marketing because it regularly places the Colliers brand in front of prospects. Real estate transactions may be few and far between for many clients and when they are finally ready to make a deal, Colliers wants to be front of mind.

"People can subscribe to an office report to get automatic e-mails on a subset of our markets," Fost says. "This is the bread and butter of our renting business. We have featured properties that are rolled into one unified database on the main site. But if you go to each location site, you will see more properties. For some markets, there are as many 10 types of market reports." According to Fost, Colliers publishes several hundred individual market reports, all available on the Colliers Web site. Many people subscribe to multiple reports to keep up with different markets. "There are roll-up reports from the specific locations to regions as well," Fost says. The roll-up reports are ideal for those with a bigger picture interest. "We do investment services," he adds. "When people want to manage property or invest money, we also help with that."

Real Content from All Over

Fost faced a significant challenge in designing the back-end systems for a firm with strong local as well as global content requirements. The most important aspect, he says, was to make certain that each office could post content directly to the site and that each local section was culturally appropriate. "We wanted a back-end system to make it easier for marketing people to control content on the site," Fost says. "Each page includes some images, which are people and real-estate related. We set up the pages so the marketing people can choose the best colors, people, architecture, and city skyline that are most

Each local office selects culturally appropriate people, images, and colors.

appropriate for their market." Because Fost spent so much time in the design requirements phase, he nailed down issues like site navigation and information architecture form the start. "The content management system provides enough flexibility to provide as much freedom as they had previously with their own site," Fost says. "But now we have the same look and feel across the world. Comparing the Warsaw and Sydney offices shows the different use of images but it still hangs together as one company."

The amount of localization found on the Colliers International site is quite remarkable. "The site is multilingual," Fost says. "There are 15 languages represented, all in the same look and feel of the international site." Content is at the heart of the site and with real estate, the descriptions, photographs, and specifications are critical to putting properties in the best light possible. "Each market creates property descriptions," says Fost. "We have a workflow process to bubble-up featured properties for use on the international site. Case studies, news releases, and properties are the main forms of content." Surprisingly, there is very little top-level editing that takes place across the organization according to Fost. "We allow each office to define workflow," he says. "Some offices are more rigorous about editing."

While other organizations with valuable content like Colliers' market reports would be tempted to charge for or limit distribution, Colliers makes it all available for free on the open Web. "We don't ask people to register unless they want to receive market reports because we need an e-mail address," Fost says. "Otherwise the content is all open." Colliers' use of what many would say is proprietary content that should be controlled in some way is a hallmark of the site's value. While many business-to-business sites only provide valuable market research reports through direct connection with a salesperson, or by filling out lengthy forms for later approval, Colliers has chosen to be open. In the end, Colliers generates more interest and more leads with freely available content.

Fost faced an interesting challenge when it came to the creation of truly international content that would be displayed on the main site home page. "This is an organization where 90 percent of the content comes from local offices," he says. "The headquarters office staff consists of only 13 people in an organization of 8,800. To show the full amount of activity and the true value of the content, we have to use content from the offices because we don't create much here at headquarters."

Case studies, news releases, market reports, and property descriptions are the main forms of content featured on the Colliers site.

With all of the content included on the Colliers site, what more could they possibly add? "We had one really great idea we couldn't fit in," Fost says. "We wanted to do an e-zine, kind of vibey, hipified bit of content that you'd want to check each month. That was a completely new content idea. We want to do it, but the challenge is who would do it and how. How would it get written? We want to circle back to it."

$$$$$$$$$$$$$$$$$$$$ Cashing In $$$$$$$$$$$$$$$$$$$$

Ultimately, the tremendous investment in the Colliers site has to help the firm to transact more business. A major component is its huge listing of properties—a critical set of content. It all comes down to each of the local markets according to Fost. "The local market is only one click away from every page," he says. "The two navigation coordinates are location and service. When people put the two together by clicking, they reach the right person."

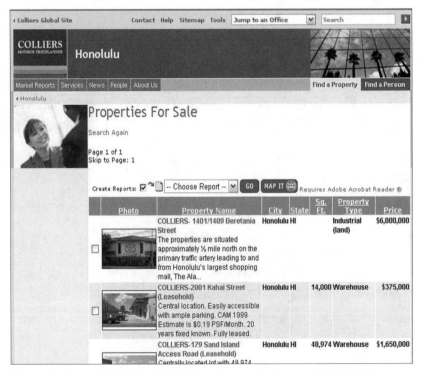

Real estate bread and butter: Colliers has thousands of properties listed from offices all over the world.

All of the content includes contact information for local brokers just a click away. As big ticket items with very long sales cycles, commercial real estate is clearly not a likely e-commerce item. "We think it is rare that people will actually buy a property online via the site," Fost says. "Instead, we see the site as part of the sales process. Many people have heard of Colliers because they see our ads on buildings. People want to get a sense of who we are before they contact us, so they go to the site. They have heard of us or seen our signs on a building locally, but then they see we're much bigger than just the local market." The Colliers Web site is the tool that demonstrates that Colliers is much bigger and broader than just a local real estate office, while at the same time never loosing sight of the fundamentally local perspective of real estate.

There's no doubt that the site now presents a much more unified picture of Colliers as a multinational firm. "The new site has brought our company together in a big way," Fost says. "There is an incredible cross pollination of the offices now, which brings the partnership much closer together. People now put colliers.com on their business card rather than the local office URL. That's important for us because we can show we're bigger. We're lowering the borders between offices and showing that everyone is a peer."

"My personal view is that if clients express that it is easier to find what they want and we show potential clients that we are more unified, and that it's easy for both to get in touch with us, then we are a success," says Fost. For such a massive global undertaking, the site's objectives can be reduced to a simple proposition: "A big win for us is to have people contact a broker from the site."

CHAPTER THIRTEEN

Booz Allen

Career Content

➤ **Organization**
Booz Allen Hamilton Inc.
www.boozallen.com

➤ **Interviewed**
Alicia Mallaney, Recruiting Manager
Lois Remeikis, Director of Web Communications

What's For Sale

Booz Allen, a global leader in strategy and technology consulting, uses the Web to recruit and hire the most qualified people from over 100,000 candidates per year who submit profiles online.

What's So Interesting

As a leading international consulting company, the Booz Allen product consists of the brainpower of the 16,000 people who work there. The company recognizes that its services are only as good as the quality of its employees and is committed to using the Web as a tool to recruit this key component of its success. Content on the site points people to the careers section and once there, potential employees are presented with a wealth of information on what it's like to work at the company, descriptions of hundreds of open positions, and interactive tools that allow them to apply.

Why You Should Care

While most companies bury the careers section (if they have one at all) deep in the bowels of a corporate Web site, Booz Allen promotes careers extensively on the home page and then supplies content targeted specifically at select applicant groups, such as experienced professionals, MBAs, and recent college graduates. The site generates thousands of qualified applicants each month for the firm's open positions at a cost that's much lower than using a team of recruiters. Booz Allen cashes in by hiring the best person for each job—adding to its valuable brain trust—in an efficient and cost-effective manner.

Consulting firms sell brainpower. This requires constantly and consistently recruiting the best and the brightest candidates to maintain a quality service offering. At Booz Allen Hamilton Inc., a global leader in strategy and technology consulting, the need is particularly acute because of the size and scope of its operations. The firm generates over $3 billion in annual sales and staff numbered more than 16,000 people across offices on six continents. Clearly, the services Booz Allen provides to clients are only as good as the Booz Allen people. The company offers expertise in fields that include Strategy, Organization, Change Leadership, and Information Technology, and it must continually hire top experts in these areas to remain competitive. Thus, hiring the very best people is an essential element of the Booz Allen corporate strategy.

Most firms view the Web as an afterthought for recruiting. On most organizations' Web sites, potential employees have to do some hunting just to find the careers pages—which might be in "about us," "contact us," or any number of other locations; it's usually not a distinct link right on the homepage. Once a job-hunter hunts down the careers section, they are likely to find little more than rudimentary job listings with perhaps a diversity policy and an e-mail address to send a resume. Most candidates feel reluctant to submit their credentials into what they perceive as a "black hole" of an e-mail address on a stark site.

Booz Allen puts careers front and center both as a corporate strategy and on its site. Right at the home page, you'll find several links to careers, including an extensive drop-down menu of content. Candidates can choose to learn more about work/life balance, Booz Allen culture, or opportunities for newly minted MBAs. "We look at our site as the way to get our message out as an employer of choice," says Alicia Mallaney, Recruiting Manager for Booz Allen Hamilton Inc. "The careers tab is a means to drive traffic to the careers section. We want people to fill out profiles and apply for employment, but we also look at it for branding purposes. We want people to see what Booz Allen offers to the marketplace. It's an initial step in the education about Booz Allen."

The Right Fit for You?

Once people land at the careers section, they're presented with multiple content paths to follow. Self-select paths include a choice by the type of opportunity (such as Experienced Professional Opportunities, College Opportunities, and MBA Opportunities), as well as sections about what it's like to work at Booz Allen (A Great Place to Work, Benefits, Career Development, Culture/Core Values, and Work-Life Balance). On any given

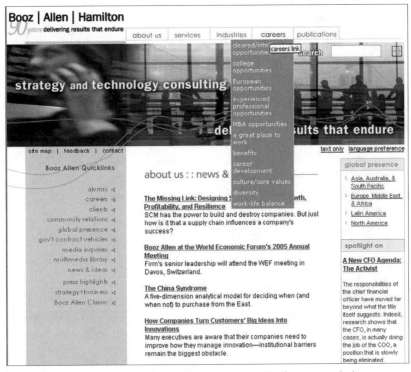

The Booz Allen Web site has links to the careers section from several places on the home page and includes an extensive drop-down menu.

day, feature articles might include such topics as "Upcoming U.S. Recruiting Events," "Booz Allen Receives Business Community Partner Award," and "African American Heritage Month at Booz Allen."

"When we first implemented the applicant tracking system, we made entryways for the types of people we wanted to attract," says Mallaney. "The content is specific to the individual audiences. We want to show whether Booz Allen is a place for them and explain why they might want to work at Booz Allen. We also want people to tell 10 of their friends: We want people to say we have a good Web site and we're actually hiring." The provision of content in all of these areas and more marks the Booz Allen site as a standout in the recruiting world.

Applicants can choose content based on the type of employment opportunities available at Booz Allen or they can learn more about what it's like to work at the company.

We Want You to Work Here

But the employee-centric focus isn't limited to the Careers section; much of the site's content exists to provide potential job candidates with information about Booz Allen. The idea is to get people interested in the company, show them what it's like to work there, and then have them apply for a job by submitting an applicant profile. "We have a value proposition that's focused around the important reasons why Booz Allen is a great place to work," explains Lois Remeikis, Director of Web Communications for Booz Allen Hamilton. "We want people who want to work here to know about us. Career development is important; we want people to know that they can grow within Booz Allen." According to Remeikis, Booz Allen is consistently ranked as a top consulting firm for programs of importance to employees such as training, which is promoted on the site. "We want people to know they will grow in their careers," Remeikis adds.

Content is developed in-house by a team of professionals from both the Web Development and the Human Resources groups. "We look at the whole

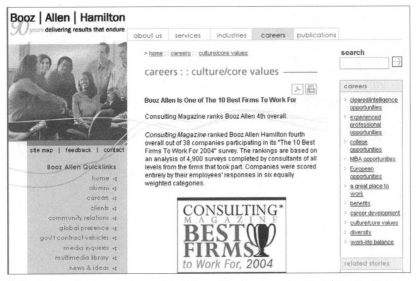

Potential employees can learn about Booz Allen's core values—and more— to see if the company is a good fit.

life cycle of the employee," says Mallaney. The content presents Booz Allen in realistic terms without a lot of fluff, according to Mallaney. "We lay it all on the line and tell it like it is," she says. "You can get a picture of the culture of Booz Allen on the site. People want to know what it would be like to work at Booz Allen and we show them what the organization is about. Our core values are important to the organization and we want that to come through."

Mallaney and Remeikis work together with their teams to create content specifically targeted at the different types of people they want to attract and write in terms intended to appeal to them. "We want to tailor news stories to each group," says Mallaney. "For example, with MBA students, we help them to understand the whole interviewing process."

Please Complete Your Profile

The ultimate goal of all this content is to get candidates to fill out and submit a profile. "We're constantly looking at the candidate experience," says Mallaney. "We try to empathize. Many companies want you to supply information but in our case, we want to supply content up front so they feel comfortable submitting information."

15,000 candidates per month fill out a personal profile on the Booz Allen site.

By every measure, the Booz Allen site is phenomenally successful in generating candidates. According to Mallaney, 73 percent of people who visit the site fill out profiles. "We are getting about 15,000 profiles a month," says Mallaney, "considering about 16,000 people work for the company now, that's a lot."

Mallaney and Remeikis work to constantly increase the site user experience. They evaluate at each step of the process and work to enhance content and functionality based on input from candidates. "We look at feedback about the experience of submitting," says Mallaney. "Usability is important. We interview people who got jobs on the site in order to make the site better." As many marketers know, a challenge in creating any type of Web form is asking for the right information. People in charge of Web sites are constantly tempted to ask for everything they always wanted to know. However, asking for too much overwhelms people and they abandon a form in frustration. "We're also looking at how to make the number of forms and fields they fill out as few as possible."

"It seems like a continual improvement process," adds Remeikis. "We're constantly upgrading the site and the usage increases. It's not like we wait for content to get stale." The team looks at all aspects of improvement, no matter how seemingly mundane. "We consider simple things like when people don't understand why they have to do something," says Remeikis. For example, when people don't answer a particular question on the site, it triggers a content review. "Even subtle changes are important," Remeikis says.

On any given day, there can be nearly 1,000 open positions posted on the Booz Allen site and its search engine makes finding positions easy for candidates. The search capability includes simple keyword searching or advanced search using criteria such as geographical location, department, job level (such as Director or VP), and full- or part-time. Once a candidate has filled out a profile, he can apply for specific positions found as a result of searching or browsing.

Career Content Creation

Remeikis works with the Human Resources department and other groups to source content for the site. With the broad goals of educating potential employees about what it's like to work at Booz Allen, selected content might be a speech by an executive, an article about the company from a magazine,

Hundreds of job postings are listed and searchable.

or an essay on work/life balance. "The recruiting team produces content and then we go over it to make it Web-friendly and to tighten it up," says Remeikis. "We have conference calls about what should be updated and how, and a weekly editorial meeting where we talk about news stories and so on."

Because content located in all areas on the Booz Allen site will be read by potential employees, the team pays attention to the entire site, not just the career pages. "We have 'Our People' right on the home page, which is updated regularly and helps in the recruiting process," Remeikis says. Candidates see the human face of Booz Allen and are more likely to connect with the organization and want to join. "Based on statistics, 'Our People' is well read by those who then visit the careers section."

$$$$$$$$$$$$$$$$$ Cashing In $$$$$$$$$$$$$$$$$

"The most important thing is that providing good information is the best way to improve the site," Remeikis says. When tracking the actual number of employees hired through the Web site, the focus on career content is considered a great success for Booz Allen. Global consulting firms recruit employees in many different ways: university job fairs, referrals, executive recruiting firms, etc. According to Mallaney, an average of 24 percent of Booz Allen hires come from the site.

When recruitment succeeds on the Web, tremendous tangible and intangible benefits occur. An immediate benefit for recruitment includes an increased pool of applicants at a lower cost than hiring executive recruiters or traveling to university job fairs. Equally important is the tremendous good will built up among the hundreds of thousands of potential employees who learn about Booz Allen through Web content. These people, even if they are not hired, will remember the experience and provide excellent word-of-mouth and viral marketing, which are critical for a service business. Some people may even be in positions to hire consulting firms in the future. If they had a positive experience with Booz Allen during a job search, they might think of Booz Allen first for their projects.

The Booz Allen executive management team is encouraged by the results. "We send out a report to all the marketing people and partners of the firm that has statistics on the site," Remeikis says. "The partners provide very positive feedback. They're very encouraged by the success of the site. We use the Web and the tools in a strategic way to impact the business."

CHAPTER FOURTEEN

UPS Investor Relations

Delivering Stock

➤ **Organization**
UPS
www.ups.com, www.shareholder.com/ups

➤ **Interviewed**
Paula Norton, Director of Investor Relations

What's For Sale

UPS, with $36.6 billion in revenue in 2004, is the world's largest package delivery company and a leading global provider of specialized transportation and logistics services. The company's Investor Relations site serves as a window into how the company is run, promoting UPS stock as a solid investment.

What's So Interesting

Founded in 1907 as a messenger company, for the first 92 years UPS was employee-owned. But in November 1999, the company went public in what then was the largest initial public offering in the history of the New York Stock Exchange. The IPO instantly put the company under intense scrutiny by investors worldwide. The UPS Investor Relations site provides visibility into the finances of a company that had historically been rather mysterious.

Why You Should Care

In the post-Enron era, open governance and financial visibility signal corporate health and directly influence a positive reputation. At the time of its massive IPO, UPS didn't have an extensive public financial history, so it launched a site to serve as a primary credibility tool for investors. The UPS Investor Relations site provides a model for any public company: Open and visible information on how a company is operated helps make its stock attractive to the investing public.

I magine being in charge of Investor Relations for one of the biggest companies in the world just as it is about to go public in what, at the time, was the largest initial public offering in the history of the New York Stock Exchange. Your job is to communicate to potential investors throughout the world about the structure, organization, and financial history of your company as well as provide details about how the company is being managed.

Investors make decisions on the basis of publicly available information and a company's financial performance track record. As a privately held business, UPS didn't need to provide investor visibility for the first 92 years of its history and, as a result, didn't have a visible financial track record. But that all changed when the company decided to go public; the transformation posed a tremendous challenge for the UPS Investor Relations team.

From the time of the IPO, the company's communications strategy has been one of providing open and visible corporate governance and other shareholder information. A major communications vehicle for UPS has been the provision of valuable content on the UPS Investor Relations Web site. "Initially the site was put up quickly in conjunction with the IPO in November of 1999 to provide some basic information," says Paula Norton, Director of Investor Relations. However, since it went live in 1999, Norton and her team expanded the UPS Investor Relations site significantly, supplying the information required by both professional and individual investors. "We want to clearly describe how we run the company," Norton adds. "The goal of the UPS Investor Relations site is to provide the newer investor, and particularly the individual investor, a user friendly and comprehensive look at the company."

Corporate governance has taken on greatly increased importance in the wake of the many financial scandals that rocked the business world at the turn of the 21st century. Norton describes how UPS tackled these communications challenges: "We redesigned the entire corporate site and, in conjunction, we upgraded the Investor Relations site by adding a lot of content around corporate governance, particularly in response to the Enron issues." UPS worked with investor relations content specialists at Investors Relations (IR) communications firm Shareholder.com to build the investor relations section of its site at www.shareholder.com/ups to seamlessly link to and from its main site at www.ups.com.

In its broadest form, corporate governance can be defined as the relationship between a corporation and its shareholders. In particular, corporate governance often refers to how a company promotes and communicates corporate fairness, transparency, and accountability to its stakeholders, particularly

Corporate governance information provides the transparency and visibility that makes an investment such as UPS stock attractive.

investors. At UPS, an entire section of the Investor Relations site is devoted to corporate governance, providing the company's code of conduct, its relationship with varied constituencies, management values and philosophies, and other information used by investors to understand what makes a company tick.

At the top level, the Investor Relations site has tabs for Financials, Company Information, Governance, and Sustainability. The Governance section provides detailed information on how the company is run. Written in no-nonsense, easy to understand language (with abundant links to additional information) prospective investors and shareholders alike can make their own decisions about the company and its management philosophies. The main navigation of the Governance section features a highlighted sidebar, calling out the following content sections:

- The UPS Charter

- Governance Guidelines

- Board Committee Charters

- Code of Business Conduct

- Corporate By-Laws

- Articles of Incorporation

Within each section, drill-down options allow you to get to more detailed content appear as you click through. For example, within the Code of Business Conduct section, additional content links include:

- Statement of Policy

- Preface

- Chairman's Message: On Leading with Integrity

- Our values, our management philosophies

- Checklist for Leading with Integrity

- The UPS Business Conduct and Compliance Program

- Asking Questions and Voicing Concerns

- Retaliation

- Our People

- Our Customers

- Our Shareowners

- Our Communities

- How to Suggest Changes to the Code of Business Conduct

When companies provide content about the ways that the business operates, the details send a clear signal to the market: "We have nothing to hide," and, by extension, "We can be trusted." After headline-making scandals from companies like Enron, Worldcom, and Tyco, UPS uses content to position itself as a leader in promoting honest forthright governance as an important corporate attribute.

Airplanes and Those Funny Brown Trucks

The Investor Relations site serves a set of constituents quite different from those that hit the UPS site. However, the content within different sections of the two sites serve each other's constituents through a well-designed map of cross linking. "We work very closely with Public Relations people and we

Content is linked between Investor Relations and other sections, including Public Relations.

link our sections of the Web site," says Norton. "There is a seamless flow of Public Relations information on the Investor Relations section of site."

Clearly, when someone investigates UPS stock as a potential investment, the content found in the Public Relations section is also very important. Things like press releases, management biographies, and other content originating within the Public Relations section of UPS.com is organized to mingle seamlessly with the Investor Relations site. The PR content offers fascinating tidbits—such as UPS employs 369,000 people, drives a fleet of 88,000 vehicles (including the trademark brown delivery trucks), and operates an air force–sized flock of 569 planes worldwide—all of which might influence a would-be investor.

Norton and her team continuously refine the UPS Investor Relations site and look for additional content of value to investors. "We're undertaking a project to add more content to the site," she says. "Over the past several months, I've been saving a lot of materials about how to evaluate and build a great Web site. I'm looking at other large company investor relations Web sites for ideas and I'll consider what experts say are best practices. I already know I want to increase the corporate governance section to make it even more all-encompassing."

Norton also relies on her constituents to help determine valuable content and to analyze site statistics and other data. "We look at the questions that come into us from the site," she says. A "Contact Investor Relations" link appears prominently at the top of all the Investor Relations pages. "I also gather input from others at UPS such as the public relations team," Norton adds.

Environmentally Friendly

UPS is committed to protecting the environment and makes information about its activities in this area a major part of the Investor Relations site. Sustainability is one of the first tabs a visitor sees at the site and, with a single click, they can read the company's sustainability statement, which begins: "At UPS, we believe our business success depends upon balancing economic, social, and environmental objectives . . . "

It's significant that a huge company devotes prime real estate to describing things like Corporate Culture, Employee Health and Safety, Greenhouse Gas Emissions, Recycling and Waste Management, Globalization, and Outsourcing in the sections of its investor site. "The sustainability section

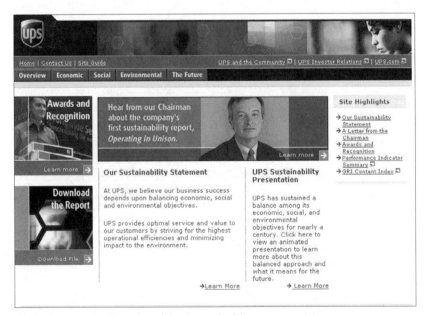

A good corporate citizen translates to a valuable company.

describes the softer side of the company and is an increasingly important part of the site," says Norton. "I think that five years from now sustainability and corporate citizenship will be a big issue for all companies." Norton's focus on providing all kinds of content about the company in order to drive the interest of investors is quite different than the financial-only approach of many companies' Web site investor relations sections.

As a so-called mega-cap company (with market capitalization hovering in the $100 billion range), UPS stock is held by many institutional investors. But as Norton describes, the Investor Relations site is built to serve different audiences: "We focus on the individual investor because the larger money managers have extensive information at their disposal at their firms," she says. "We think about retail investors vs. institutional investors."

"Another huge audience for us is UPS employees," says Norton. "Our employees and retirees own 50 percent of the company, so the information

Employee-owners visit the Investor Relations site frequently, especially if the stock is going up.

about the stock is very important to them." Employees and other investors alike all have access to materials such as SEC filings, quotes and charts, and financial tables. "It's very important to include the stock quote and stock chart. People are more likely to want to learn more about the company after they see the quote," Norton adds.

On-Time Delivery

"We write all of the content in-house," Norton says. "Good communications is the key. Even the smallest company can look like the largest by communicating well." With a great deal of existing content on the Investor Relations pages and more added all the time, it could be easy to ignore content fundamentals, like keeping the site content fresh. "The importance of keeping the site up to date may seem obvious, but it's so important," Norton says. "We want to change the home page of the Investor Relations site every now and then. Every few months we add additional content to the Investor Relations front page to make certain people know that we're always doing new things."

$$$$$$$$$$$$$$$$ Cashing In $$$$$$$$$$$$$$$$

Norton and the Investor Relations team might be tempted to look at the UPS stock chart each day and use that as a measure of their success. That approach wouldn't be entirely off base, as a great Investor Relations Web site certainly adds to the likelihood that a potential investor will buy a certain stock. But she also measures success in other ways. "Outside recognition is important," Norton offers. The UPS Investor Relations site has won awards and has been featured in best practices articles and reports. But then after a pause, she adds, "Not getting complaints is also good because that means the site works for our audience."

PART 3

Nonprofit, Education, Healthcare, and Politics

CHAPTER FIFTEEN

CARE USA

Content Fights Global Poverty

➤ **Organization**
CARE USA
www.careusa.org

➤ **Interviewed**
Toby Smith, Internet Strategist

What's For Sale

CARE USA receives millions of dollars in online donations from people who want to help poor communities throughout the world.

What's So Interesting

CARE is one of the world's largest private international humanitarian organizations, committed to helping families in poor communities improve their lives and achieve lasting victories over poverty. The CARE USA Web site provides a comprehensive window into the organization's activities in dozens of countries, which allows potential donors to understand exactly where their money will go and how it will be spent. As one of the most responsibly managed nonprofit organizations, the CARE USA site communicates that funds go where they will help the most and that less than 10 percent of expended resources go toward administrative and fundraising expenditures.

Why You Should Care

Unlike for-profit commercial enterprises, CARE USA doesn't sell a product or service on its Web site. Rather, it uses content to educate and explain its role in helping improve the lives of people around the world. The Web-based content is used by the organization to sell and market its good works in order to solicit online donations. The "product" CARE USA sells—fighting global poverty—presents an unusual sales and marketing challenge. CARE USA successfully uses Web content and serves as an excellent learning model for any organization marketing an intangible service, whether nonprofit or commercial.

C ARE, one of the world's largest private international humanitarian organizations, is committed to helping families in poor communities improve their lives and achieve lasting victories over poverty. Founded in 1945 to provide relief to survivors of World War II, the organization's reach and mission has greatly evolved and expanded from the simple CARE package of 60 years ago. CARE USA is a part of CARE International, a confederation of 11 CARE organizations that strives to be a global force and partner of choice within a worldwide movement dedicated to ending poverty. Each CARE organization (including CARE USA) that is part of the global consortium stewards country projects in offices around the world. As an independent organization, CARE USA is accountable to its donors and those it helps around the world. With a budget of half a billion dollars, CARE USA has a strong record of fiscal responsibility; the organization uses less than 10 percent of budget funds for administrative and fundraising expenditures.

As a global consortium, individual CARE Web sites have been created by the independent organization members in multiple languages including German, French, and Japanese. The consortium constructed a portal (www.care.org), which simplifies access to each of the available sites and languages, including the CARE USA site. The CARE portal and sites serve varied constituents around the world. However, for people who contribute funds and for those who are considering making a donation, the CARE USA site functions as an educational tool that shows how funds are used in the field. With a staff of nearly a dozen professionals (including two photographers) in charge of content, CARE USA's site provides a fine example of how content can drive online contributions for a nonprofit organization.

"I think of the Web as a fundraising tool, a community tool, and an educational tool," says Toby Smith, Internet Strategist for CARE USA. As part of a nonprofit organization offering people an opportunity to fight poverty by donating money, the CARE USA site is a key component in the organization's efforts to help the world's poor. "We want to educate our constituents about the issues surrounding global poverty and to get people involved so they feel they are part of the global poverty fight," Smith says. "The reality is that we ask for money. It's important for our constituents to have concrete stories about our work around the world. The Web helps to connect donors to the work in the field. It's been a progression, but the end goal of our site is really to raise money because it's important to raise funds in order to do our good works."

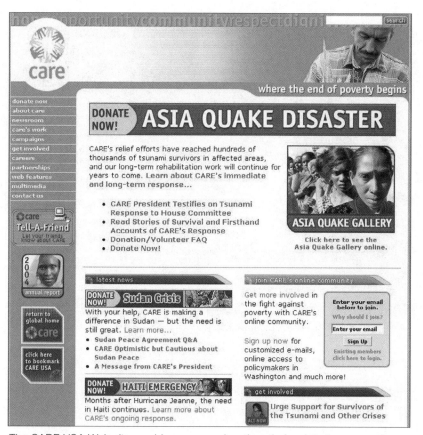

The CARE USA Web site provides a comprehensive window into the organization's activities in dozens of countries around the world.

Content to Drive Donations

As the person responsible for the content strategy on the CARE USA Web site, Smith's challenges are quite different than the straightforward business transactions that occur on most commerce sites. "In the for-profit world, you get something for your money—a product or a service," Smith says. "With a nonprofit, there's an altruistic component you need to articulate. We need to explain what you get for your money, because it's not tangible." Smith uses Web content to detail the work of CARE USA for its online donor community.

Smith's views on site design for a nonprofit organization focus on using content to drive action. These views reflect the influences of his early career experiences working with for-profit corporations. "There are a number of

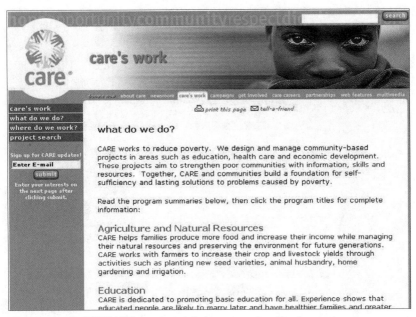

As a nonprofit, CARE USA must explain how your donation is spent.

distinct differences between a nonprofit site and a commercial site," he says. "For-profit sites are trying to sell a good or a service. We're doing the same thing, but with a larger education component. Like a for-profit, we are trying to explain and market our products and services. But the biggest difference is the education component; for us education is important to change the world."

The CARE USA site includes vast quantities of information about the work CARE USA does throughout the world. This well-organized site includes pages for those who want to get a broad view of a region (such as Asia) or a specific issue (children living with AIDS, for example). The site makes use of navigation architecture to provide ample opportunities for people to drill down from any of the sections to see details of the hundreds of individual projects in progress at any one time around the world. "There's a multiplatform component that doesn't appear on most for-profit sites," Smith argues. To explain, he describes how each page of content has multiple ways to link in and link out to facilitate exploration by users. He contrasts what he's built for CARE USA with what he describes as the much more linear and straightforward sites of commercial organizations saying, "There's a more streamlined approach in the

Donors are astute about international affairs and want details about the projects their money supports.

for-profit sites. We need a holistic feel. For-profits can talk about the product, but we must talk about the problems we solve."

The ability to dig deep into the issues surrounding global poverty is critical to the site's success, according to Smith. "People who are astute about international affairs want to go into detail on the Web," he says. "A highly educated group of people give to international relief nonprofits. We need to educate these people and keep them aware of what's going on in the world."

Comprehensive Content in a Soundbite World

Smith says that, for his team, attention to detail is critical in the provision of CARE USA's Web site content. "In a soundbite world, where things can be explained in a few sentences, CARE doesn't fit in," he says. "Our message is complex and we have to use content to explain our messages to donors. CARE is about the root causes of poverty. That's not a soundbite; it's about detailed and useful content. We need to educate, which takes time."

CARE USA's Virtual Field Trips provide an excellent example of the sites' detailed and comprehensive content that educates and informs. Web

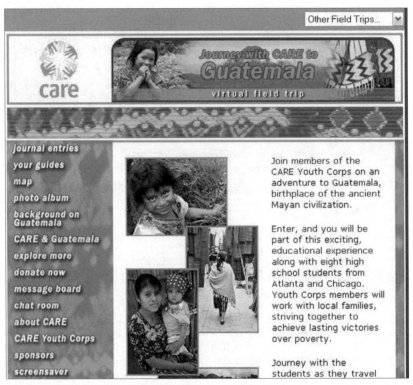

CARE USA Virtual Field Trips educate about CARE USA works around the world, generating more donations in the process.

site visitors can explore fantastic photographs and well-written and detailed stories from places like Guatemala, Ecuador, Kosovo, and Haiti. Through words and images Field Trips vividly illustrate CARE USA projects around the world, generating donations in the process.

Get Involved with Content

Not limited to fund-gathering, the CARE USA site also mobilizes constituents to support the fight against global poverty in other ways. Interested visitors can get involved by contacting government agencies and elected officials through the site. "There's a tool for people to e-mail government leaders on a particular topic, bill, or other issue," says Smith. For example, you can click to 'Voice your Support for Critical Programs that Fight Poverty.' When people use the CARE USA interactive system to send e-mails, Smith tracks that information. "If people send lots of e-mails through the system, that's important for us to know so we can use that information to market to them." A database of constituents who use the site for outreach provides incredible demographic information for marketing purposes. Smith learns the issues of importance to site visitors who use the e-mail tool; this information, combined with each person's online donation history, creates a detailed personal record for the most involved supporters.

Few organizations, for-profit or not, devote the extensive resources to content creation that CARE USA does. "We have a publications unit that's dedicated to writing content for our site," Smith says. "We have people who travel the world to write content and take photographs for the Web." The CARE USA content team is comprised of about a dozen people including two staff photographers, four publications staff, and a press office. According to Smith, the team writes feature stories, special reports, and other educational information on subjects of key importance to CARE USA. CARE has adopted a "show, don't tell" approach to marketing on the Web. CARE USA shows the

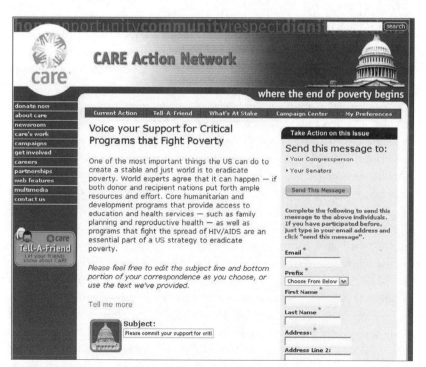

CARE USA offers ample opportunities for constituents to get involved, such as sending e-mail to government officials on important issues.

organization's results through the photographs, projects in the field, and reports. According to Smith, people are more likely to donate when they can see and interact with the results of their financial contributions.

With its dedicated team, CARE USA has also focused on building databases of content that can be used on the site when necessary. "We get content from the projects in the field," Smith says. "Each project has a database and much of the content appears on the site in the projects works section." Besides the articles and project reports, CARE USA also maintains a photo library of over a million photos, according to Smith.

Given the subject matter of the CARE USA site, Smith faces some unusual obstacles in obtaining content. "We have challenges in getting information back from the field in a place like Bangladesh," Smith says. "It is a real trick." To collect content, CARE USA relies on a variety of high-tech and traditional technologies. Of course, Web and e-mail deliveries to the site are ideal; however, in some cases, content needs to be hand-carried to a larger town and faxed or even mailed to Smith in order to be edited and placed on the site. With content coming from many continents, often originally written by those in the field—many with English as a second language—Smith and his team face unique challenges in trying to maintain editorial consistency. "It is a challenge to edit content so that it feels like it comes from one voice," he says. "Many of the reports are written by scientists, so the publications unit edits to make things compelling."

With vast amounts of content available, Smith spends a great deal of time on content selection and its placement to facilitate both searching and easy browsing. "Because we have lots of different areas of content, we make it easy to stay on the surface or drill down very deep into an issue or a project," Smith says. Smith uses a content management system to link content at the back end to facilitate an intuitive browsing experience. Another challenge for CARE USA is to show all of the compelling content both in the best light and in a variety of useful contexts, and technology helps. "It's difficult to strip out the different parts of what the Web can do, because the Web does so much," he says. "It is a collective whole. It is difficult to separate the content from the technology."

While Smith certainly makes use of technology, he's keenly aware that without interesting and informative content, back-end systems don't really matter. "Content is the meat of a site," he says. "Yes, Flash is pretty but does it do something? Meaning has to come from words and pictures. If you don't have that, you have nothing. The end goal of our site is to help save the world through education. We use the Web to build communities and constituencies to help eradicate poverty."

$$$$$$$$$$$$$$$$$$ Cashing In $$$$$$$$$$$$$$$$$$

As part of one of the largest nonprofit organizations, CARE USA manages a half-billion dollar budget. A major part of the organization's funding comes from over $100 million in direct public support. As Smith and his team continue to build the educational components of the CARE USA Web site, more and more donations are made directly online. "Our donors get detailed reports on where their money goes," Smith says. Indeed, the donation pages on the site include a breakdown of how money is spent, including details on the less than 10 percent spent on fundraising and administrative purposes. Potential donors can dig much deeper and are even provided with an opportunity to download the CARE USA federal tax returns from the site.

Much like a subscription service or companies that rely on repeat-business, CARE USA develops relationships with donors who contribute money on a regular basis. "We must cultivate customers, unlike some for-profits that just sell something once," Smith says. CARE USA uses the content on the site and specific targeting approaches based on people's interests. Smith explains, "There's a back-end database that helps us to cultivate people with content geared towards their interests and history," he says. "We use Customer Relationship Management systems and databases to capture information to manage the relationship over time. We have a large, complex set of back-end databases we use to market to donors. If you contribute and you're interested in the work we're doing for people living with AIDS in Thailand, we'll send you appropriate content via e-mail on AIDS and Thailand."

Smith is under constant pressure to show the value of technology to the mission of CARE USA around the world. Clearly, Web technology itself is not the answer to eradicating poverty, but there's no doubt that it enables content to help raise donations, which fund CARE USA works. The technologies Smith employs help present an impressive array of content, in a variety of ways, to donors and potential donors; this robust mix of content and technologies is intended to drive donors and potential donors to fund the CARE USA efforts. "Nonprofits are nonprofits," Smith says. "Every dollar that comes in here goes out the door. The level of investment that we put into the Web is a constant struggle."

Smith speaks for all nonprofits as he describes what he faces every day. "We have a difficult mission and a considerable challenge to convince nonprofit organizations to spend money on the Web and technology," he says. "Resources are a constant challenge for all nonprofits. We spend money on eradicating poverty, not on the Web and technology."

People donate millions of dollars online to support CARE USA's efforts to help the world's poor.

Interestingly, Smith has discovered that the CARE USA Web site tends to reach different people than do more traditional direct mail approaches. "We have a number of communities and constituents," Smith says. "The direct mail profile is a bit older person, more traditional-style givers. On the Web, we have a much different profile—a younger set of people, who are well-educated and global. We can reach different people online compared to those who already contribute through the direct mail programs."

The immediacy of the Web also offers CARE USA the opportunity to provide content and solicit donations for quickly developing crisis situations. For example, when the December 2004 tsunami devastated many parts of Asia, a region where CARE is actively funding many projects, the CARE USA home page was quickly updated to feature educational information and specific donation requests to support the victims of the tsunami's devastating effects. The fast development of tsunami-related content posted soon after the disaster ensured significant donations via the Web that would not have been possible with direct-mail solicitations.

While nonprofit organizations are often reluctant to spend money on technology, CARE USA's results highlight the effective implantation of technology to facilitate compelling content. For example, the organization secures dona-tions from younger people than CARE USA had traditionally reached through direct mail by its use of various Web-enabled technologies and targeting. "We use constituent relationship management tools to coordinate all of our con-stituent outreach," Smith says. "One the biggest values of technology is to maximize communications. In the end, the grand goal is to have satisfied con-stituents. We want our constituents to feel part of a community." The CRM systems allow Smith to measure his impact. "We watch e-mail signups and want people to be part of the communications to help eradicate poverty," he says.

According to Smith, Web donations still comprise only a small percentage of the overall donations to CARE USA. "The reality is that fundraising on the Web is in its early stages," he admits. "We have a long way to go. But many nonprofits see the future on the Web." CARE USA appears to be building the right model. With terrific content that's organized for browsing and supported by robust back-end systems, Smith and his team make a real impact. "We want an educated constituency," Smith adds. "We want people to get involved and interact with the Web site regularly. If people are delighted with our con-tent and our site, they will open their purses and wallets to donate."

CHAPTER SIXTEEN

Tourism Toronto

Hit the Site and Hit the Town

➤ **Organization**
The Toronto Convention and Visitors Association (Tourism Toronto)
www.torontotourism.com

➤ **Interviewed**
Kathy Barnett, Director of Content Development

What's For Sale

Tourism Toronto, the public face of the Toronto Convention and Visitors Association, is the official destination-marketing organization for this Canadian city. Hotels, restaurants, and others catering to the tourist trade have millions of Canadian dollars at stake and an obvious interest in promoting the city. Tourism Toronto, a membership organization for businesses in the travel and tourism trade, provides a significant promotional vehicle through its Web site.

What's So Interesting

Tourism Toronto promotes the city to several distinct buyer demographics, including individuals who plan their own journeys, those who book travel for groups, and representatives from organizations interested in booking conventions. The Tourism Toronto site provides excellent content specifically targeted to meet the needs of each buyer type. In 2003, Toronto faced a crisis of epic proportions when the world's media focused on the city's SARS epidemic, but the site's content helped the city face and transcend the crisis. Tourism Toronto works to build renewed interest in the city as a destination.

Why You Should Care

The Tourism Toronto site features self-select paths based on the type of potential visitor that quickly lead to appropriate content. Both those in the leisure trade and convention organizers can find appropriate content that builds interest in planning trips to this exciting city. The content speaks directly to people in each demographic and moves them along the sales cycle to the booking stage. Any organization with multiple diverse audience-types can learn from the well-organized and targeted content found on this site. Additionally, organizations recovering from a PR crisis can learn from Tourism Toronto's use of Web content to reeducate potential buyers.

Tourism Toronto, the public face of the Toronto Convention and Visitors Association, faces several challenges. First, the site must speak intelligently not only to the individual traveler who researches destinations on the Internet, but also to professional group planners and convention organizers. Too often, organizations fail to recognize and serve multiple audiences with specific content and end up with a dumbed-down one-size-fits-all site that serves nobody well. Not Tourism Toronto. The well-organized site includes multiple self-select paths that quickly lead each demographic directly to content created especially for them. In fact, content navigation is so seamless that many people might not even realize that the site serves diverse needs other than their own.

To compound the challenge of building a quality site, in 2003 the city of Toronto faced a PR crisis and is still emerging from the debilitating effects on its tourism industry. When the world's media targeted Toronto for scrutiny over a number of SARS deaths in the city, thousands of individuals, many group meetings, and several world-renowned artists, including Elton John, canceled plans to visit the city. Toronto faced an image problem of monumental proportions; hotels, restaurants, and other businesses suffered terribly. Tourism Toronto has led the charge to reenergize the city as a tourist and convention destination in the wake of the SARS scare and the site's content acts as an essential educational and informational tool.

Kathy Barnett, Director of Content Development for the Toronto Convention and Visitors Association, sums up the role of the Tourism Toronto Web site saying, "The site is a portal for visitors to the city." As the official destination-marketing organization for Toronto's tourism industry, Tourism Toronto focuses on promoting and selling the greater Toronto region as a remarkable destination for tourists, convention delegates, and business travelers. "The primary goal is to drive visitors to Toronto," Barnett says. "It's a service bureau—the first contact to the public. Somewhere around 90 percent of people who travel research the city via the Web site before they go to any other method, such as books, so the site needs to be really good."

Officially operating as a not-for-profit agency, Tourism Toronto boasts more than 900 members and is a partnership of public and private sectors. The Web site serves the needs of the members by showcasing the city, as well as its many attractions, hotels, restaurants, galleries, and shopping. According to Barnett, members also have opportunities to create content to be considered for site inclusion. "The Web site is the channel of first resort," says Barnett, "the first public touch, the first opportunity to communicate with potential visitors."

This primary portal for visitors to the city of Toronto serves several buyer demographics with self-select paths and compelling content for each.

Individuals, Groups, and Conventions

According to Barnett, the Tourism Toronto site serves several buyer demographics through the content. "Part of the audience is the individual traveler," she says. "But a big part is group travel including conventions and events and also group leisure travel such as church groups. We have navigation across the top of the home page to make it easy for each group to find a place to go. These are separate sections within the site to make it more relevant to each group."

Once a site visitor selects from the top-level navigation, they enter a specific section of the site with content created and organized especially for them. "For meeting planners, we make it easy to learn about the facilities and hotels but for leisure travel, we focus on exciting things to see and do in the city," Barnett says. "And for each group there is a separate home page. So it's almost like we have five separate sites." The site includes sections such as 'Five Reasons to Choose Toronto' written specifically for each of the target markets.

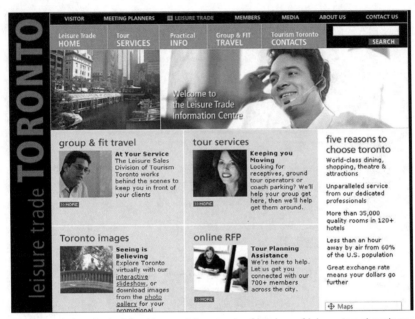

This home page is designed to meet the needs of leaders of leisure travel such as church groups.

Content to Book Trips

Barnett focuses much of her attention on the needs of the individual traveler who's surfing the Web in search of an interesting place visit. She describes how it works, "There are a lot of people who research starting with 'I want to go on a trip but I don't know where to go' in their mind. The experience pages on the site help these people. The content draws people in. The experience menu is broken down into different themes, such as sports and recreation, and nightlife, so people can experience a unique aspect of the city. We use those pages to give visitors more of a window onto the city. The other sections are fact-based, while this is more around feeling."

Toronto has a tremendous amount to offer visitors but until very recently, the city's charms remained a well-kept secret. Barnett describes the situation she faced, "Over the past 10 years, travel to Toronto has been in decline because the city hasn't been promoted that much. But we are going through a rebirth now: Art galleries and the theater scene have picked up. The distillery district is catching on. The nightclub scene is one of the best in the world. But many people don't know about all these things. So we're in the middle of a huge

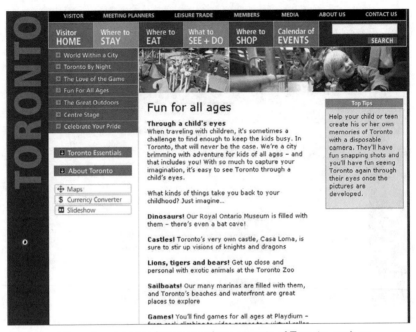

Dinosaurs! Experience pages focus on unique aspects of Toronto, such as interesting things to do with children.

exercise to re-brand the city to the world. The site content needs to show the world how great we are. We're trying to change the fact that we're a secret."

The individual traveler could spend hours reading all of the interesting content promoting the city, particularly the experiences sections. For those seriously considering making a trip to Toronto, site content ultimately steers them toward the decision to book the journey. When potential travelers are ready to commit, the site then also facilitates the transaction. So after the softer, feelings-based content does its job, hard data takes over. "When they know they want to come to Toronto, the fact-based information on hotels, restaurants, and local attractions becomes valuable," Barnett says.

Recovering from SARS

In 2003, Toronto experienced a major crisis when the world's media began intensively reporting on the cases of SARS that led to several deaths in the city. The effect was magnified because Toronto was singled out as one of the first locations outside of Asia with a SARS outbreak. The effect on tourism

Research and book your hotel while you're still intrigued by content about the city.

was immediate and devastating. "SARS hit Toronto very hard," Barnett says. "Many people didn't realize the impact of tourism on the city until the SARS effects were felt throughout the economy. Thousands and thousands of people are employed at hotels, restaurants, and in entertainment; many companies went belly up and people were left without work. The SARS issue was a very scary time, and not just for health professionals, but for the whole of the Toronto economy."

Tourism Toronto's Web site has served as a major vehicle for promoting the city after the SARS crisis. The primary goal, of course, is to encourage individual tourists as well as groups to visit the city. The entire tourism industry has banded together to support the city's promotional efforts. "Through a 3 percent destination marketing fee payable on all hotel bills," Barnett says, "we now have a budget to help promote the city. This was a voluntary initiative of the hotels."

The investment is paying off, according to Barnett. Throughout and since the SARS crisis, the Web site has been a unifying force to bring visitors back. "The Web site is one of the best vehicles to show the city's renewal," Barnett says, "because 90 percent of people who are thinking of visiting a city will view the site."

Content Voyage

Barnett and her team work very hard to make the content appropriate to each of the targeted demographic groups. "Our content needs to be a true representation of our city and the services we offer," she says. "It needs to be a resource for people. If you're a meeting planner, we need to have the information you need and if you're a visitor, we need to answer your questions."

Barnett's team writes much of the content for the site, but Tourism Toronto also relies on its hundreds of members for input. "Because our organization is member-based, we use content from the members," says Barnett. "When you see a feature on someone or something, it's by a member. This controls the specific content. For general content, we focus on what's important for all the groups. I write the general content so I can provide one voice and a consistent message."

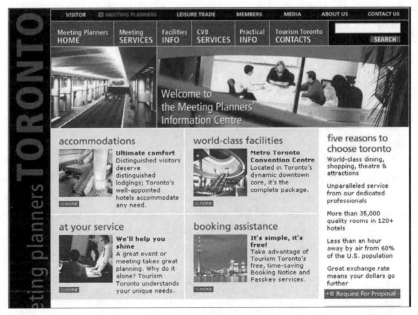

Meeting and convention planners find everything they need in one convenient place.

The sheer volume of material available to Barnett in one of North America's largest cities is stunning. She says, "We've got 6,000 restaurants in Toronto of all ethnic varieties" and any one of the restaurants could be featured on the site. Barnett's team also pays close attention to seasonal variations when posting content. For example, they carefully consider when to post photos and stories about winter sports. The winter travel content needs to be available when people are considering a winter holiday, prior to the onset of winter. "Features are seasonal," Barnett says, "and offers are appropriate. The content has to be relevant for a large number of visitors."

Interactivity and Small Bits of Content

In late 2003, Barnett and her team completely redesigned the site. "This site is drastically different from our old site," she says. "We did lots of best-practices research on how people use content on Web sites and what they need in a destination Web site. So the new site reflects that extensive research." Because Barnett focused so much effort on studying Web content strategy prior to executing the new design, the site works on all levels.

With extensive research into content development and a site that is living up to its goals, Barnett's Tourism Toronto site is a great example of best practices itself. For example, Barnett points out: "A Web site is not a publication. It is more like an online news site so it must always change." In addition, Barnett likes to offer tools to engage the user with the site. "Interactive stuff like a currency converter, interactive maps, calendars, slide shows, and so on is all important," she says. The site includes an online Request for Proposal (RFP) form that promises to "do the legwork" for group travel planning.

In order to appeal to varied readers, Barnett focuses on providing content that is organized logically, navigates well, varies in length, and has an appropriate shelf-life. "Smaller bits of content—a paragraph or two on a topic—are more important than dense text," she says. "The text keeps them engaged and clicking for more and it cannot be static. A site needs fluidity." Interestingly, while many sites that promote destinations include extensive advertising, Barnett has resisted the additional revenue ads could bring in. "We have no advertising on the site because it doesn't make a good visitor experience," she says.

$$$$$$$$$$$$$$$$$$$ Cashing In $$$$$$$$$$$$$$$$$$$

So—with extensive content appealing to diverse demographics and a redesign that serves to deliver that content effectively—does Barnett consider the site a success? "The feedback has been extremely positive so far," she says cautiously. "Comments from all audiences have been overwhelming strong." The ultimate reward, of course, is bringing more visitor-dollars to the city of Toronto. Barnett focuses success metrics on two objectives: "One is to drive visitors to the city," she says. "If the site can help increase the number of visitors, then it is successful. Two, provide the information people need. For example if you're a meeting planner, we want you to have your needs met with the content on the site." With success, the Tourism Toronto site helps its members to gain more business.

Although it's a little too early to tell for certain the extent of the site's impact on Toronto's tourism industry, things are looking up for the city. There's a fresh feeling in the air and visitors are returning. Barnett concludes that, with the site, "We want to show the world that the city is going through a renewal and that it is a great place to visit."

CHAPTER SEVENTEEN

Kenyon College

A Literary Tradition on the Web

➤ **Organization**
Kenyon College
www.kenyon.edu

➤ **Interviewed**
Kimberlee Klesner, Vice President for Development

What's For Sale

Kenyon College, as one of the nation's finest liberal arts colleges, uses its site to boost donations and attract the best students.

What's So Interesting

Kenyon College has a long-standing history of academic excellence and literary achievement. But this college of only 1,550 students is located in tiny Gambier, Ohio and must fight for national recognition. The Kenyon site was rebuilt in 2003 with the specific goals of raising the college's profile, attracting more donations, and increasing the number and quality of applications for admission. The site was designed from the ground up to use content to tell the college story and accomplish its objectives.

Why You Should Care

Kenyon's site is organized specifically to appeal to the different groups of people the college needs to reach, including high school students (for admissions), alumni, and parents (for donations) as well as students, faculty, and the local community. The site tells the college story through numerous profiles of Kenyon College graduates, students, and faculty, including high achievers from business, the arts, and academia. Organizations that are lucky enough to possess strong offline content can learn how to leverage it for the Web by studying Kenyon's site.

K enyon College is one of the nation's finest liberal arts colleges. The school has a long-standing literary tradition and its learning environment succeeds because it is rigorous and collaborative at the same time. According to *Kaplan/Newsweek*, Kenyon is one of the country's "hottest colleges," and according to *U.S. News & World Report*, it's among the top liberal arts colleges in the nation. But have you even heard of Kenyon College? How on earth can a small college in the middle of a cornfield in Ohio with only 1,550 students stand out on the Web? Not by giving the world a basic overview of its academic and student life—the college tried that approach and it didn't work out so well.

Kenyon performed a comprehensive site overhaul in order to focus on content. The college started the redesign by convening a cross-functional working group that included faculty, staff, and students; the group was charged to analyze needs for the site. Kenyon chose to use an outside firm to help with the rigorous planning process that took nine months.

After the analysis, what Kenyon came away with was both a simple and eye-opening concept: A college, just like a Web site, is all about content. A college is not just a collection of ivy-covered buildings with students throwing Frisbees on the quad nor is it about biology labs or other facilities. A college is its content. Kimberlee A. Klesner, Kenyon's Vice President for Development, sums up the thinking this way: "A successful Web site is about three things: good content, good content, and good content. And that's what Kenyon College is about— good content."

But portraying the content of a college through the content on its Web site is not easy. Yet as the team analyzed the college and the new Web site design, a major aspect of Kenyon's personality emerged: the strong sense of community at the college. Thus, the site was organized to place front and center the many and varied individuals who make up the college community and let these individuals' stories tell the tale of the college.

"Because of Kenyon's location and setting, we have an unusually strong sense of community," says Klesner. "We felt that if we were going to portray the vibrancy, intellectual curiosity, and sense of community of the college through the Web site, the only way we could do it effectively was through content—not technology—so that's what the focus is on. And one of the best ways to describe the community is to talk about Kenyon people on the site."

Kenyon is certainly fortunate to have some fascinating people with interesting stories to tell. And the message is loud and clear on the home page: If you choose to study here, you'll become one of them. Through the Meet

A college is about content and community, and at Kenyon, its people tell the story.

Kenyon People section, you'll learn about graduates: Allison Janney, class of 1982, has a leading role in TV's top-rated "The West Wing"; Mark C. Rosenthal, class of 1973, is President and Chief Operating Officer of MTV Networks; E. L. Doctorow, class of 1952, is an award-winning author; John Snow, class of 1961, is the U.S. Secretary of the Treasury; and Rutherford B. Hayes, class of 1842, was the 19th President of the United States. Kenyon's message is that its graduates are lifelong learners who lead productive and interesting lives. "The home page cycles each time you click. We have not only alumni, but students, faculty, and others who appear," Klesner says.

Klesner launched the people profiles site with about a dozen profiles and is gradually adding more; profiles cycle through when the page is refreshed. Initially some profiles were reproduced from the college's print publications, including the alumni magazine, but since the site's been live, the majority of the profiles have been written by staff from the college's small Public Affairs department. Now, according to Klesner, staff has a "Web-first mentality" where profiles start on the site and then migrate to print.

The Right Way to Rebuild a Web Site

Kenyon's site redesign was undertaken as a major college initiative. The team that took on the project worked for nearly a year and did it right—studying the weaknesses of the existing site and bringing together representatives of groups to get user input. "The old site was organized and structured like the college was," says Klesner. "Academic was located in one place, student life in another. When we started looking at what makes Kenyon distinctive, we wanted to communicate directly to alumni and to prospective students the content that would be important for them." In other words, the Kenyon team knew that the previous site had been organized from college administrators' perspective, but the new site needed to be organized from visitors' varied perspectives.

The team realized early on that they would need outside help to build the new site and the process for selecting an outside partner was rigorous. "We started by researching Web consulting firms and submitting requests for proposals to 15 organizations," says Klesner. "Then we invited four to come in and present to us so we could make our selection."

By first understanding the needs of the college, then initiating the Web consulting selection process based on the identified needs, Kenyon was able to find the best partner for its project. The college chose mStoner, a firm with extensive experience in working for educational institutions and nonprofits. Then the real work began, because Klesner had a hard deadline she had to meet. "We wanted to have the new site up to help with admissions for the 2004 academic year," she says, "so we worked intensively for nine months." And Klesner succeeded in this goal—the site went live in early July 2003, just as the incoming class for the 2004 year was about to enter its senior year of high school.

A Site That Speaks to All Constituents

The Kenyon site needed to speak to several distinct visitor groups and required compelling content for each. For external audiences, the sections for alumni and for prospective students are the most important and much attention was focused on these areas. But there's more, as Klesner explains, "We decided to deliberately view parents as a separate group and build content for them. We have a very committed and involved group of parents and, unlike other schools, we don't treat parents as an extension of alumni. Instead we have a separate gateway on the Kenyon site for parents that includes content such as 'demystifying financial aid.' We learned that parents have different needs on the site. Just like when they take our campus tour, parents want to go to a different place than their children, the prospective students."

As an educational institution, Kenyon's site also needed to serve the needs of current students, faculty, and staff. But the content for these groups didn't need to be front and center on the home page like the content for alumni, prospective students, and their parents. Klesner says they solved the problem by using hidden gateways. "We have a lot of people within the college who come to the site. Many sections are important to students and faculty but not to outside audiences, such as the College Registrar's section. These sections of the site are within a gateway that we don't feature on the main pages." The Office of the Registrar's site (http://registrar.kenyon.edu) has a utilitarian feel, providing quick no-nonsense access to essential information for students.

When the site development team spent time with different groups, they learned a great deal of surprising information and the real-life input made the site significantly more usable. For example, Klesner explains how the Current Student gateway, which is accessible from the home page, was created with student help: "We wanted to know exactly what content students wanted to be one-click away from. For example, we learned that it was important for students to have easy access to the local movie schedule. The students really got into the process and we all learned a great deal about how to serve them with the site." The team also built a Community section where local residents could learn about campus events open to the general public.

Another challenge in creating the new site was that it required a system for content on the site to be "owned" by varied groups, departments, and other individuals; each is responsible for keeping their section's content fresh. Kenyon chose to deploy a content management system for the site to make it easy for non-technical people to update content. The site is overseen by the College's Public Affairs department and one person is dedicated full time to site content, but there's no way that one person could do it without the use of the CMS and having each department responsible for specific content. Klesner knows the challenge involved in managing many different content originators. "We've talked about how to evaluate if content is getting stale," she says. "The site needs to constantly have new information so it is fresh and pertinent, but we have to balance that against the resources available."

Literary Content

Kenyon has a world-renowned English department and the college is the publisher of the prestigious *Kenyon Review*. As a premier literary journal,

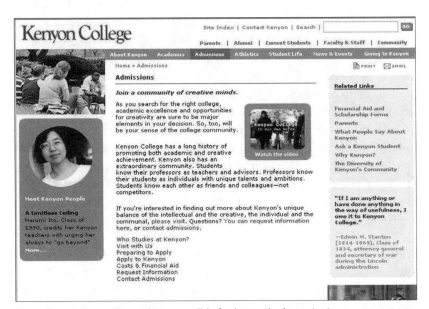

Each department or group is responsible for its section's content.

Klesner and the team knew that the *Kenyon Review* needed to occupy prime real estate on the new site. But there was a distinct challenge in making use of the fabulous content found in the *Kenyon Review* and a host of other print publications such as the *Kenyon Alumni Bulletin;* the team knew the content would be compelling for the new site, both because of its quality and its literary reputation, which enhances that of the college. They also recognized the limitations of print; according to Klesner, "We needed to change the approach to print content repurposed on the site. The print publications are great but they are in a different medium, so the content must be rethought for the Web." One important consideration, according to Klesner, was the length of the print stories and profiles migrating to the Web. The Public Affairs staff aimed to have longer pieces shortened to a target of 250 words when repurposed from print to online.

The main Kenyon site includes distinct sections for showcasing print publications as well as Kenyon's literary tradition. For example, the *Kenyon Review* section includes a bi-weekly feature, where visitors can read an essay, story, or poem from the journal. The main Kenyon site features people who've published books. "One of my favorite pages is the Kenyon author section,"

Quality print content from the *Kenyon Review* is repurposed for the Web site.

says Klesner. "This is really important to showcase the talents of Kenyon people, both faculty and alumni authors."

$$$$$$$$$$$$$$$$$$$$ Cashing In $$$$$$$$$$$$$$$$$$$$

As a small liberal arts college with a relatively modest endowment, Kenyon relies on funding support alumni, parents, and foundations. The Web site features content specifically for alumni and includes a "Give Now" button to allow anyone to quickly donate money online. To encourage giving, the site features news stories about major gifts and information on how to name Kenyon in your will.

Now that the site has been live for a while, the team is focused on measuring and analyzing feedback and remains committed to making changes as required to continue to meet the original goals. Initially, they used surveys to learn how people were reacting and in particular, focused on the site experiences of alumni and newly-admitted students. "We've gotten some universally positive feedback," Klesner says, but she knows that's only part of the picture. The college has also looked at its WebTrends data to learn how people navigate through the site. "The alumni online community pages are much more popular now than before," she says. "People are going deeper."

Major gifts to the college are featured on the site in part to put Alumni in the giving spirit.

The college has taken initial steps to analyze the site based on the original objectives of driving donations and increasing the number and quality of applications for admissions. "We compared people who visit the site to those who give to the college and learned there is a strong correlation between the two." And applications are up: Kenyon received nearly 3,800 applications for the class of 2008, an increase of 13 percent from the year before.

But Klesner and the team realize that a true analysis will take time. In fact, it will take years before Kenyon knows how successfully it is using the site to influence the college admissions process because of the very long lead times required for students to select a college. Klesner describes the dilemma, "When students visit colleges in person, they tend to be juniors and seniors in high school. But we learned that when students first visit college Web sites, they're freshman or sophomores so the Web site is often the first place that a student comes into contact with the college." It will be years before the students using the site today are ready to send in an application and Klesner projects site analysis going even further into the future. For example, she says, "I want to know if there is a correlation between the academic department home pages and the student's choice of major."

Asked how Kimberlee Klesner would sum up the most important things about the Kenyon College Web site, her response is simple, "It's all about the content."

CHAPTER EIGHTEEN

Sharp HealthCare

Putting Patients in Control with Content

➤ **Organization**
Sharp HealthCare
www.sharp.com

➤ **Interviewed**
Kelly Faley, Director of Marketing Technology

What's For Sale

Sharp HealthCare, San Diego's leading healthcare system, includes seven hospitals, three medical groups, a health plan, and a full range of facilities and services.

What's So Interesting

Sharp HealthCare's site empowers patients with information, including Web-enabled disease-specific self-assessments. The site is organized throughout to move patients from the information-gathering phase to choosing a doctor and making an appointment at a Sharp facility. While most healthcare sites are little more than online brochures, Sharp leads the way to a more interactive info-centric future with innovative use of Web content; strong content has helped the organization become number one in the San Diego healthcare market.

Why You Should Care

Leaders in the healthcare profession are beginning to understand and appreciate the value of a strong Web strategy. Sharp HealthCare has been named one of the "Most Wired" hospitals and health systems in the nation by *Hospitals & Health Networks*, the journal of the American Hospital Association, while *Modern Healthcare* magazine named Sharp the "best integrated health-care network" in California. Its objectives of informing and assisting existing and potential patients via the Sharp site before a doctor visit helps Sharp increase patient loyalty, develop viral marketing opportunities, and significantly increase the number of new patients. Service businesses of all kinds can learn from the Sharp approach.

W hen a person doesn't feel well or has been diagnosed with an unfamiliar ailment, information becomes critical in making healthcare choices. The more serious the medical condition, the more urgent the need for knowledge becomes. For years, Web sites have been catering to patients who have an intense need to learn about illnesses and make informed healthcare decisions. In the late 1990s, health information portals built on advertising-based business models emerged to provide comprehensive information. One of the more famous founding healthcare portals, www.drkoop.com, was launched by C. Everett Koop, M.D., former Surgeon General of the United States. Since then, as more and more people take an active role in managing their health, hundreds of sites have emerged to provide content on healthy living, health issues, diseases, and concerns specific to each stage of life or lifestyle. But until recently, hospitals and healthcare organizations left the creation and provision of this content to advertising-supported portals and specialty sites that focused on a single disease, a particular type of cure, or unusual philosophical approaches to treatment and medicine.

Professionals at Sharp HealthCare realized that patients look to the Web for information. Because Sharp didn't want its patients surfing just any old healthcare site, it dedicated significant resources to create a site that would provide its own end-to-end health experience—from the information-gathering stage all the way to doctor or hospital visits and treatment selection. A pioneer in the provision of comprehensive healthcare content to help patients make informed decisions, Sharp HealthCare was named among the nation's "Most Wired" by *Hospitals & Health Networks Magazine* for five straight years.

Sharp HealthCare, an organization described in marketing materials as "designed not for profit, but for people," is San Diego's leading healthcare system with seven hospitals, three medical groups, a health plan, and a full range of facilities and services. The organizations' more than 14,000 nurses, employees, physicians, and volunteers are committed to offering the best healthcare possible and that includes content. "We want patients to be able to look up information from a reliable source," says Kelly Faley, Director of Marketing Technology for Sharp HealthCare. "When people look for information, they are looking for specifics on a disease, a condition, or an organ. We want to give our patients and San Diego consumers a place for quality information that they can rely on."

While the content provided to consumers on the Sharp site is freely available to anyone, there's no doubt that one of the company's objectives is to profit from its relationships with new and existing patients. "The goals of the Sharp site are to educate the San Diego market on Sharp HealthCare as well as to build physician referral and the selection of a Sharp physician," Faley says.

I Need to Know Fast

The Sharp site provides content on specific illnesses, but its intelligent design delivers much more, including interactive self-assessments and links to profiles of physicians who practice in the Sharp network of facilities. Easy-to-navigate drop-down menus, which include Adult Health, Kids Health, and Teen Health, help direct visitors to appropriate content by type. To illustrate the Sharp difference, say your child had trouble with her eye. With most healthcare systems, you'd probably have to either telephone a primary care physician or surf the Web to locate an unfamiliar site of questionable authority and reliability in an attempt to learn more. With Sharp, everything—including information gathering, selection of a doctor, making an online appointment, and getting driving directions to the facility—happens seamlessly within its Web site. "We think content is the hook," says Faley. "We know that people who are on the Internet are looking for general health information. We want to capture them

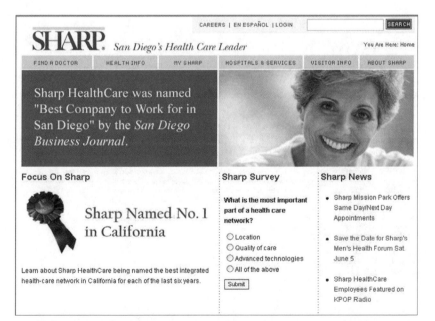

The Sharp site provides healthcare information for San Diego residents from a reliable source.

and meet the immediate need to help them with the disease, but then we want to provide them with information on who will help them and how."

The effect of the Sharp site's organizational approach is to take a process that might require several steps, simplify it, and make it all happen in one place in order to convert the information-seeker into a patient at Sharp. "In the full spectrum of healthcare Web sites, we're on the high end with what we provide," Faley says. "Most healthcare organizations don't have the level of integration we do. For example, at the Sharp site, after you read all about cardiac care, we link to Sharp cardiac facilities and Sharp cardiac physicians. We also have links to interactive tools."

Viral Healthcare Content

Faley and her team focus on the many ways that the Sharp site serves as a marketing program for the many services of the Sharp system. "We average 300,000 visits per month and 10 minutes per visit," she says. "This is great marketing for us when you consider the average impression that people would see in life is much less—say a billboard on the highway for 10 seconds or a TV commercial for 30 seconds. It's amazing that they're with us for 10 minutes."

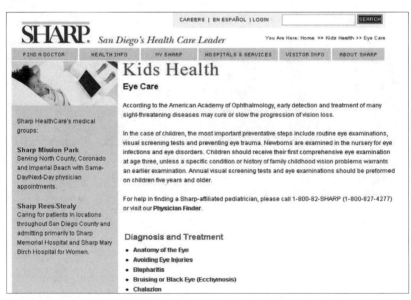

Comprehensive information on illnesses and conditions is conveniently organized.

While a major goal of the site is to market to potential new patients, Faley also recognizes that it is important to provide content for those who already use Sharp services as well. "We also want to build relationships with our patients," she says. "It's the small things that are important. For example, we have door-to-door driving directions to every facility and every physician. We're trying to add more interactive forms and billing information." Faley also concentrates on things that might lead to viral market success such as providing content on the site intended to be shared with friends and family. "We include things like newsletters and a baby gallery," she says.

The baby photo as viral content marketing—e-mail to a friend and promote Sharp at the same time.

The baby gallery provides an interesting example of viral marketing using content. New parents receive their own complimentary page on the Sharp site, which includes a photo and birth details for their new bundle of joy. Other fun facts are listed on each baby's page such as "this day in history" and "famous birthdays." New parents eagerly e-mail the link to family and friends, promoting Sharp HealthCare in the process. "We try to link from content to other things," Faley says. "For example, on the baby gallery, we list the physician's name and link back to the physician's profile. When people are in the baby gallery, they browse a lot. They might learn about our newborn classes, breast-feeding classes, and other information."

A particularly impressive aspect of the Sharp site is its comprehensive set of interactive tools and calculators. These useful ways to learn about health also serve to directly link users to appropriate Sharp HealthCare professionals. Examples of tools and calculators include:

- Could You or Someone You Know Have a Drinking Problem? - Find out whether your drinking patterns are normal or indicate a serious problem.

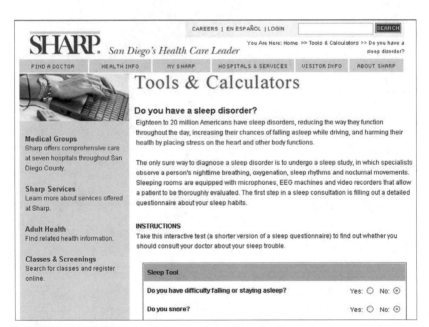

Interactive tools allow you to learn about your own health and make appointments to use Sharp HealthCare services.

- Physical Exam Reminder - Let Sharp remind you to schedule your annual physical.

- Body Mass Index (BMI) - The medical standard for obesity can be a useful tool for all people managing their weight.

- How Much Do You Know about Women's Risk of Heart Disease? - Think you know everything about heart disease? Test your knowledge with this interactive quiz.

On the same page where interactive results are posted, the tool or calculator provides links to obtain more information or to schedule an appointment with the appropriate Sharp HealthCare professional. "The tools and calculators are kind of a fun way to keep people interested and using Sharp services," says Faley.

Healthy Demographics

Faley and her team take care to understand the demographics of the San Diego community as well as users of the Sharp site in order to create appropriate content to reach them. "Over 75 percent of healthcare decisions are made by women," Faley explains. "Women are the primary decision makers when choosing doctors, choosing the healthcare provider, and more—so the site must appeal to women." One way Sharp targets women is through specific pages and newsletters covering women's health issues. And to meet the needs of another demographic—southern California's large Spanish-speaking population—Sharp created a Spanish language version of the site.

Studying site demographics has led to some interesting discoveries. For example, Faley describes how the site reaches teenagers, one of the most wired demographics. It turns out that teens won't go to a kids section, so Sharp needed a section of the site designed just for teens, which includes essays on Adolescent Health problems, Cognitive and Relationship Development, and links to a variety of resources. In addition to broad site design, Faley also analyzes details on specific pages based on usage details she's gleaned over the years. "We know that some people choose physicians based on their photo," she says. "It's not the best way to choose, but it happens. So we have to provide physician photos on the site."

As a non-profit organization focused on the health of the San Diego community, Sharp HealthCare faces distinct challenges when it comes to how it sets itself apart from the competition. "Most healthcare organizations including Sharp are not-for-profit," Faley says. "At Sharp we want to provide the best

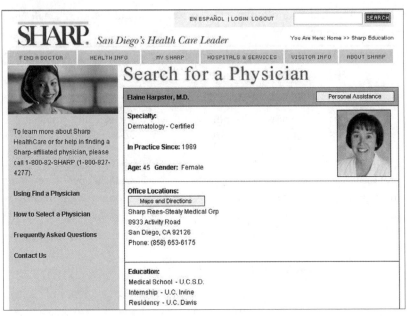

Choose your physician based on their qualifications, practice location, or even photo.

healthcare available, but that doesn't mean we want the competitors to be less good, because we want all people to be as healthy as possible." As much as Faley wants everyone to be happy and healthy, she's serious when it comes to competing for patients online. "We watch our entire competitor sites in San Diego locally and also we benchmark against sites all over the country," she says. "We look at San Diego groups because we don't want the San Diego competition to get a leg up."

Creating Compelling Healthcare Content

When it comes to creating a terrific Web site fueled by valuable content, Faley is fortunate to have financial support within Sharp HealthCare all the way to the top of the organization. "Senior management believes in the Web site and provides resources to use," Faley says. "We create our content in-house. Because we're focused on it and have dedicated—not outsourced—resources, we can provide a great site." According to Faley, some of the more basic and general health information in both English and Spanish comes from a health content syndication company called Greystone.net. "Everything else we write ourselves," she added. "For example, we feature things such as breast health information. We write the tools, services, hospital information, and much more."

$$$$$$$$$$$$$$$$$$$ Cashing In $$$$$$$$$$$$$$$$$$$

As Faley creates increasingly targeted content and interactive tools on the Sharp site, it becomes easier to measure the specific impact of the programs and resources and collect information about users. Thus, being able to quantify the results is a new focus for the site. "There's been a Sharp Web site for many years," Faley says. "Until very recently, we hadn't asked for much in the way of user demographics. But now that has changed as we provide services. For example, to book an appointment online, patients need to give their information."

According to Faley, another way to measure results is through content targeting. "We write newsletters because we want to target our customers with purpose-built information," she says. "For example, we focus on recent studies or something timely and we add related content on the site. For breast health month, we have links to things like reminder tools for mammography and links for how to do self exams."

The dedication and efforts of Faley and her team are being noticed by management. Besides the awards like "Most Wired" that Sharp HealthCare has won, demographic data is proving the organization can cash in with content. "We've been having discussions about success recently," she says. "In the past, we used to just look at visitor numbers, now we focus on our referral network from the site. We want to know if users turn into patients. From a business perspective we want to get more patients. Whenever they have a choice, we want them to choose Sharp."

CHAPTER NINETEEN

Dermik Laboratories

More than Skin-Deep Content

➤ **Organization**
Dermik Laboratories
www.skinhealthsolutions.com

➤ **Interviewed**
Robert Partridge, Director of Corporate Communications

What's For Sale

Dermik Laboratories provides skincare products marketed to dermatologists and other healthcare professionals as well as directly to consumers.

What's So Interesting

In an environment where drug makers saturate the airwaves and print media with advertisements that drive consumers crazy with choice, Dermik Laboratories uses the Web as the medium for its message. By launching a site called Skin Health Solutions, Dermik has chosen to educate consumers and health care providers through the provision of content rather than by force-feeding sales messages compressed into 30-second TV spots. Interestingly, Dermik did not build the Skin Health Solutions site with its own original content. Rather, the site is comprised of links to more than 300 other sites (including competitors) to offer the very best of skincare content, all reviewed by an independent professional advisory board. Dermik wants Skin Health Solutions to be the first place both doctors and patients go for information on dermatological conditions.

Why You Should Care

Dermik made an interesting and unusual move by choosing to launch a site independent from its corporate site (www.dermik.com). The Skin Health Solutions site includes links to all kinds of other sites with information on skin conditions, which makes this a fascinating example of Web content marketing. Yes, you can link from Skin Health Solutions to Dermik's products, but you can just as easily link to a competitor's products. Skin Health Solutions' strategy of building awareness around a market category first and Dermik's own products second makes the site a Web content innovator worth watching.

Dermik Laboratories, a leading maker of dermatological products, faces a marketing challenge similar to thousands of other companies: Its competition includes many better-known brands, which makes it difficult for the smaller Dermik to raise awareness. This is compounded by the fact that the company's market category is not well known to the average consumer. The marketing professionals at Dermik realized that traditional awareness-generating tactics such as advertising and direct mail could work to raise brand and product recognition with patients and healthcare professionals, but knew that it would be also be very expensive. Rather than deploy the traditional marketing methods of its competitors, Dermik embarked on an unusual strategy: The company launched skinhealthsolutions.com, a Web portal designed to be the destination for finding the best Web content about skin, nail, and other dermatological conditions.

Dermik Laboratories, a wholly owned subsidiary of Aventis Pharmaceuticals, markets its dermatological products, including treatments for skin and nail conditions, to healthcare providers and directly to patients. With its Skin Health Solutions site, the primary goal is to establish Dermik as the leading

Skin Health Solutions: finding credible and reliable online skin, hair, and nail medical information made easy.

resource for credible, reliable, and current information on any dermatology-related topic. "Dermik takes a strategic view of the skinhealthsolutions.com site," says Robert Partridge, Director of Corporate Communications for Dermik Laboratories. "Dermik has been a dermatology presence for over 50 years. We're the big fish in a small pond of dermatology. Dermik is already widely known to dermatologists, but we want to become better known to the large number of other doctors who prescribe dermatology products. With conditions like acne and other types of skin conditions, treatment is often provided by doctors other than dermatologists, such as primary care physicians or pediatricians."

While Dermik does want to inform consumers (who are increasingly involved in requesting specific products for treatment), the most important audience Dermik hopes to reach with its site is healthcare professionals outside of the dermatology specialty. As doctors and nurse practitioners search or browse the sections on skin conditions and quickly find information they need, Partridge and his team hope they will come to remember and rely on Dermik. "Our main focus is to have all kinds of professionals turn to Dermik," Partridge says. "Physicians tend to think of the big pharmaceutical companies first but we want them to use our site first when they are thinking of dermatology." Partridge describes the strategy as a sort of "unbranded branding." By providing the leading portal for information on skin care, Partridge hopes to raise the status of Dermik.

Imagine a primary care physician confronted with an unfamiliar skin condition. She might be inclined to turn to a large pharmaceutical company for answers because she has worked with them on other medical issues in the past. Before Skin Health Solutions, that's exactly the situation Partridge faces. "When we try to go to the bigger offices such as primary care physicians and pediatricians, we don't have much voice because we compete with the huge pharmaceutical companies like Novartis," Partridge says. "We wanted to create a way for people to come to Dermik first for dermatology— everyone, not just dermatologists." Of course, the site's goal of increased awareness about the dermatological gamut is ultimately intended to sell more Dermik products as people become increasingly interested in and informed about treatments for dermatological conditions.

Aggregating the Best of Available Content

Unlike many other sites cashing in with content, Partridge and his colleagues at Dermik decided from the beginning to keep content creation to a

The Skin Health Solutions Web site includes valuable information on many conditions such as acne.

minimum by aggregating existing sources on the Web. "Our goal was not to put together a site with lots of original content," Partridge says. "We wanted a site that would include content from many sites. We don't have answers for everything, but we want people to think about Dermik as a place to find answers." For the technical aspects of creating Skin Health Solutions, Partridge worked with I-SITE, an Internet design and development firm.

Like any information portal on a specific topic, the volume of traffic is critical; if people don't visit, Dermik won't see results. Skin Health Solutions maximizes traffic flow through search engine optimization and links from other sites. The entire site is designed to be found by search engines; much of the traffic to Skin Health Solutions comes from professionals and patients who are searching for information about specific skin conditions on the Web. Visitors to Skin Health Solutions also come through links from other health-care sites.

Dermik Laboratories includes the skinhealthsolutions.com URL in much of its offline marketing promotions. "All our materials now reference both Web sites," Partridge says. "We want to change the order of prominence so skinhealthsolutions.com is the primary site." Partridge adds that, over time, he expects that Skin Health Solutions will be referenced much more than the corporate site in most marketing materials and promotions. "We want to shift traffic to skinhealthsolutions.com from Dermik.com so that Skin Health Solutions is the place people go to first," he says.

When visitors hit the site, its organization and indexing makes it feel like an information portal rather than a corporate or sales-oriented site. Sure, Dermik products are listed first in each reference category, but the Dermik offerings are posted using the same fonts and size as those of the competitors. In other words, the site structure, design, and architecture are organized to specifically avoid overhyping the site's sponsor, Dermik Laboratories. "We've got it indexed so we get noticed," Partridge says. "But because we include sites that compete with Dermik, we feel users can trust us because it's not just a corporate site."

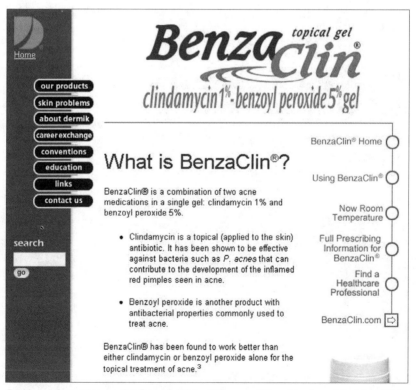

Product information on the Dermik Web site has a different look and feel than Skin Health Solutions to maintain independence and crediblility.

People can link from Skin Health Solutions to the Dermik Laboratories site to learn more about Dermik products, but they can visit Dermik competitors just as easily. Interestingly, when visitors click on a link to a site outside of skinhealthsolutions.com, a pop-up window informs them that they are leaving Skin Health Solutions; when they return they are prompted to rate the site they just visited. This is designed to maintain the integrity of the information portal and to make certain that it is providing the best information, no matter the source.

Maintain Integrity

Dermik has established a professional review board to help select the very best content for the Skin Health Solutions site and to help maintain the integrity of Skin Health Solutions as a market resource. As an information portal sponsored by a pharmaceutical company, potential conflict of interest issues are rife and the review board helps maintain editorial independence for the site. "The review process includes two levels," says Partridge. The first level includes detailed appraisal by Dermik people before going to the second level of outsiders.

When you leave the Skin Health Solutions portal to visit the Dermik corporate site (or click through to any other site), you're given a pop-up notice.

Partridge explains the steps in the first review, which is performed by Dermik professionals from a variety of departments and roles. "Normally we have a promotional review committee of Dermik people, including those representing legal, regulatory, product, and marketing," he says. "All content is reviewed by this committee. The committee gives the best advice before any materials goes out to the public."

In the highly regulated world of pharmaceutical marketing, government review of some initiatives is also required. "In some cases, the FDA needs to see the latest campaign," Partridge says. "The committee tends to be conservative in its approach because of the regulatory environment. But the FDA focuses on TV ads rather than Web sites."

According to Partridge, the next part of the review process means the most to the independence and integrity of the site's information. "The second set of review involves expert physicians in each area," says Partridge. "The doctors rate the site, and we hope this is a more democratic way to rate how well the site meets the needs of the people who visit. We don't use Skin Health Solutions just for promoting Dermik."

Drive Interest in the Category

As awareness of the skincare and dermatology issues found on Skin Health Solutions builds, Dermik believes it will help the company sell more products. However, in marketing, it is certainly a leap of faith to believe that generating awareness in the category as a whole will increase sales of one specific player. "Content is to draw people to us first," Partridge says. "We want people to see tangible examples of Dermik helping them, even if it doesn't involve Dermik products. We're not going to try to squeeze people into the wrong solution. So we would rather push them to something outside Dermik than give wrong or nonuseful information."

The site's dual market targets are medical professionals and everyday consumers—both with very different comprehensions of skin health problems. To serve both groups, Skin Health Solutions includes self-select paths to direct visitors to appropriate content within its vast resources. So, as Partridge builds the Skin Health Solutions portal, he works on specifically targeting certain demographics in both the consumer and professional categories. "There are a number of customers we speak to—not just doctors," Partridge says. "We're talking about anybody with whom Dermik would interact. Those people can range from high school students writing a paper to a parent who's concerned about an acne outbreak on her child's face."

Dermik provides specific content sets targeted at teenagers and preteens including its animated AcneBeat site (www.acnebeat.com), which links to the Acne section of Skin Health Solutions. AcneBeat tells the story of a teen band that works together to help each other overcome acne. Kids select a band member and follow his or her story leading up to a big gig. The teenage characters on the Web site educate consumers that acne is a treatable condition and advise teens to visit a physician to learn about treatment. Additional features of the site include a downloadable educational brochure on acne and a link to information on how to treat acne. Users are encouraged to complete a brief survey at the end of a music video to help Dermik track the impact of the messages on site visitors.

While consumers are becoming more proactive in requesting specific medical treatments, it's the healthcare community that writes prescriptions. Partridge explains: "We focus on healthcare professionals including nurse practitioners and physician assistants (who can prescribe dermatology products in many states), pharmacists (who may look for mixing instructions and interactions), and physicians." Dermik is already well known to dermatologists, but it is working hard to educate general practitioners who also prescribe dermatology products. "The podiatric community is another one we're

Skin Health Solutions has a varied audience and reaches teenagers directly with a separate "AcneBeat" site.

focused on," Partridge says. "Podiatrists prescribe skin care products for certain types of conditions."

The Right Stuff

In any market in which content needs to speak to professionals and consumers at the same time, it's a challenge to target individuals within a single portal. "Our customers include healthcare professionals so we can't go to the lowest common denominator and only speak to consumers," Partridge says. "But we also can't aim too high because we don't want to turn off consumers." Partridge accomplishes the goal of appealing to various groups partly by creating separate sections of the site for professionals and consumers. "To appeal to dermatologists, patients, and others, we have lots of information links," he says. "We have to account for all audiences so we don't turn any one audience off. The site is accessible to all people, but how they use it is up to the individual."

$$$$$$$$$$$$$$$$$$$ Cashing In $$$$$$$$$$$$$$$$$$$

Dermik has taken a calculated marketing risk with its approach to pharmaceutical promotion. "We'd like to think that this is a novel approach to use the Internet as a way to build customer relationships," Partridge says. "Marketing for pharmaceutical sites almost always needs to show immediate return on investment. But Dermik has an overriding mission to increase awareness over time, so we don't have that immediate need to show results."

Of course, nobody at Dermik is interested in pouring money into a project that isn't showing signs of success either. "Traditional measures include hits and visitors and we're really pleased so far," Partridge says. He cites other Web-based marketing initiatives he and his team have done as benchmarks for Skin Health Solutions. "A few years ago, we did a back-to-school campaign that was a big success," he says. "The number of unique visitors can be astounding based on a particular program." Considering his past success and current numbers, Partridge is very optimistic about Skin Health Solutions. He sees positive signs in other places. "Nontraditional measures include surveys of the sales force and customers who have commented on the site." But this is just the beginning of Dermik's evangelical mission to raise the awareness level of an entire product category. "Dermik has taken a more courageous measure of success," Partridge says. "We see results down the line. Dermik is in it for the long term. It's a significant investment on the part of the company to build a site that isn't guaranteed to show a measurable return on investment for a while."

CHAPTER TWENTY

Dean for America

Internet Presidential Politics–The New Grassroots

➤ **Organization**
Dean for America
www.deanforamerica.com or www.blogforamerica.com

➤ **Interviewed**
Mathew Gross, Director of Internet Communications

What's For Sale:

Howard Dean's use of Internet content in his run for the Democratic nomination for U.S. President in the 2004 election pioneered a new way for candidates to communicate, build community, and raise significant campaign funds.

What's So Interesting:

Dean didn't win his party's nomination for President in 2004, but his influence will be felt in political campaigns for decades to come. The Dean campaign pioneered the use of the blog as a grassroots political communications tool, gathering online credit card contributions from ordinary Americans along the way. This idea was quickly copied by candidates for offices big and small all across the United States.

Why You Should Care:

A little-known governor from one of America's smallest and least populous states registered 640,000 supporters and raised $50 million on the Internet in a little over a year. With content updated continuously—including a wildly active blog—the Dean campaign kept supporters engaged throughout the run of the presidential nomination process. Along the way, Dean built the largest grassroots organization in the history of the Democratic Party by using Web content. Dean for America's trailblazing tactics provide insights and ideas for all markets, industries, and organizations.

(Note to readers: www.deanforamerica.com became static once Howard Dean withdrew from the nomination race; however, Dean for America site archives are available. Dean then launched www.democracyforamerica.com and operated it together with www.blogforamerica.com until he was elected Chairman of the Democratic National Committee in February 2005.)

U.S. presidential politics have been profoundly impacted by each generation's new media. Franklin D. Roosevelt's fireside chats in the early 1930s pioneered the use of radio for political communication. John F. Kennedy's ease and natural appeal on television in the 1960 debates instantly made him appear more in control than his opponent, Richard M. Nixon. In the 2004 Democratic nomination race, Internet content and community took center stage. Howard Dean dramatically changed the face of politics by creating the largest grassroots political organization ever seen in the history of the Democratic Party—and he did it through his pioneering use of the Internet as a political force. In the process, the Dean campaign built a huge Web-based money-making machine that generated $50 million. These were mostly small contributions paid through supporters' credit cards. Other candidates learned quickly and emulated Dean's approach. While Dean didn't win any primaries, his organization both mobilized more people and raised more money than the other Democratic candidates.

Politicians had Web sites for years before Dean's remarkable rise. For the most part, political sites were just places to publish long and boring position papers, display endless press releases, and post photos of the candidate shaking factory-workers' hands and kissing babies. Until Dean, sites weren't interactive, the content was static, and as a result, people might visit once but never return. The Dean for America site differed because it delivered a formidable quantity of content, much of it interactive and updated minute-by-minute, creating an imperative for interested individuals to visit often and get involved.

The sheer volume of information made available on DeanforAmerica.com was a first for political sites. With Web logs (blogs), contribution pages, a comprehensive events section, press information, poster downloads, a photo gallery, and even wireless content availability, supporters could read and interact on the site for hours each day. With its numerous and varied ways to get involved—or contribute money—Web content drove the Dean campaign forward. Mathew Gross served as Director of Internet Communications for the Dean for America organization from February 2003 until Dean left the race in February 2004. Gross was in charge of the content and how it was delivered. "I'd come in early and post a morning news roundup," Gross says. "Then we'd update the site with press releases, news reports, and of course, the blog."

Unlike many candidates, Gross says that Dean was engaged in his site and had a personal interest in the content. "I'd often get e-mails from Governor Dean offering suggestions about the content," Gross says. "For example, when he released the Disability Rights Platform, he sent an e-mail requesting

Dean for America—join the campaign, contribute money, meet others like you, and post your thoughts for all to see.

prominent display on the site because it is an issue he's passionate about." In his work, Gross spent considerable time with other departments, such as political and finance, to focus on how the Internet could help with the communication of all types of information.

The Dean for America site included content created and posted by the Dean campaign, such as photos and reports from the campaign trail, and position papers and press releases focused on the issues. It also linked to hundreds of unofficial sites, in particular the independently operated supporter sites created by geography (Alaskans for Dean), demographic (Students for Dean), or special interests (Unemployed for Dean). By encouraging groups all over to create unofficial sites and then facilitating linking to the official site, the site allowed supporters to interact in a vast network of content.

Dean for America pioneered the use of the political blog in national politics. Its blog delivered a steady stream of information from the campaign, such as reports from the campaign trial, comments from members of the campaign staff, reminders of upcoming events and rallies, and links to stories in the media. With this robust content, the Dean campaign's BlogforAmerica.com became the center of the candidate's grassroots support.

Howard Dean was fully engaged with the content that appeared on his site.

Introducing the Presidential Blog

Gross personally changed the face of presidential politics. He oversaw an awesome communications infrastructure and was instrumental in pioneering the blog as a grassroots political communications tool. "I believe in the power of the written word to change people's lives," Gross says. "It seemed to me that this new medium could reach political supporters, but it has been amazing to me how radically the Internet has changed presidential politics."

The origins of Blog for America can be traced to work Gross had been doing prior to joining the campaign. "In February 2003," says Gross, "I was living in Utah and writing for a political blog in my spare time. I was writing a lot about Howard Dean—he was the favorite grassroots candidate on the Internet—but the Howard Dean official site was static at the time. So I flew out to Vermont, walked into the Campaign headquarters, and handed Joe Trippi [Dean's campaign manager at the time] a memo about how we should engage people directly. Joe turned around in his chair and said: 'You're hired'."

Gross moved into a hotel and began work on the site almost immediately. "On a snowy March night Joe said 'let's start the first Presidential Campaign

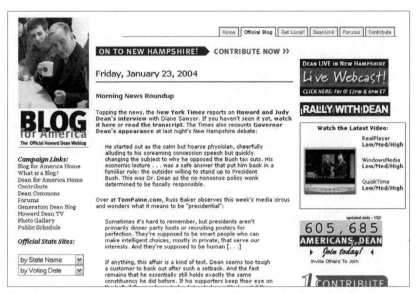

Dean's Blog for America engaged hundreds of thousands of grassroots supporters and was updated thousands of times a day during the campaign.

Web log'," Gross recalls. They were off and running, adding considerable value to the campaign almost instantly. Blog entries included statements from Governor Dean, calls to action, reports from volunteers and staff across the country, news roundups with links to national and campaign news stories, and dispatches from the campaign trail.

From the start, the Dean for America Web program was a calculated and strategic campaign tool. "At campaign headquarters, the Internet team was right outside the Campaign Manager's door, which illustrates the importance Joe Trippi placed on the rapid response capabilities of the Internet," says Gross.

Making Readers Feel They Have a Stake

Importantly, Blog for America included the ability for anybody to post comments. Dean posted messages, but the majority of threads were started by campaign staffers, including Trippi, Gross, and others. Threads on the official blog encouraged anybody to post comments 24 hours a day. During busy periods, content was updated several times per hour by the Dean staff. Remarkably, many of the items appearing on the blog had hundreds or even thousands of comments as part of the thread. The blog was constantly well read, regularly drawing tens of thousands of people per day. "DeanforAmerica.com was among the top sites in the world," Gross says. "We had a tremendous amount of blog traffic."

The Dean campaign took a calculated risk by allowing anybody to directly post unedited messages to its blog. The blog was operated with a simple rule, which was posted on the site for all to see: "We encourage you to stay on topic, but we do not edit comments with which we disagree." The connection between candidate Dean and his supporters was strengthened by the freedom of the blog, though the campaign surrendered a degree of control over its message. Of more than 200,000 comments posted to the blog during the course of the campaign, off-message (and off-color) postings certainly appeared. Some were purposeful disruptions contributed by rival campaigns. Dean campaign staffers made light of the dirty posts by describing the practice in a link on the site, even going so far as encouraging more donations as a part of the fun:

> **"What is a troll?**
>
> A troll is someone who deliberately disrupts the discussion in the comments thread. (It comes from the fishing term—a troller drops his lure hoping someone will bite.) We encourage commenters to stay on the thread's topic, but trolling is inevitable and, let's face it, sometimes amusing.
>
> **What do I do if I think I see a troll?**
>
> Please remain seated. Do not panic. If trolls are making posts that violate the comment policy, the best thing to do is ignore them. Responding to a troll simply prolongs the disruption of the discussion. Web team staff will delete comments that are rude, derogatory, discriminatory, libelous or offensive. Some bloggers have begun the tradition of discouraging trolls by contributing to the campaign through the 'Troll Goal' whenever trolls are present."
>
> *Source: DeanforAmerica.com*

The use of humor by Dean's staff was an important component of the content in its Web campaign. Fun things like making light of trolls kept people interested and coming back for more. Dean even appointed Kasey, a mop-like pooch with pointy ears and big eyes, as the campaign's director of canine outreach. With his own Web page, Kasey maintained the Pets for Dean gallery, which included photos, poems, and other information about the pets of Dean supporters. Humor had its place, but content on the Dean for America site was not all fun and games. The blogs tended to focus on strong messages delivered in an informal and personal way and, according to Gross, the campaign made a point of keeping important information such as position papers and press releases serious.

Members of the Dean campaign realized early on how powerful a force an Internet community of supporters can be. "Howard Dean understood how the site and the blog could reach people," says Gross. The Dean organization treated Internet supporters as an extended staff—empowering them to raise money, organize themselves, and communicate with one another with little external direction from the campaign. A steady flow of content was created by Gross and the others on the Dean staff—including messages sent to an e-mail list of over a half million, the blog, official statements, photos and reports from the campaign trail, as well as the constant challenges to raise money. This varied and steady flow maintained a personal and informal tone, well-suited to a grassroots community audience. Even Gross was surprised by the level of human connection the campaign made. "An older couple came from California all the way to Vermont and asked for Mathew Gross rather than Howard Dean," he says. "They wanted to take their picture with me. That was the first time I realized how people are really engaged with what I do."

Everyone was invited to support Dean for President, even dogs.

Meetup with Other Supporters

A major outreach component of the Dean for America site included vast listings of meetings, rallies, events, and other gatherings that supporters could attend in person. The Dean campaign was by far the largest user of Meetup.com, the for-profit Web site contracted to facilitate meetings and organize all kinds of events and groups.

Using Meetup, a supporter could enter a ZIP code or use the search tool to display opportunities for (and information about) local involvement. Nearly 200,000 people registered on the Meetup system to find out about or attend Dean for America gatherings in their area. Events ranged from coffee at a neighbor's house, where a handful of people would discuss the candidate's positions, to major rallies, where Dean himself would speak. The online Meetup system got people away from their computers and out into their communities. Meetup entries and the blog allowed supporters to efficiently work toward specific goals; when the campaign needed to promote a financial goal or to publicize a particular event, the Internet content machine would kick in. For example, in the months leading up to the Iowa Caucuses, Dean for America launched a separate site specifically to educate supporters and volunteers about the all-important first state to vote in the primary season. Many

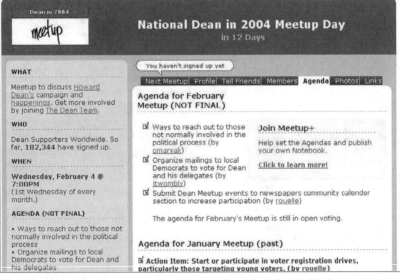

The Dean campaign encouraged people to get out from behind their computers and Meetup with others in person.

Dean supporters traveled to Iowa from all over the country to work for the candidacy; the Internet, including Meetup events, served as their organizational tool. By logging on to the Meetup section of the site, supporters would discover exactly when and how they were needed (perhaps to go door-to-door or to help stage a rally). While Dean didn't win the Iowa Caucus or any of the primary races, it certainly wasn't because of poor organization, weak financial support, or a lack of available information.

The Dean campaign utterly blindsided the political establishment by pioneering sophisticated use of the Internet, particularly digital content, as a grassroots political tool. At a time when other candidates were buying mailing lists and sending out expensive and often dull one-way communications in hopes of getting a vote or a check, the Dean team engaged supporters on the issues through interactive content, using the Web to raise millions.

Internet Content: The New Grassroots

As Dean's candidacy basked in frontrunner limelight in the winter of 2003–2004 (leading up to the disappointing Iowa Caucuses in mid-January), Gross became famous for pioneering Web content as the new grassroots. He

Internet content served as the tool to organize an army of supporters.

was interviewed for dozens of newspaper and magazine articles in publications from around the world including *Newsweek*, the *Washington Post,* and the United Kingdom's *Guardian.* In fact, Gross became a celebrity in his own right. "It's certainly been incredible," he says. "This is a moment in history that we lucked into. I see myself playing a role with this far in the future. The Internet can change presidential politics." Gross plans to write a book about his experience with the Dean campaign, and his practical skills as an Internet political strategist are in high demand by candidates of all stripes.

$$$$$$$$$$$$$$$$$$$$ Cashing In $$$$$$$$$$$$$$$$$$$$

While other candidates hosted endless rubber-chicken events to raise money at $100 a plate, Dean's $50 million war chest was amassed by people contributing $50 or $100 through credit card transactions on the Dean for America site. To raise the same amount of money using traditional methods, the Dean campaign would have had to host 500 separate $100-a-plate dinners for 1,000 people each—a nearly impossible task given the short primary cycle and limitations on the candidate's time.

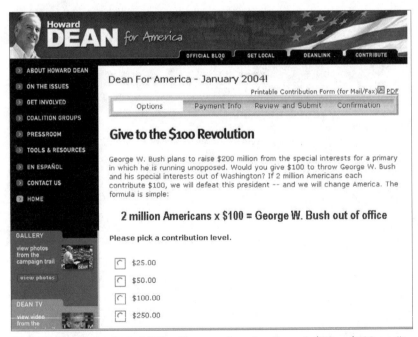

Dean for America collected $50 million, mostly online through $50 or $100 credit card contributions.

Contrast Dean's online campaigning and fundraising tactics with that of Vice President Dick Cheney, one of the Republican Party's most prolific fundraisers: Cheney would board Air Force Two and fly into a city, ride to an exclusive event in a Secret Service protected motorcade, and meet with a few hundred big-time donors. He'd be gone from Washington, D.C. for most of the day and raise a few hundred thousand dollars. In a vastly different strategy, Dean would set a goal such as "$700,000 by Sunday for Wisconsin" and put his Internet machine to work. E-mail messages would fly and the blog would light up with appeals. Credit card contributions would then pour in from Dean's army of supporters in relatively small increments. Many people would contribute more than once, responding to a number of particular appeals. As a result, Dean raised more money online without leaving his office than the Vice President of the United States would at the expense of an entire day away from the capitol (not to mention prohibitive travel costs). And Dean wouldn't even have to pay for renting a hall or providing food and drink for the donors.

The low cost of its appeals for donations greatly contributed to the campaign's bottom line. Traditional fundraising involves expensive marketing pieces sent through the mail or campaign meet-and-greet events that require the candidate's direct participation—both labor and money intensive. However, an Internet-enabled appeal costs almost nothing (given the efforts of a relatively small group of volunteers) and can bring in big money. The money raised goes directly for campaign expenses or advertising rather than to the expenses incurred through traditional fund appeals.

With Dean for America, for the first time, micro-contributions leveled the playing field against big money—all as a result of Web content. The Dean for America fund-raising success has made every candidate rethink the long-held beliefs about raising money. Dean for America proved that traditional strategies such as direct mail, phone solicitation, and personal press-the-flesh events are not the only way to obtain contributions. Gross and his fellow staffers at Dean for America pioneered a new way to blend compelling Web content about a candidate with effective fundraising. As Web-site content creators, Gross and his team knew the difference between the old one-way force-feeding of static content and the more effective give-and-take of the interactive Internet community.

Dean and Gross realized that a presidential campaign could cash in with content and created Dean for America as the largest online campaign contribution site on the Internet. "Blogs are making a difference because they talk about what people are interested in," says Gross. "The Internet really made Dean's campaign."

PART 4

Putting Content to Work

CHAPTER TWENTY-ONE

Best Practices from Innovative Web Marketers

W hen I set out to write *Cashing In With Content*, one of my primary objectives was to profile as wide a variety of successful content-savvy sites as possible. I felt it was important to select examples from smaller and less well-known organizations, older established companies with extensive offline businesses, and companies formed expressly to exploit the Internet. Since this is the first book presenting the stories of how organizations use content to cash in, I felt it was critical that the marketers tell their tales directly. Their candid insights were gathered throughout a year of research, conversations, and e-mail exchanges. As individual marketers related the information they deemed critical to the success of their sites, a series of fascinating best practices emerged.

Originally, I thought that the content techniques would differ by the type of organization; I assumed that a corporations' use of content would not resemble the nonprofits and that e-commerce would be different than business-to-business. While each site has its own distinct flavor, this collection of profiles actually reveals a remarkably consistent set of best-practice ideas and tips. As I composed the profile chapters, I came to realize that the strategies and techniques used in one type of industry or organization can also benefit others from very different industries. This chapter distills the concepts that emerged through the profiles and shows how you can put these best practices to work in developing and deploying your organization's content strategy.

Marketing with Web Content

There are a dozen best practices included here and each possesses the potential to benefit you, your Web site, and your larger organizational goals and objectives. While I have put together what I believe are the top 12 best practices based on my research, this is not intended to be an all-inclusive list of each and every content best practice. However, the focus is not on basic Web site content best practices such as paying close attention to spelling and grammar, keeping the site updated and fresh, including an About page and FAQ page, and removing any dead links; these are too obvious to warrant focus here. It's also important to note that these best practices provide valuable information for engaging visitors once they *arrive* at a Web site, so I have chosen not to detail any search engine marketing strategies that are designed to drive traffic *to* sites. Rather than spend time on basic techniques or search engine marketing strategies that are outlined in many "how to" books on Web site creation and marketing, this chapter focuses on higher-level content strategies that fuel successful sites.

These best practices are numbered for convenience but the enumeration does not denote any priority ranking. While many or all of these practices can or should be employed together as part of a holistic content strategy, the best practices do not necessarily build upon one another, so each one may be read (and applied to your site) in any order, or as you see fit.

It's important to note that the best practices contained here are drawn directly from the interviews and profiles featured in this book. If you've already read the profile chapters, there's bound to be a bit of déjà vu as you read the best practices. In each case, the companies that focused on some aspect of the best practice from that category are identified at the end of the section so you can do a Content Cross-Check and revisit the appropriate chapters to learn more. Sites that aren't listed may well employ a particular best practice, but the chapters listed are from those marketers who specifically focused on the given best practice as being integral to their site's success.

As you begin to read these best practices, remember that you will learn from the ideas presented here even if the original concepts are derived from a very different market, industry, or type of organization than your own. E-commerce companies may draw from the experience of nonprofits and established business-to-business companies can learn from politicians and educational institutions. The level of overlap in the strategies of these varied sites is indicative of the power certain content strategies possess.

Drawing best practice ideas from industries that differ from your own should prove an enlightening experience that may also lead to unexpected success. Just imagine: While your competitors are busy copying one another's Web sites, you will be implementing innovative strategies for cashing in with content, derived from some of the most successful sites on the Web.

Best Practice #1: When launching a new site, start with a comprehensive needs analysis

It may sound painfully obvious: When designing a new Web site (or planning an extensive redesign), start with a needs analysis. Yet many marketers just jump right into site aesthetics or begin to write content before taking time to analyze how the site fits into a larger organizational strategy; they neglect to determine what the site needs to do and what content visitors will require to support the larger strategy. The reality is that, for many successful sites, the needs analysis and planning phase may take significantly longer than actually building the site.

When Kenyon College began working on a major site redesign to focus on content, the team charged with the project convened a cross-functional working group of people. The group included faculty, staff, and students who worked to analyze visitor needs. This rigorous planning process took nine months. Colliers International adopted a similar approach when it set out to build the new Colliers site. The site had to represent the varied requirements of marketers from offices all over the world, so the firm established a committee of stakeholders that met frequently for more than a year to hash out different aspects of the site. Colliers even created a design prototype to validate its extensive planning.

Hanley-Wood Interactive used research demographics to drive the creation of its ebuild site. The company learned that 95 percent of construction professionals visited ebuild expressly to research products, and so designed the site to cater to this specific audience need.

As you work on your own site—analyzing market requirements and drawing from the expertise, talent, and opinions from within your own organization—try to think a bit more like a publisher. A publisher carefully identifies and defines target audiences and then develops the content required to meet the needs of each distinct demographic. Although graphical elements, colors, fonts, and other visual manifestations of the site are important, they should take a back seat during the content needs analysis process. For example, Laurel Touby, CEO & Cyberhostess of mediabistro.com, drew heavily from her prior work experiences on magazines such as *BusinessWeek* and *Glamour* when designing her site. Touby's training as an editor drove her to consider as a primary concern: Who are potential readers and what content will be valuable to them?

Editors and publishers obsess over readership and so should you. Figure out who your site visitors are or should be. Determine if they are varied and whether they should be sliced into discrete target markets. If so, develop different types of content that will specifically appeal to each of these target groups. In addition, craft more generalized content that will work across demographics. To do this, consider problems your visitors face that you can help solve through content offerings. Done well, a needs analysis drawing from your research, the knowledge of a cross-organizational team, understanding of your market demographics—combined with the diverse opinions and knowledge of your internal stakeholders—will form the basis of a successful site. Needs analysis and planning are important in order to maximize the value of your site and your organization should invest significant up-front energy to this phase of site planning and content development.

Content Cross-Check for Best Practice #1

Chapter Four: mediabistro.com
Chapter Ten: ebuild
Chapter Twelve: Colliers
Chapter Fourteen: UPS
Chapter Seventeen: Kenyon College

Best Practice #2: Speak with one voice to create a consistent site personality

A common theme heard from the marketers interviewed for this book is the importance of creating a distinct, consistent, and memorable site; these characteristics can often be attributed to the tone or voice of its content.

Design Within Reach specifically focuses on its site's personality as content is created. The objective is to ensure that visitors to the DWR site have a memorable experience derived from the character of its content—whether the content is in the form of text or images. DWR readers want to know about living in a world filled with good design and the company creates content that consistently delivers. Booz Allen Hamilton Inc. pays close attention to the tone of its site because, for people who are job searching, corporate culture will be one of the deciding factors in choosing to apply. Booz Allen banks on communicating its culture through content in order to generate recruits. The company also believes that, by creating a site that is indicative of the organization's personality, it will receive applications from candidates who are more likely to fit if they are eventually hired. The mediabistro.com site walks a fine line to maintain its hip and cool—but not too hip—tone, which appeals to the media professionals that comprise its audience.

As visitors interact with the content on your site, they should develop a clear picture of the organization behind the site. Is it young and playful or solid and conservative? For newer sites, the first task might be to define a personality. For example, since Alloy and Esurance were both launched as new businesses on the Web, they didn't have an offline personality, so they had more flexibility in creating site personalities. Because Alloy targets teenage girls, the company hired people who were pop-culturally aware to write content and establish a tone for the site. The company chose a team of marketers and editors who had worked in the teen target demographic for publications like *Seventeen Magazine*. In order to maintain the veracity of its voice in the ever-changing teen vernacular, the Alloy team constantly monitors the words and phrases that teenagers use on the site to make certain the Alloy.com is using the latest language and pop culture references appropriate for the teen market.

Esurance began its personality-creation with the premise that automobile insurance was inherently boring, so the site was specifically conceived to have a somewhat playful and humorous tone. The site's personality was intended to make the process less tedious and to build an amicable relationship with site visitors. Web site visitors aren't nameless faceless numbers; they're people like you and me. Most people enjoy a bit of humor here and there and many sites make use of the lighter side of content as an important personality component. For a commodity as traditionally dull as auto insurance, Esurance livens things up with some fun, contributing to the site's charm. For example, an article called *Don't Take a Ride on the Wild Side*, which discusses auto-deer collisions, both educates and entertains. At Esurance, the company mixes business with humor to create a distinct voice for its content and site personality.

The use of humor by Dean for America staff was an important component of the content in its Web campaigns and added to the Dean campaign's pioneering online image. Dean appointed Kasey, a mop-like pooch with pointy ears and big eyes, as the campaign's director of canine outreach. With his own Web page, Kasey maintained the Pets for Dean gallery, which included photos, poems, and other information about the pets of Dean supporters.

Defining and maintaining personality, voice, and tone is just as important for established companies with offline brands as it is for online-only upstarts. However, the existence of an offline business means there's less room for creating something new online, although using an established personality can also be a starting point for a new site. Alcoa is a large multinational company that manufactures aluminum products used in applications from aerospace to beverage cans; the company employs a review process to make certain that the content is appropriate to its site. The Alcoa site is written for the involved and intelligent business professionals that are the company's customers but also with the concern of an organization that cares about the environment and the communities it touches. Marketers at Alcoa carefully consider how Web content reflects upon and affects offline businesses and the community, and creates content accordingly. Professionals at CARE USA carefully edit content sent from the field because much of it is originally written by scientists and others who speak English as a second language. It is important to the marketing people at CARE USA to rewrite content so that it comes from one consistent—powerful, caring, and trustworthy—online voice that will communicate its informed, benevolent message in order to generate donations.

Keep in mind that Web site visitors may be well-educated (or at least well-informed) in their areas of interest or they may come to your site knowing little or nothing at all. Marketers who produce content for the Web need to take audience-members' knowledge into consideration and create content accordingly. For example, on the Aerosmith site, content is written to suit two demographics with very different knowledge levels: newcomers interested in learning more about the band as well as die-hard fans that have every album and may have seen the band dozens of times in concert. On the Crutchfield site, marketers write copy appropriate for both buyers who know very little about electronics as well the company's core group of electronics enthusiasts.

Both the Online Journal and CARE USA target online users as a demographic distinct from offline audiences and create content accordingly. On the Web, CARE USA writes to a relatively young and well-educated market. The Online Journal is written for people who know what specific information they are looking for on the Web versus an often serendipitous informational approach taken with the print version of the *Wall Street Journal*. Both the CARE USA site and the Online Journal are written with the intelligence required to appeal to the well-educated online market these sites target.

Whatever the personality, the way to achieve consistency is to make certain that all of the written material and other content on the site conform to a defined tone that has been established from the start. Although this might seem easier for companies with a dedicated content creation team, there are often overlooked content components of a site like error messages, help files, and FAQ sections. It is important that even relatively mundane site content speaks with one voice. A strong focus on site personality and character pays off. As visitors come to rely on the content found on your site, they will develop an intellectual, emotional, and personal relationship with your organization. A Web site can evoke a familiar and trusted voice, just like that of a friend on the other end of the telephone; users know from experience who's speaking and welcome the interaction. A site builds this relationship through its tone and style. Just like the welcome and familiar phone call, well-executed Web site content will be perceived as a trusted friend and resource.

Content Cross-Check for Best Practice #2

Chapter Three: Design Within Reach
Chapter Four: mediabistro.com
Chapter Five: Esurance
Chapter Six: Aerosmith
Chapter Eight: Alcoa
Chapter Nine: Weyerhaeuser
Chapter Thirteen: Booz Allen
Chapter Fifteen: CARE USA
Chapter Sixteen: Tourism Toronto
Chapter Twenty: Dean for America

Best Practice #3: Dedicate editorial resources to create consistent and informed content

Speaking with a consistent and intelligent voice becomes a whole lot easier when an organization employs a dedicated content resource for its site. Nearly all of the sites successfully cashing in with content maintain editorial control by maintaining in-house resources to create, contribute, or edit Web content. The number of people involved varies tremendously from site to site, but no matter if one person spends a few hours a week or hundreds are involved full time, editorial ownership is best entrusted to a dedicated person or group. In other words, content on the Web site should be treated as a primary business tool requiring a focused effort, rather than as an afterthought. For some sites, editorial ownership might be a part of someone's wider role within the organization or even belong to the very top level. Rob Forbes, Design Within Reach's founder, takes a personal interest in his site's content, writes much of it, and oversees its consistency. In the case of Aerosmith, band members themselves have final say on any significant new content that gets posted on the band's fan site.

Not surprisingly, a traditional publisher that leads the way on the Web boasts the biggest content resource of the organizations profiled: The Wall Street Journal Online publishes more than 1,000 news stories per day with a dedicated news staff of more than 60 editors who draw from the Dow Jones network of nearly 1,600 news staff. Yet not every organization has—or remotely requires—this scope of editorial resources. While quantity may be nice, quality and consistency are essential.

At CARE USA, content is contributed by writers from all over the world, many of who are scientists. Thus, the site employs a dozen professionals focused on smoothing out linguistic issues, unifying the editorial tone of the content, and selecting photos for site inclusion. Since Alloy must keep up to the minute on teen interests and lingo, they choose to populate the editorial and marketing team with individuals who had worked at some of the leading teen magazines. Alcoa outsources some of its site design work, but employs two full-time people to make certain that all content is appropriate and reflects well on the business as a whole. While Dermik doesn't create content for its www.skinhealtsolutions.com site, it aggregates what it says are the best sources on the Web for skin heath information. To live up to this claim, the organization established a professional review board to select content for the site.

Establishing a dedicated person or group to "own" site content is one of the best ways to ensure quality, consistency, and personality. At a large site, you may have several full-time staff writing original content specifically for the site. In a smaller organization, a focused individual might select, rewrite, or repurpose content already available from marketing brochures, public relations materials, or even at other sites. But no matter how large or small their resources, the best marketers don't treat content as an afterthought. A dedicated commitment—and commensurate resources—to create and maintain quality content will allow your organization to reap benefits.

Content Cross-Check for Best Practice #3

Chapter One: Crutchfield
Chapter Two: Alloy
Chapter Three: Design Within Reach

Chapter Four: mediabistro.com
Chapter Five: Esurance
Chapter Six: Aerosmith
Chapter Seven: The Wall Street Journal Online
Chapter Eight: Alcoa
Chapter Nine: Weyerhaeuser
Chapter Eleven: ServiceWare
Chapter Thirteen: Booz Allen
Chapter Fourteen: UPS
Chapter Fifteen: CARE USA
Chapter Eighteen: Sharp HealthCare
Chapter Nineteen: Dermik Laboratories

Best Practice #4: Encourage browsing by using appropriate self-select paths

To best leverage the power of content, you need to help users find it—which means facilitating browsing. The clearest way to create a browser-friendly site is to design navigation and use links that coincide with the way site visitors think and thus lead them to content appropriate to their needs. When a new user visits, the site makes its first impression and the user quickly decides: Does this organization care about me? Does it focus on the problems I face? Or does the site only include information describing what the company has to offer from its narrow perspective? Too often, site navigation simply mimics the way the company or institution is organized (by product, geography, or governmental structure, for example). Unfortunately, the way audience members use sites rarely coincides with businesses' internal priorities, which leaves site visitors confused about how to find what they really need. One way to facilitate browsing is to create a series of self-select paths for each group of people to follow based on their interests, level of knowledge, or specific needs.

Prior to its browsing-optimized revamp, the Kenyon site was organized and structured like the college with separate sections that mirrored the institution, such as academic and student life. The new site incorporated self-select paths specifically targeting the distinct needs of audiences such as alumni (How do I keep up with my classmates?) and prospective students (Should I apply to Kenyon?). Each path includes detailed content-sets created especially to meet the needs of these site visitors.

ServiceWare created a set of links organized around potential customers' problems, offering job-function-based paths to allow visitors to benefit from ServiceWare's back-end knowledge management solutions. In the case of Colliers International, with its huge listing of commercial real estate, the ability to navigate the content based on user needs (including type of property, geography, and other criteria) are all important, but regardless of individual priorities, visitors reach their chosen location quickly through well-designed navigational paths.

When considering the type of self-select paths that would best lead visitors to the point where they are ready to spend, donate, join, or whatever your objective might be, marketers should consider each specific target market and identify the needs of that demographic, then offer solutions to meet these needs. A "target-problem-solution" approach ensures that a site speaks appropriately to the markets it serves rather than simply creating a one-size-fits-all design or navigation that mimics the organizational structure behind the site.

Within the career section of the Booz Allen site, self-select paths include choices by type of job opening, such as those for the experienced professional or college or MBA graduates, as well as more generalized sections about what it's like to work at Booz Allen. The company's self-select paths are specifically designed to provide entryways for the target profiles of the different types of employees Booz Allen wants to attract and each includes specific content. Dermik Laboratories includes sections for its two very different demographic groups on skinhealthsolutions.com—one for consumers and another for health care professionals.

The Tourism Toronto site serves several buyer demographics: It needs to work for individual travelers, people who book group travel including conventions and events, and also people who plan group leisure travel like church groups. The site includes self-select paths and navigation intended to make it easy for the targeted demographic to find appropriate information—with the ultimate goal to get visitors to Toronto. Weyerhaeuser recognizes that it serves a variety of constituents with different needs, including customers, the media, and investors. The site also includes a section for those who would like to use Weyerhaeuser land for recreational purposes like camping or hunting.

The Wall Street Journal Online Network of service-oriented sites includes content-specific free sites such as CareerJournal.com, OpinionJournal.com, StartupJournal.com, RealEstateJournal.com, and CollegeJournal.com, which each present content for people browsing those specific topics while drawing these distinct users into the larger Online Journal family of sites.

A major component of cashing in with content is knowing your demographics. This knowledge allows you to segment distinct user groups and help them find the information they need. Navigation must be created to reflect the way that visitors think and interact with the site. Recognizing different types of visitors and making targeted content easy to browse are hallmarks of useful (and successful) Web sites. Sites with well-defined, content-rich self-select paths succeed in segmenting visitors into defined categories, which organizations can better serve and sell.

Content Cross-Check for Best Practice #4

Chapter One: Crutchfield
Chapter Three: Design Within Reach
Chapter Four: mediabistro.com
Chapter Seven: The Wall Street Journal Online
Chapter Eight: Alcoa
Chapter Nine: Weyerhaeuser
Chapter Eleven: ServiceWare
Chapter Twelve: Colliers
Chapter Thirteen: Booz Allen
Chapter Fourteen: UPS
Chapter Fifteen: CARE USA
Chapter Sixteen: Tourism Toronto
Chapter Seventeen: Kenyon College
Chapter Nineteen: Dermik Laboratories

Best Practice #5: A separate URL or blog facilitates providing targeted content

Using multiple URLs and topic- or interest-specific blogs can make it easier to provide targeted content beyond that available on an organization's primary site. An excellent example of this is the Wall Street Journal Online Network of service-oriented sites, which includes content-specific free offerings such as CareerJournal. com, StartupJournal.com, RealEstateJournal.com, and CollegeJournal.com. The Network of sites is used to gain the interest of those who are part of specifically targeted demographics, but who haven't yet signed up for a paid Online Journal subscription. By demonstrating the organization's expertise in specific areas of interest, the company hopes to cash in when readers look to the network for other informational needs.

Dermik Laboratories built its entire skinhealthsolutions.com strategy through making the site separate and distinct from the company's corporate dermik.com site. The company also created a site specifically for teenagers struggling with acne at acnebeat.com. Each site maintains a distinct personality with content intended to serve its targeted demographic.

Aerosmith also employs separate sites—aeroforceone.com for hard-core fans and Aerosmith.com for casual visitors. The main site also serves to funnel self-selected intense fans to Aero Force One, with the hopes that these fans will ante up for premium content and other offerings.

In addition to its primary site, www.ups.com (which averages a remarkable 145 million hits per day), UPS built a separate site targeted at investors. Because stock buyers and owners have very different needs from customers shipping packages, the separate site focuses on the investor demographic, but smoothly links to and from content on the main UPS corporate site. The seamless interaction between the two sites could influence an investor's impression of the company as a whole.

Crutchfield Corporation launched CrutchfieldAdvisor.com as a companion site to its more advanced information and e-commerce oriented Crutchfield.com site in order to supply specific content useful to those in the early stages of the buying process. An added benefit of Crutchfield Advisor as a separate site is that it provides an alternative "front door" to the consumer electronics shopper who is in research mode and not yet ready buy. Although there are two separate sites, visitors easily click back and forth between Crutchfield.com and CrutchfieldAdvisor.com depending on their point in the research and purchasing process. A separate site that seamlessly links to a primary or corporate site provides an ideal way to deliver segmented information to a distinct target demographic, while maintaining its role in the larger organization.

Another way to provide targeted content, without requiring the creation and maintenance of a distinct site, is to include a Web log (blog) as part of your overall site content. Blogs are emerging as an important way for organizations of all types to quickly and efficiently add highly focused content and encourage interaction with visitors. Dean for America pioneered the use of blogs in Presidential politics when it launched a blog as a means to deliver a constant stream of information that was highly personal in tone. With reports from the campaign trail, comments from members of the campaign staff and the candidate himself, reminders of upcoming events and rallies, links to stories in the media, and much more, the Dean campaign's BlogforAmerica.com became the center of the candidate's grassroots support; it was a major factor in Dean raising some $50 million in contributions through the Internet. BlogforAmerica.com was constantly well-read, regularly drawing tens of thousands of people per day. In fact, the Dean campaign started a major trend. Today, political Web sites of all sorts feature blogs, many of which include posts directly from the candidates.

mediabistro.com took the innovative approach of building a series of sister sites like TVnewser.com as blogs rather than traditional Web sites. These blog-sites are quick to launch and modify, which also makes posting highly relevant content an easy task for nontechnical people.

Using separate URLs or blogs allows an organization to take content in different directions that will appeal to specific target demographics without negatively impacting the strategy and content of its primary Web site. As a way to experiment, to test new ideas, or to reach narrow niche markets, smart marketers make use of fresh sites with new URLs or highly focused blogs. Of course by using hyperlinks, you can create seamless interaction between independent Web properties, but on the other side of the equation, if your experiment fails, you can simply shut down a distinct URL with little or no negative effect on your main site.

Content Cross-Check for Best Practice #5

Chapter One: Crutchfield
Chapter Four: mediabistro.com
Chapter Six: Aerosmith
Chapter Seven: The Wall Street Journal Online
Chapter Ten: ebuild
Chapter Fourteen: UPS
Chapter Nineteen: Dermik Laboratories
Chapter Twenty: Dean for America

Best Practice #6: Push content to users to pull them back to your site

Web content is only valuable if somebody reads it. To provide alternate content routes, many companies use digital delivery methods like e-mail newsletters and RSS feeds to push content directly to audiences, with the intention of drawing them back to the site and the organization behind it. As an added bonus, this approach allows firms to multipurpose content, which can be created for a newsletter, posted on a site, and then channeled into RSS feeds, which are an increasingly popular form of digital delivery that pipes content directly to users desktops via an RSS reader or into e-mail in boxes. When a site visitor subscribes to an e-mail newsletter or RSS feed, they demonstrate significant interest in whatever you have to offer—getting your foot in the door right from the get-go.

Certain types of customer groups require a longer consideration cycle or need to establish a rapport with an organization before committing to purchase, join, or donate. An e-mail newsletter can help build this type of long-term relationship and encourage return visits to a site.

Event-specific e-mail notifications can help keep valued customers up to date on the latest news: Sharp HealthCare provides a reminder service for a patient's annual physical checkup or for doctor appointments; Aerosmith sends out notifications to fans when an upcoming tour is announced, ensuring that members of the fan community receive first dibs on the best seats. Weekly or monthly e-mail newsletters can also serve to maintain awareness. For example, real estate marketer, Colliers International, regularly sends users city market reports via e-mail based on their specific cities of interest. The e-mail ensures that the Colliers name is in front of the potential customer throughout commercial real estate's long sales cycle.

Design Within Reach's founder demonstrates his commitment to the power of e-mail newsletters by writing many of the feature articles himself. The firm banks on the newsletter's ability to demonstrate its expertise as well as to help establish a connection with potential buyers. The added personal touch of see-ing the founder's by-line on well-crafted articles about good design creates a loyal following of people who regularly purchase from the company.

Registered users of mediabistro.com can get a Daily Media News Feed, which provides a roundup of targeted stories and links to other content and offers on the site. Through the registration process, mediabistro.com gathers information about its readers and draws readers back to the site via click through. The Online Journal started its free e-mail newsletter called Best of the Web Today with modest expectations: It uses the free e-mail newsletter to intro-duce people to the editorial page and the unusual content of the *Wall Street Journal*. The experiment proved tremendously popular as hundreds of thou-sands of people, many of whom are in a very different demographic than tradi-tional print readers, have subscribed to daily Best of the Web Today e-mail.

Smart marketers at nonprofit organizations that rely on donations use e-mail newsletters to cultivate repeat contributions. CARE USA uses Customer

Relationship Management systems and databases to capture information. The system helps to manage the relationship with donors over time, and allows the organization to create e-mail newsletters specific to donor interests. Dean for America made use of e-mail newsletters to solicit repeat donations, often tied to a specific event such as an upcoming primary or caucus. Dean for America also provided an RSS feed, so users could keep track of updates at Dean's Blog for America without having to repeatedly visit the site, or if they saw something in the feed of particular interest, they could choose to click through for more.

E-mail newsletters and other direct digital delivery methods that push content directly to readers can significantly aid in building and fostering long-term and more meaningful (and lucrative) relationships with customers. When your target audiences see your messages via e-mail or feed on a regular basis, they associate a positive experience with your brand without even visiting your site. Done well, the e-mails will come to be seen as a welcome informational tool to users and can serve to build site traffic, brand reputation, and ultimately help your organization to cash in.

Content Cross-Check for Best Practice #6

Chapter Three: Design Within Reach
Chapter Four: mediabistro.com
Chapter Six: Aerosmith
Chapter Seven: The Wall Street Journal Online
Chapter Twelve: Colliers
Chapter Fifteen: CARE USA
Chapter Eighteen: Sharp HealthCare

Best Practice #7: Don't forget images—original photos are powerful content

Content is not limited to words. Innovative marketers make use of nontext content—including cartoons, charts, graphs, audio feeds and video clips—to inform and entertain site visitors. Photographs play an important role for many sites. For example, Kenyon College prominently features photos of students and faculty as well as famous alumni like actors Allison Janney of TV's The West Wing and movie star Paul Newman. By showing the varied faces of current students and including some famous alumni faces, Kenyon communicates that it strives to continue to produce impressive graduates and becomes increasingly appealing to potential students.

Sharp HealthCare provides photos of physicians as part of the profiles on its site because the hospital network found that some people are significantly influenced in their choice of physicians based on appearance. The organization also includes a Baby Gallery on its site that features photos of the newborns delivered in the Sharp network facilities. This service is very popular among new parents and serves to promote Sharp, as links to the Baby Gallery are sent out to family and friends. In its "Looks We Love" section, Alloy provides photos of movie, TV, and rock stars with direct links to the Alloy store where teenagers can purchase outfits similar to the ones their idols are wearing.

Photographs are powerful content when the images are recognizably an integrated component of the Web site. However, generic "stock" photographs may actually have a negative effect. Users appreciate original photos such as Aerosmith in concert, the wonderful places to visit included on the Tourism Toronto site, buildings for sale or lease by Colliers, and illustrations of the aluminum products offered by Alcoa; all contribute directly to the content appeal of these sites. But imagine a rock band site with a stock photo of a random concert by a faceless band. Or a tourism site with generic shots of buildings that aren't even in the city featured on the site. Too often, marketing people (many who are influenced by advertising agencies) fall back on stock photographs to "add visual interest" instead of ensuring that the images have meaning in the context of the other content. Think carefully before you put a stock photo or art on your site. Consider alternatives to non-descript clip art images or stock photos.

Some large organizations even have the benefit of in-house or on-staff photographers. The CARE USA Web site includes many beautiful photos taken from around the world by its team of staff photographers. These photos help to communicate the value of the CARE USA humanitarian projects to donors. Dean for America employed a staff photographer to shoot pictures of the candidate as he participated in rallies and events all over the United States. While a professional in-house photographer may be beyond the budgetary reach of many companies, simple digital snapshots can often be very effective. For example, on mediabistro.com, visitors enjoy hundreds of party photos from the company's offline events and the Dean for America Pets for Dean gallery was comprised of amateur shots of supporters' pets.

A particularly interesting way to cash in with photos exists on the ebuild site. Companies listing building supply products in the ebuild directory have an opportunity to enhance the free-for-inclusion basic information provided.

ebuild makes good money by selling photo listings to companies as a form of online advertising that actually enhances the user experience.

While photos, charts, graphs, and other nontext content make great additions to any site, be wary of very large image sizes and using distracting multimedia content like Flash Video. Visitors want to access content quickly, they want sites that load fast, and they don't want to be distracted from the information they seek. A number of marketers mentioned that they specifically avoid excessive use of overbearing technologies and images that would diminish the value of the actual content. In many cases, they actually went against well-meaning expert advice.

Photos, images, and illustrations help tell your organization's story. When used as a component of an overall content strategy, photos enhance and add context to text-based information. Even in complex business-to-business applications, such as Weyerhaeuser's wood and paper products and Alcoa's aluminum components, photos are critical to more complete understanding. In virtually any marketplace, charts, graphs, and especially original informative photos help visitors to grasp what you're selling, making them more likely to buy.

Content Cross-Check for Best Practice #7

Chapter One: Crutchfield
Chapter Two: Alloy
Chapter Three: Design Within Reach
Chapter Four: mediabistro.com
Chapter Six: Aerosmith
Chapter Eight: Alcoa
Chapter Nine: Weyerhaeuser
Chapter Ten: ebuild
Chapter Twelve: Colliers
Chapter Fifteen: CARE USA
Chapter Sixteen: Tourism Toronto
Chapter Seventeen: Kenyon College
Chapter Eighteen: Sharp HealthCare
Chapter Twenty: Dean for America

Best Practice #8: Consider making proprietary content freely available

The more valuable a piece of content on a Web site is perceived to be, the better the site is in the eyes of visitors. This is not to say that a site that sells premium content should always give away the store, but even successful content providers like the Wall Street Journal Online give away select valuable content as an enticement to opt in for premium information. All sites that offer valuable content are more likely to cash in. However, organizations often shy away from posting much of their best content they possess because it is deemed "proprietary." On many sites, even information such as detailed product specifications and price lists are available only through direct connection with a salesperson, by completing a lengthy registration form with approval mechanisms, or by requiring visitors to pay a fee. Yet this is exactly the sort of free content that would move people closer to a purchase if it were readily available.

Many marketers have enjoyed success by defying those in their organizations who wish to lock away proprietary content. Alcoa makes more detailed product content available on its public site than do many other business-to-business companies and, in many cases, the content directly drives sales for Alcoa. Colliers International provides proprietary content in the form of comprehensive real estate market reports in PDF format on the site without any registration requirement beyond a user's e-mail address.

In some cases, the actual site design and organization are conceived of expressly to reveal propriety information developed over long periods of time. This strategy demonstrates the depth of an organization's expertise. For example, ebuild has developed a comprehensive taxonomy of several hundred thousand building products and makes the hierarchy available on the site. Other companies might be tempted to create the back-end architecture required to surface the content, but hide the underlying taxonomy to visitors. The ebuild approach might be considered risky by some marketers because the product organization structure would be considered a "trade secret" that could be freely copied. The construction of the ebuild taxonomy required significant effort on the part of Hanley-Wood; however, the company created ebuild to be as valuable as possible to users, even if the result was the opening up of its infrastructure to potential competitors.

Every marketing professional, whether working at corporations, government agencies, or nonprofits, struggles with determining what content is appropriate to post on its site. After all, that's the subject of this book. The struggle may be even more challenging when dealing with well-meaning executives who worry about corporate image, with legal departments who have a reflexive tendency to say "no," and with salespeople who feel it is easier to sell when they're the sole source of knowledge. These groups make it difficult to gain the necessary approvals to post "proprietary" content.

But consider the other extreme: CARE USA has a policy of showing its donor constituents that it is responsible with the money it raises. To support this policy, it posts perhaps one of the most proprietary documents there is— its tax returns, listing everything from executive salaries to revenue by source. CARE USA has a policy of the utmost transparency in its finances, operations, and activities, but the practice contributes greatly to allowing CARE USA to cash in; its contributors feel good knowing exactly how their donations are spent. The more valuable the content available on your Web site is perceived to be, the more valuable your Web site and your organization will be perceived to be.

Content Cross-Check for Best Practice #8

Chapter Seven: The Wall Street Journal Online
Chapter Eight: Alcoa
Chapter Six: Aerosmith
Chapter Ten: ebuild
Chapter Twelve: Colliers
Chapter Fifteen: CARE USA

Best Practice #9: If you serve a global market, use global content

The Web has made reaching the world far easier, but global marketing adds incredible complexity to the creation of the marketer's message. For some global marketers, it may be appropriate to create and offer local content to help an organization better serve both local and global audiences.

On some sites, organizations feature a local content presence for each market served. For example, the Alcoa site includes a network of nearly 100 country-specific sections in multiple languages. With so many different permutations of content appearing in one vast network, content management is critically important for the Alcoa site's success, which has hundreds of updates coming from the field per day.

Global content is also a key component of the Colliers International site. With 247 offices in 50 countries and 15 languages represented on the site, globalization posed a challenge. Designed with one look and feel, site content consists of real estate descriptions, photographs, and specifications. Since this content is critical to putting properties in the best light, Colliers' marketers make it a priority to include both local details and a view of the larger organization at work. The CARE USA site features vast quantities of information about the work CARE U... ...roughout the world. The site makes use of navigation architec... ...ample opportunities for visitors to drill down to learn n... ...the hundreds of individual projects going on at any one time... ...llenge for editors since the content comes from contributors in... ...might literally be little more than a field, posing significant tec... ...es) whose English language and writing skills vary widely. Ho... ...ntent is critical in demonstrating the global impact of the org...

The Online Journal... ...e global content, publishing more than 1,000 news stories... ...staff that draws on the Dow Jones network of business and... ...42 global news bureaus spanning the Americas, Asia, Eur... ...and Africa. The factors affecting businesses occur e... ...line Journal creates content appropriate to its global...

Of course, not ever... ...ol of dedicated content resources of staff locate... ...the world. But many global organizations, particularly those headquartered in the U.S., often make the mistake of including site content only derived from (and reflective of) the home market. Basic approaches to get your site up to global standards might include offering case studies from customers in various countries or spec sheets describing products with local country standards. Or an even simpler approach might be to highlight the speaking engagements or tradeshows your organization is attending in different countries. For example, Aerosmith posted a series of updates from the Japan leg of its 2004 tour with lots of photos of local fans. Sometimes the little things make a difference. For example, don't forget that the rest of the world uses the standard A4 paper format instead of the U.S. letter format, so having fact sheets and other materials that print properly on both formats is useful to users outside the United States.

Providing content in local languages can also help show the global aspect of your business, though this need not mean a wholesale translation of your entire site. A simple Web landing page with basic information in the local language, a case study or two, and appropriate local contact addresses and phone numbers will often suffice. Many global sites make use of country flags to clearly denote links to localized content. If your product or service is global, your site must reflect that. As innovative marketers have shown, an attention to global content adds significantly to a site's appeal within local markets.

Content Cross-Check for Best Practice #9

Chapter Six: Aerosmith
Chapter Seven: The Wall Street Journal Online
Chapter Eight: Alcoa
Chapter Nine: Weyerhaeuser
Chapter Twelve: Colliers
Chapter Thirteen: Booz Allen
Chapter Fifteen: CARE USA

Best Practice #10: Include interactive content and opportunities for user-feedback

Interactive content tools that get people involved with a site provide an ideal way to engage visitors, build interest, and move people through the sales cycle. For example, Sharp HealthCare's comprehensive set of interactive tools and calculators—like its physical exam reminder, body mass index calculator, and heart disease risk quiz—provide useful ways to learn about health; they also serve to directly link users to appropriate Sharp HealthCare professionals. On the same page where interactive results are posted, the Sharp tool or calculator provides links for more information or to schedule an appointment.

Weyerhaeuser provides a calculator that determines the linear footage in a roll of paper to make it easy to buy the right amount. CARE USA includes a tool for users to create e-mail messages about humanitarian concerns to send directly to government officials. Tourism Toronto offers a currency converter and interactive maps that smooth the path in deciding to visit Toronto.

At the Esurance site, interactive content drives visitors right to the point of purchase. Its interactive insurance quote tool is the most important part of the site because it's where the actual purchase transaction starts. Esurance reports that 70 percent of consumers decide on auto insurance based on price alone. Using its site, customers can generate online quotes by entering data like the state they live in and the kind of car they drive; an interactive calculator uses this data to generate a live quote. The Esurance quote tool provides fast auto insurance quotes making the online purchase experience quick and painless.

Tools aren't the only way to get users involved with your site. Aerosmith provides an opportunity for fans to create reviews or contribute artwork for posting on the site. Alloy includes many interactive components for girls such as quizzes, chat rooms, and message boards—all designed to draw readers in and make them part of the community. Interactive content is also important at mediabistro.com where users share information on topics of interest on the online bulletin board.

The Dean for America site allowed anybody to post comments to the official Dean blog. The campaign took a calculated risk with the practice, relying on the community to weed out "trolls" who posted content intended to deliberately disrupt the topic thread. The open availability of posting rights resulted in over 200,000 comments contributed throughout the campaign. Posts were from people totally immersed in the Dean for America content and each became a likely source for the millions of dollars in campaign contributions raised on the site. In the case of Dean for America, interactive content contributed directly to moving visitors through the cycle until they were ready to donate.

Another form of interactive content—providing a mechanism for site visitors to send comments and suggestions—serves as a terrific way to learn what visitors want, to improve content, and to develop and maintain a relationship with visitors. Yet, remarkably, most sites fail to provide any feedback mechanisms beyond a basic "e-mail the Webmaster" link.

Alloy targets a very specific market, teenage girls, so it employs a mall-rat dialect, perfect for its target audience. This trend-obsessed market is sensitive to the slightest tone of nonauthenticity as well as any missed fashion trends. It's critical for Alloy to keep content just right, so it relies on its site visitors to help. The teenagers communicate with marketers at Alloy via e-mail and chat rooms, which helps keep the company up-to-date with the lexicon and what's important to users.

Crutchfield Corporation uses multiple methods to gather input, comments, and suggestions from customers. Each page has a "rate this page" link to give a quick "thumbs up" or "thumbs down" as well as opportunities for more detailed written customer comments. Crutchfield uses feedback to develop content that helps customers to better understand the electronic products it offers. So, ultimately, Crutchfield.com sells more. Dermik Laboratories does not create its own content, but instead aggregates what it states are the leading sites in the dermatological field; it uses a "rate this site" feature on its Skin Health Solutions site when visitors are taken to external content sources. This allows Dermik to consistently evaluate site resources through the users themselves.

Interactive content and feedback mechanisms serve a dual purpose for your site—maintaining users' interest and gathering feedback. Interactive components give visitors a chance to become immersed in site content, which could lead them through the sales consideration cycle to the point where they are ready to spend money. The second purpose is to gather feedback from visitors, both direct and indirect. Of course, the direct feedback mechanisms like "rate this" buttons and opportunities to post comments provide valuable information, but the indirect data you get from interactive tools and usage analysis can be even more valuable. The simple knowledge that large numbers of visitors use a certain interactive tool on your site provides vital marketing information about what's working for you. Tools need not be intricate or time consuming. For example, a simple calculator to determine the best product for a prospect is a great starting point in the sales cycle. Interactive content leads directly to sales for many companies and provides essential user feedback, so carefully consider adding some tools that will help you cash in.

Content Cross-Check for Best Practice #10

Chapter One: Crutchfield
Chapter Two: Alloy
Chapter Three: Design Within Reach
Chapter Four: mediabistro.com
Chapter Five: Esurance
Chapter Six: Aerosmith
Chapter Eight: Alcoa
Chapter Nine: Weyerhaeuser
Chapter Thirteen: Booz Allen
Chapter Fourteen: UPS
Chapter Fifteen: CARE USA
Chapter Sixteen: Tourism Toronto
Chapter Eighteen: Sharp HealthCare
Chapter Nineteen: Dermik Laboratories
Chapter Twenty: Dean for America

Best Practice #11: Use content to trigger viral marketing

Content provides terrific fodder for viral marketing, which is the phenomenon of people passing on information about your site to their friends and colleagues or linking to your content in their blogs. When content proves interesting or useful, visitors tend to tell friends, usually by sending them a link. This may sound straightforward, but creating buzz around a site to encourage people to "talk it up" isn't easy. Certainly it is helpful to include an "e-mail this page" link, but there are other ways to optimize your content for maximum pass-along.

Booz Allen's strategy is to show that the company is a great place to work with plenty of job opportunities, so that visitors will not only apply there themselves but also tell their friends about interesting jobs. Alloy relies heavily on the way teens communicate with each other about "what's in" and "what's out" and hopes that alloy.com is a site that teens tell their friends about.

However, many sites specifically create content with the purpose of having it linked to or e-mailed. For example, the Esurance site uses a special section to showcase the many positive customer comments it receives on its site. The Esurance content team obtains permission from the people who submit these comments to post them on a special section of the site. As it turns out, many Esurance customers forward links to their posted comments to family and friends, which results in a viral marketing effect for Esurance. Since mediabistro.com spends no money on marketing, the entire site is set up to optimize viral marketing opportunities. Pictures from its networking parties, job boards, and courses all provide opportunities for people to mention the site to a friend or colleague who works in the media businesses.

The Baby Gallery on the Sharp HealthCare site is an excellent example of viral marketing content at work. New parents receive their own complimentary page on the Sharp site that includes a photo and birth details for their new bundle of joy and Sharp makes it easy for new parents to e-mail the link to family and friends. Sharp has found that when people visit the baby gallery, they browse a lot. To promote Sharp HealthCare, links from the Baby Gallery to newborn classes, breastfeeding classes, and other information builds interest among other potential customers who might be seeing the Sharp site for the first time via the Baby Gallery. For Sharp HealthCare, babies are good business and baby photos make great viral content; they help recruit new patients.

Viral marketing can be tricky to trigger, however. Many companies will "bring in the experts" (which usually means an advertising agency) when it is deemed time to "try to get some viral marketing." But the whole concept of viral marketing—creating content that has a pass-along value—is not something you can create with any degree of certainty because it happens more organically. There are a few things you can do to help the process, though. When creating site content, think carefully about what content might be something a user would want to pass along and then make that content easy to find and link to. Make the actual URLs permanent so that people don't find dead links if they visit months later and consider adding "e-mail to a friend" buttons within the site. The bottom line to be successful with viral marketing is to say something interesting and valuable and make it easy to find and share.

If visitors think the content you have is intriguing, they will tell their friends and colleagues and your organization will benefit.

Content Cross-Check for Best Practice #11

Chapter Two: Alloy
Chapter Three: Design Within Reach
Chapter Four: mediabistro.com
Chapter Five: Esurance
Chapter Six: Aerosmith
Chapter Thirteen: Booz Allen
Chapter Eighteen: Sharp HealthCare

Best Practice #12: Link content directly to the sales cycle

To cash in, marketers at many sites specifically design content to support the sales consideration process or draw a potential buyer into the sales cycle. People considering a purchase always go through a thought process prior to making a decision. In the case of something simple and low cost, say buying a new umbrella, the process may be very straightforward and only take seconds. But for major financial commitments—such as where to go to college, what car to buy, and for many business-to-business sales—the sales cycle may involve many steps and take months or even years to complete.

Effective Web marketers take Web site visitors' sales consideration cycle into account when writing content and organizing it on the site. People in the early stages of the sales cycle need basic information on the product category. Those further along in the process want to compare offerings and need detailed specifications and lists of features and benefits. Of course, those ready to whip out their credit cards need easy mechanisms linked directly from the content so they may immediately buy (sign up, donate, etc.).

To supply content to those in the early stages of the buying process, Crutchfield Corporation launched CrutchfieldAdvisor.com as a companion site to Crutchfield.com. Crutchfield Advisor is designed to be the equivalent of a trusted friend who knows a great deal about electronics. When customers are ready to buy, the Advisor site seamlessly links to Crutchfield.com, which includes the detailed product information, product comparisons, and a store front.

The Toronto Convention and Visitors Association found that many people who are early in the sales consideration cycle start out on the Tourism Toronto site (and other travel-related sites) knowing they want to go on a trip some-where. At this point they haven't narrowed their choice down to a particular country or city. The Tourism Toronto site includes "experience" pages with content designed to draw people in at those early planning stages. The Tourism Toronto experience menu is broken down into different themes, such as sports and recreation, and nightlife, so people can discover particularly appealing aspects of the city. Once people have decided to book a trip to Toronto, content appropriate to the latter part of the sales cycle, like informa-tion on reservations for hotels and activities, are readily available.

mediabistro.com views each bit of its content as a vehicle to bring cus-tomers into the sales funnel. All the free content on mediabistro.com is one step away from people paying money. ebuild created a site that links appropriate news and articles directly to the over 250,000 product listings on its site. As peo-ple browse products, they seamlessly link to news articles that help them move through the sales cycle. ServiceWare also focuses on the sales cycle by offering white papers appropriate for each step in the sales consideration process.

Kenyon College faces a daunting challenge because of its long sales cycle. When students visit colleges in person, they tend to be juniors and seniors in high school, but marketers at Kenyon learned that when students first visit col-lege Web sites, they're freshman or sophomores. So the Web site is often the first place that a student comes into contact with the college and must cater to an audience that won't be ready to apply for admission for two or three years. Because the Web marketers at Kenyon know that the college Web site is pro-viding information at the very early stages of a long sales consideration cycle, they create appropriate content to develop a lasting relationship. Content includes Kenyon student profiles that help high school students get a sense of what college life would be like if they were to attend Kenyon.

As you know, this book is about using Web content to get browsers to buy. While each best practice adds to the ability of a site to cash in, linking content directly to the sales cycle is perhaps the most important. The goal should be to make certain that appropriate content is created, posted, and designed with links to the point of purchase. This is a particularly critical best practice—don't ignore it! After all, if your site isn't optimized for your ultimate goal—getting people to buy, subscribe, join, or donate—then you're missing a tremendous opportunity. In my experience, the vast major-ity of sites are little more than online brochures. Don't let the opportunities that the Web offers pass your site by. Help your prospects along the path to opening their wallets by offering content directly linked to the buying con-sideration process.

Content Cross-Check for Best Practice #12

Chapter One: Crutchfield
Chapter Four: mediabistro.com
Chapter Five: Esurance
Chapter Eight: Alcoa
Chapter Ten: ebuild
Chapter Eleven: ServiceWare
Chapter Fifteen: CARE USA
Chapter Sixteen: Tourism Toronto
Chapter Seventeen: Kenyon College

Practices Make Perfect

The constant throughout each and every profile in the book, and the resulting best practices included in this chapter, is the focus on using content to drive action. In every case, content is created, organized, and deployed to drive visitors to do something—be it to purchase, subscribe, invest, join, or donate. The marketers profiled here turn browsers into buyers and their best practices provide useful ideas to anyone charged with creating a great Web site that will cash in with content.

When looking back at the 12 best practices, it will certainly seem a daunting task to apply each one to your own organization's Web site. The fact is that trying to make use of all of the ideas at once would be next to impossible. But you don't need to implement them all (or at least not at the same time). For one thing, not all best practices are appropriate to every site. For example, the use of new URLs or the addition of global content may not make sense for you and your organization's strategy. It's also important to reinforce that these best practices do not necessarily build on one another. There's no need to make use of the best practices in any particular order; you can pick and choose what's important for you and implement each of those best practices independently.

Importantly, the best practices are not strict "either/or" propositions. You don't need to remove some aspect of your existing site and replace it with the best practice. Rather, the best practices may in many cases be added to and built on top of the Web site you already have in place. For example, if you have focused on text-based content in the past, you may find that you can now enhance it through the addition of original photos or interactive tools. Many best practices can be added on top of the content that already appears on your site, making the task of deploying these ideas a far less overwhelming process.

One of the beauties of the Web that makes these best practices straightforward to implement is that sites are created over many months and years through an iterative process. Rather than trying to do everything at once, you might choose a particular best practice idea and quietly implement it. You can then test to see if it has helped you to cash in, modify it as appropriate, and move on to implement another best practice.

Hopefully, these best practices will get you and others in your organization thinking more about content than you had in the past. Taking the power of content into consideration is particularly important as design modifications and Web site upgrades are being considered and planned. Content is also a great starting point for brand new sites or those that have stalled and need reinvigoration. As your colleagues argue about color, design, and technology, step up with content strategies. While everyone else thinks like a designer, you have an opportunity to present the ideas of a publisher. You can directly contribute to your organization's ability to cash in on the Web, and content is your tool.

CHAPTER TWENTY-TWO

Lessons Learned

My goal in writing *Cashing In With Content* was to demonstrate through the experiences of marketers at diverse successful organizations how content is conceived, created, and then published on the Web in ways that prompt visitors to buy, subscribe, apply, join, invest, or contribute. Throughout the book, I've explored how content turns browsers into buyers—be it buying a product or service or buying into a philosophy or image. The power of content has been related through the opinions and successes of the marketers who make and use content in ways that directly contribute to the bottom line of the organizations they represent. Now that the stories are told and the collective best practices catalogued, content can take its rightful place as a major contributor to Web site success.

OK, fine, you might say, but what about me and my own organization? How do I take all of this information and put it to work? How and where do I begin?

You're a Publisher Now, So Think Like One

Publishers are the old-school kings of content. Until the Web, it is unlikely that most other organizations would have even used the term "content" to describe the data, information, and expertise they possess. Yet, in order to implement a successful Web strategy and truly cash in, marketing people need to think more like publishers. Marketers at the most enlightened organizations recognize the fact that they are now purveyors of content and they manage it as a valuable organizational asset—with the care a publishing company does.

One of the most important things that publishers do is start with a content strategy and then focus on the mechanics and design of delivering that content. Publishers carefully identify and define target audiences and consider what content is required in order to meet their needs. Publishers consider questions like: Who are my readers? How do I reach them? What are their motivations? What are the problems I can help them solve? How can I entertain them and inform them at the same time? What content will compel them to purchase what I have to offer?

Publishers also set out content as a significant line item in an overall business plan. On the other hand, consider the *average* marketing budget: It likely includes line items for advertising, collateral production, direct mail, and other tactical programs. Many marketing budgets also have specific categories for Web site design and programming, but very few specifically earmark funding for content of any kind, much less Web content. One of the first steps in thinking like a publisher when creating a marketing strategy is to allocate resources for content in the marketing budget.

What would you include in a content marketing budget? If you're responsible for a larger site, you might want to include the hiring and training of dedicated writers and/or editors devoted exclusively to your site. If your organization isn't large enough to hire full-time Web content staffers, you might factor in the costs of repurposing existing print content for your Web site; many organizations have content available in other divisions like product marketing, public relations, or investor relations that can be repurposed for the Web. However, repurposing content often requires editing to make it serve the needs of various target users. Perhaps purchasing syndicated content or dedicating an individual or team to scouring the Web for the best aggregation of links would be suitable for your industry or marketplace. Or, you might earmark funds to work with a technology company on content optimization, taxonomy creation, or white paper distribution. For sites large or small, if your business plan doesn't contain a line item for content, it will forever take a back seat to the other programs that are already "covered" in your budget. And if content is treated as an afterthought, your site and your organization may suffer the same fate in the minds of consumers.

Make Content the Focus of Your Site

As anyone involved in building and maintaining a Web site certainly knows, many factors contribute to success; a site is made up of much more than just content. Appearance and navigation are important: Interesting graphic design consistent with site goals and objectives ground users in the experience. Appropriate text choices on the site regarding both color and fonts make everything easy to read. To encourage browsing, an intuitive menu and clear navigational options make the site usable to those who don't know exactly what they're looking for. A good search engine is required to ensure that visitors who already know what information they are looking for can easily find it. Reliable technology and back-end infrastructure make the site perform flawlessly 24/7. Easy-to-locate Contact Us, About Us, and Frequently Asked Questions (FAQ) pages highlight the company or institution behind the site and provide a quick-to-find overview. Search Engine Optimization for appropriate keywords and phrases ensures that people find your site at the top of search engine results—that will lead them to your site in the first place. Usage analytics allow you to better understand navigational and usage habits to optimize both design and content for users. These and other important factors all combine to ensure that visitors reach your site and provide a positive overall experience for them when they do. When all aspects of a site operate successfully as one seamless whole, visitors stay longer and come back again.

Thousands of books, online resources, conferences, and consultants exist to help organizations build effective Web sites. Specialized information is readily available that covers Web-based graphic design, information architecture and navigation, Search Engine Optimization HTML, XML, and various design and other programming tools. Although each of these areas can contribute to a site, one of the most important factors for site success, *content—* especially recognition of how content is used to drive action—is too often overlooked.

To move content out of the back seat into its rightful place—driving a successful Web strategy—you must make content the single most important component of your site. That might be easier said than done, particularly when parties with vested interests—from IT professionals who don't want to lose control of the site to vendors or consultants emphasizing advertising, aesthetics, or technology—exert influence to the contrary. The bottom line, however, is that these site aspects must all serve the content, which serves the user. So, when you're working on a site revision or beginning development of a new site, put your content strategy on the planning table first; then think about other elements like design, colors, and enabling technologies. Define the content strategy from the start—always with the objective of informing specific user groups—and then approach other site aspects as part of the overall content-centric site design.

Because content is so often misunderstood, you may face wide-eyed stares from your colleagues. Your advertising agency or outside design house may resist your efforts. But as the 20 organizations profiled here (and many others) demonstrate, putting your convictions about the value of Web site content on the line is well worth the effort.

Focus on Your Customer's Problems

Web marketers would be wise to emulate successful publishers who work to understand the audience first and then set about trying to satisfy their informational needs. A great way to start thinking like a publisher is to focus on your customer's problems and then develop and deliver content accordingly. This process creates content that drives action. Too often, Web site content simply describes what an organization or a product does. While simple information about your organization and its products might be valuable to a subset of your visitors, what many really want from your site is content that first describes the issues and problems they face and then provides details on how to solve the problems. Once you've built an online relationship, you can sell into the needs and potential solutions that have been defined.

The *Cashing In With Content* "target-problem-solution" approach as outlined in Best Practice #4 is worth a quick recap here. First, determine who your target audience is and figure out how they should be sliced into distinct buying segments. Once this exercise is complete, identify the situations in which each target audience may find themselves. What are their problems? What keeps them awake at night? What do they want to know? What do they need to know? Finally, after you've identified target audiences and articulated their problems, show off your expertise through information and, ultimately, how your offering provides ideal solutions to solve problems. At each stage of the target-market identification, problem articulation, and solution process, useful, well-organized Web site content will lead your visitors through the sales cycle all the way to the point when they are ready to make a purchase or other commitment to your organization.

A particularly valuable way to create content that addresses your customers' problems is to apply the "show, don't tell" rule. Novelists and actors use "show, don't tell" all the time; they use action to communicate rather than stultifying narrative. To make a reader feel that a character is happy, a novelist could tell us that the character is happy through narration or have that character use dialog to say: "I'm happy." While either one gets the point across, these approaches are not nearly as effective as words that show that the character is happy, such as: Her eyes sparkled and she danced a little jig. The same "show, don't tell" rule applies as an effective way to create content that specifically addresses customer problems. Where previously you might have listed target-market segments and the customers your organization has in these categories, you could instead create a library of customer stories that demonstrate in real-world scenarios how organizations make use of your product. You could also include photos of the product in action. Content that *shows* how your organization solves customer problems is vastly more effective than simply listing products, or even writing all sorts of copy that *tells* how your product works.

A Web Site Is More Art than Science

As you develop content marketing strategies and tactics, remember that a successful approach is often more art than science. While the ideas and best practices in this book will help your site and its users, the content you offer will have distinctive qualities. A well-executed Web site—like a quality television program, film, or published text—is an effective combination of content and delivery. But on the Web, many organizations spend much more time and money on the design and delivery aspects than on content itself.

Although many people responsible for Web sites focus more attention on aesthetics and technology than on content, the marketers interviewed in this book agree that a combination of the right content, design, and delivery is required to cash in. Perfecting that critical mix is where art comes in. There is no absolute right or wrong way to create a Web site; each organization has an individual and important story to tell. In many ways, you will be exercising your creative talents as you plan and implement a content strategy.

As you envision your content-centric site, be particularly aware of the different ways that visitors consume information. To cash in with content, you should choose the ingredients from among the techniques found in this book that will result in a recipe that satisfies the needs of your users: Encourage serendipity. Embrace easy ways to browse. Establish online newsletters. Include interesting photos, tables, charts, or interactive tools. Write and offer a free guide to something. Hire writers and an editor to keep pages fresh and content quality high. Assume that visitors may want you to tell them what to read rather than simply relying on search engines to help them find information. Ultimately, though, your creativity and dedication to the art of delivering Web content will be the single most important factor in the site's success.

Content Drives Action

A consistent theme throughout *Cashing in with Content* is that an effective content strategy, artfully executed, drives action. Sites that cash in have a clearly defined goal—to sell products, generate leads, secure contributions, or get people to join—and deploy a content strategy that directly contributes to reaching that goal. At successful sites, content draws visitors into the sales-consideration funnel and channels them toward the place where cashing in occurs. The mechanism to cash in is not hidden nor is the organization's goal a secret. When content effectively drives action, the end of the sales funnel—an e-commerce company's "buy" button, the business-to-business corporation's "please contact us" form, or nonprofit's "donate" link—are found in logical places, based on content that leads people there.

For many companies, Web content also has a powerful, less tangible effect. On the best sites, content does more than just sell product—it directly contributes to an organization's positive reputation by showing thought-leadership in the marketplace of ideas. Content brands a company or a nonprofit as an expert and as a trusted resource to turn to again and again.

A Special Note to Executives

A top-down content strategy—like any other key business initiative—will better enable an organization to build a successful site. Senior executives and CEOs make an enormous difference in their organizations when they embrace and provide support for Web content initiatives. If you're a top-level executive or other senior leader reading these words, you're taking the first step in leveraging content for the success of your organization. Congratulations! Don't stop here. Next, you should provide specific organizational guidance and insight about the power of content as a tool to drive action. Your commitment will shine through and prove inspirational to your people. In fact, entire businesses have been built by CEOs who used Web content as the driving factor. Some successful examples are profiled in this book, including Design Within Reach, Crutchfield Corporation, and mediabistro.com. And don't forget Howard Dean who forever changed the face of political campaigning with content.

As a senior executive, you also have an opportunity to publish content on your Web site under your own byline. Often the personal touch of a founder or the high-level perspective of a top manager provides the perfect way to tell a story to your market. Consider creating an online column or starting a blog to reach out to your constituents. You have an opportunity to directly contribute to your organization's online success through your personal commitment to content.

What Content Means to Marketers

If you're a marketer who has read this far, you probably have a vested interest in applying a content strategy within your organization. Terrific! But I must warn you: It is likely that in many companies, you'll be seen as a maverick. In my experience, management teams relate well to the visual aspects of a Web site: The CFO likes this logo better than that one or the vice president of sales is partial to red instead of green. You'll need to be conscious of these feelings while selling your content strategy to your organization. Content can seem abstract to those who've not had to focus on content creation or delivery before (i.e., most job functions within any type of company outside of publishing and academia) and you will need to help make both the concept and the potential impact more concrete for many members of your organization. But don't give up. There's no doubt that content drives action and helps make Web sites and those who create them successful—just ask the marketers whose organizations are profiled in these pages.

As you apply the best practice ideas from this book and dedicate your skills to the art of producing a great site based on content, I'll wager that you'll be surprised by the swiftness tangible results appear. As your site becomes more and more successful, your own personal brand reputation inside your organization is bound to grow and, in many cases, your marketability to the wider world will increase.

But if you look for job openings for your newly honed skills, you aren't likely to see specific employment categories for "Web content expert" or "Contentmaster." You'll find openings for Webmasters, internet technology specialists, site architects, and even CEOs in the technology area; interactive marketing experts, online advertising specialists, and graphic designers in the communications area; and copy writers, reporters, editors, even a vice president of content in the publishing area. However, you are unlikely to find positions that purport to directly control a Web content strategy. But fear not. Your new skills are most certainly in high demand, the world just doesn't yet know how to categorize or define them. But my guess is that as content takes its place at the forefront of both Web site and larger organizational strategies, we'll start seeing it make its way into many job descriptions and even job titles across any number of organizational types.

In the meantime, now that you understand how organizations of all kinds cash in with content, it's time to lead your site with a powerful content strategy that drives your own success.

Photo courtesy of rogovin.com

David Meerman Scott is a writer, consultant, conference speaker, and seminar leader specializing in using online content to market and sell products and services to demanding customers worldwide. His expertise is in increasing revenue by applying cost-effective content marketing programs at all stages of the sales cycle.

Prior to starting his own marketing and communications company, David worked in the news business where he held executive positions at NewsEdge Corporation, an online content leader, and for an electronic information division of Knight-Ridder, one of the world's largest newspaper chains. He's also held senior management positions at a leading e-commerce company, was a clerk on a Wall Street bond trading desk, and acted in Japanese television commercials.

David is the author of *Eyeball Wars: a novel of dot-com intrigue* and a contributing editor for *EContent Magazine*. His writing has appeared in such diverse publications as *Competitive Intelligence Magazine*, *StreamingMedia*, *North American Review*, *Metropolis*, and others. David has lived and worked in New York, Tokyo, Boston, and Hong Kong and he has presented at industry conferences and events in over 20 countries on four continents. To contact David, please visit him at www.DavidMeermanScott.com or check out his blog *Web Ink Now* at www.webinknow.com.

A

abandonment, 16
academic papers, Web-based, 8
accuracy, 56
AcneBeat site, 190
ad marketing
    on Alloy.com, 30
    effectiveness of, 4, 5
    on TV, 5–6
Adolescent Health, 179
advertising
    disclosure messages, 103
    interest-based targeting, 72
    revenue from, 160
    target audiences and, 102–104
Aero Force One fan club, 59–68
Aerosmith, 59–68
    global content for, 226
    interactive tools, 227
    multiple URLs, 218
    online voice and, 212
    photo content, 222
aesthetics
    focus on branding, 6–7
    highlighting content with, 34
    strategy and, 209, 239
    white space and, 34
age/aging
    target demographics and, 75–76,
        150
    teenage girls, 23–30, 179–180
Alcoa site, 81–88
    content review, 212
    e-commerce components, 9
    global content for, 225
    photo content, 222
    proprietary information, 85, 224
Alloy Inc., 23–30, 211, 222, 228
altruism, 143
aluminum, 81–88
alumni, online community, 169

Amazon.com, 21
answer marketing, 4, 5
appearance. consistency, 237
applicant tracking system, 125
appointments, online, 175, 180
article openers, homepages, 72
Articles of Incorporation, 134
artwork, fan contributed, 227
audiences. *see* target audiences
Audio/Video content resources, 16
auto-deer collisions, 52–53
Auto Insurance Quote tool, 54
automaker sites, 6
automobile insurance, 49–58
AvantGuild, 46, 47
Aventis Pharmaceuticals, 184

B

Baby Gallery
    photo content, 222
    viral marketing through, 177–178,
        230
backend architecture, 88, 116
bailouts, causes of, 55. *see also*
        shopping-cart abandonment
banner advertisements, 102
bargains, product-specific mes-
        sages, 102, 104
Barnett, Kathy, 153–161
Becker, Lawrence, 13–22
benchmarking, 180, 191
Best of the Web Today column,
        74–75, 220
best practices, 207–234
bill paying online, 50
biographies. *see* profiles
BitPipe network, 111
BizRate.com, 20, 21
Blog for America, 3, 195–199
blogs, 5, 46, 193–203, 218–219

Body Mass Index (BMI) calculator, 179, 227
bookmarked sites, 5
Boot Camp for Journalists, 43
Booz Allen Hamilton Inc., 123–130
   consistency of voice, 210–211
   self-select paths, 216
   viral marketing and, 230
branding
   Aerosmith, 67
   global, 113–114
   mistakes with, 6–7
   of Toronto, 157
   "unbranded," 185
Brewe, Kristin, 49–58
browsing
   content management systems and, 148
   encouragement of, 215–217
   homepage organization, 83
   serendipity in, 5
building professionals, 97–104
business news, 69–77
buy buttons, 240

C

calculators, 227, 229
calendars, 160, 179
campus tours, 167
car stereos, 14, 17
CARE International, 142
CARE USA, 141–151
   alternate content delivery, 220
   consistency of content, 214
   global content for, 226
   online voice, 212
   photo content, 222
   transparency, 225
career sites
   Booz Allen Hamilton Inc., 123
   content creation, 129–130
   job searches and, 73–74
   mediabistro.com, 39–48
CareerJournal.com, 73–74

case studies, 226
catalogs
   online, 97–104
   print, 14, 29, 33
chat rooms, 23, 24, 227
Cheney, Dick, 203
classification schemes, 101–102
codes of business conduct, 133, 134
Colliers International, 113–121
   alternate content delivery, 220
   global content for, 225–226
   needs analysis by, 209
   photo content, 222
   proprietary information, 119, 224
color choices
   branding, 7
   coordination, 100, 237
   by marketing, 117
   mediabistro.com, 48
   target audience and, 26
commercial real estate, 113–121
communication
   corporate role, 86–87
   political campaigns, 193–203
   site redesign, 165
   in a soundbite world, 145–146
   with users, 24
communities
   alumni online, 169
   building of, 72
   campus events and, 167
   company relations with, 92
   interactive tools, 227–228
   offline, 43, 200–201
   online, 39
   political campaigns, 193–203
   transfer of information within, 84
company charters, 133
company growth, 58
company history, 90, 91
company size, impressions of, 105, 106
comparison shopping, 15
competition
   comparison of sites, 135
   with larger companies, 185

monitoring other sites, 180, 183, 209
in youth media, 30
complaints, usability and, 138
confidence. building of, 18
confidentiality, 84–84
confusion, 16, 18
connections, Alloy.com, 23, 25
consistency
editorial, 10, 56, 110, 213–215
global branding and, 113–114
search functions, 116
of voice, 210–213
construction industry, 97–104
consulting, 123–130
consumer electronics, 13–22
consumers
caring about, 53
connections between, 23
education of, 53
proactive, 190
contact information, 85, 121, 226, 237
content
aggregation of, 186
alternate routes, 219–221
cost of creation, 72–73
definition, 1
focus on, 236–238
freshness of, 167
proprietary, 85, 119, 223–225
rationing information, 68
repositories of, 73
repurposing of, 168
tagging, 101–102
unedited, 198
value retention, 70
content management systems (CMS), 88, 115, 118, 148, 167
content-smart sites, 2–4
context, content and, 31–32
continual improvement processes, 128–129
contractions, written, 56
convenience, online transactions and, 54–55

core values, 92, 127
corporate bylaws, 134
corporate citizenship
company core values and, 92
environmental records and, 86–87, 89–90, 95, 136–138
sustainability statements and, 86–87, 136–137
corporate culture, communication of, 211
corporate governance, 132–133, 136
cost-benefits analyses, 114
courses, mediabistro.com, 40
Coverage Counselor tool, 54
credit cards, 194, 202–203, 231
crisis recovery, 153–161
cross-marketing, 90
cross-selling, 45
Crovitz, L. Gordon, 69–77
Crutchfield, Bill, 14
Crutchfield Advisor, 16, 218, 228
Crutchfield Corporation, 13–22, 218
currency, blogs, 46
currency converter tools, 160
Customer Relationship Management (CRM), 106–109, 149
customer satisfaction, 22
customers, relationships with, 191

D

databases
of constituents, 147
of content, 148, 149
of donors, 149, 221
of projects, 148
of properties, 117
of user profiles, 30
Dean, Howard, 3, 193–203
Dean for America, 193–203
alternate content delivery, 221
interactive tools, 228
multiple URLs, 218–219
photo content, 222
use of humor, 211

decision making
content driven, 2
doctor selection, 175
on insurance, 54
value-added content and, 16
Dell Computer, 9
demographics. *see* target audiences
dermatologists, 183–191
Dermik Laboratories, 183–191
content selection, 214
interactive tools, 228
multiple URLs, 218
self-select paths, 216
Skin Health Solutions site, 3
design
attractive, 110
consistency, 210–213, 237
content and, 84
effectiveness of, 7
external services, 87, 116
extreme, 81
Design Notes newsletter, 35–37, *36*
Design Within Reach, 9, 31–37, 210, 214, 220
designers, biographies, 31
digital cameras, 21–22
direct mail approaches, 150, 151
Disability Rights Platform, 194
disclosure messages, 103
discounts, added value of, 47
diversity
policies online, 124
of visitor needs, 85–86
Doctorow, E. L., 165
donations. *see also* fundraising
content-driven, 143–145
for content-driven, 163–171
credit cards, 202–203
"Give Now" buttons, 169
news stories about, 169
objectives driving, 170
online, 141
online voice and, 212
political, 193–203
tracking efficacy by, 149

donors. *see also* philanthropy
alternate content delivery, 221
building relationships with, 149
connections to field work, 142
Dow Jones & Company, 69
downloadable information, 93, 107–109, 194
driving instructions, 175, 177
driving safety, 53
drkoop.com, 174
Drudge Report, 5

E

e-mail
content delivery, 219–221
free addresses, 47
marketing capability, 115
mobilization of, 146–147
newsletters, 5, 35, 48, 117
from users, 24–25
viral marketing and, 228, 229
earnings reports, 88
ebuild, 97–104
needs analysis by, 209
photo content, 222–223
proprietary information, 224
sales cycle, 232
editorial content
on Alloy.com, 28
The Wall Street Journal Online, 75
editorial processes, 56
Alcoa site, 87–88
classification issues, 101–102
consistency and, 110, 213–215
content organization and, 97
language issues, 148
workflow definition, 118
editorial voice, 23
education
of consumers, 53
by nonprofits, 144
through sales cycle, 106
through site content, 141
Virtual Field Trips, 145–146

by Weyerhaeuser, 90
educators, summer opportunities, 94
elected officials, links to, 146
eMonitor, 102
empathy, with users, 127
employees, as audience, 137–137
entertainment, 25
environmental messaging, 95, 136–138
environmental records, 86–87, 89–90
error messages, 55–56, 213
Esurance, 49–58, 211, 227, 230
Ethics and Business Conduct Office, 92
events lists, 194
exclusivity, membership communities and, 61–65
experimentation, need for, 45

F

fact-checking, 56
Faley, Kelly, 173–181
fan clubs, 59–68
FAQ sections, 213, 237
feedback, 20
    benefits of, 227–229
    communication with users, 24
    complaints as, 138
    content ideas through, 53–54
    from customers, 20–21
    interactive tools, 228
    on newsletter, 37
    unsolicited e-mails, 57–58
    on usability, 128
financial statements, 88, 131
Flash Video, 148, 223
fluidity, need for, 160
Food and Drug Administration (FDA), 189
Forbes, Robert, 31–37
forest products, 89–96
forms, abandonment of, 128

Fost, Joshua, 113–121
free content, 71–75
freelancers, needs of, 40
Frequently Asked Questions (FAQs), 213, 237
freshness, 129, 167
fundraising. *see also* donations
    credit cards, 202–203
    "Give Now" buttons, 169
    for Kenyon College, 163–171
    political, 193–203
furniture design, 31–37

G

Generation Y, 23–30
global markets, 225–227. *see also* *specific* companies
glossary windows, 16
"good deals," 102, 104
goodwill, building of, 46
Google, organization of, 4–5
gossip, 25, 26
governance guidelines, 133
government agencies, 146
graphics, 26, 110
grassroots politics, 8, 193–203
Greystone.com, 180
Gross, Mathew, 193–203

H

Hamilton, Tom, 60, 65
Hanley-Wood, 98–104, 224
Hayes, Rutherford B., 165
headlines, 71, 72, 83
Health Industry Edition, WSJ, 76
health information portals, 174
healthcare, 173–181
help desk software, 106
help files, 213
home pages
    company core values and, 92
    cycling content, 165

home pages (*cont.*)
  headlines on, 71
  organization of, 83
  target markets, 46
  for visitors, 178
Hospitals & Health Networks magazine, 173, 174
"how-to-Buy" information, 17
How to See (Nelson), 37
HTML content, 93
humor, 56, 198, 211

I

I-SITE, 186
idiomatic expressions, 56
images, as content, 221–223
indexing, 187
instructions, 40, 56
insurance, 49–58, 227
integrity, 188–189
interactive features
  on Alloy.com, 23
  Auto Insurance Quote tool, 54
  company history, 91
  cross-marketing and, 90
  healthcare examples, 178–179
  inclusion of, 227–229
  sending e-mail, 146
  for tourists, 160
international companies
  Alcoa, 81–88
  Colliers International, 113–121
  cross-pollination of local offices, 121
  Weyerhaeuser, 89–96
international humanitarian organizations, 141–151
interviews, content models, 43–44
investor relations, 90, 131–138
Iowa Caucuses, 201

J

Janney, Allison, 165, 221
jargon, industry-specific, 110
job postings, 73–74
  Booz Allen Hamilton, 128–129
  company sites, 86
  cost to employers, 42
  efficacy, 124
  mediabistro.com, 39–48
  summer opportunities, 94
John B Road Reports, 65

K

Kaplan/Newsweek, 164
Kaplow, Susan, 23–30
Kasey, 198–199, 211
Kennedy, John F., 194
Kenyon Alumni Bulletin, 168
Kenyon College, 163–171
  browsing-optimized organization, 215
  needs analysis by, 209
  photo content, 221–222
  sales cycle, 232
Kenyon Review, 167–169
Klesner, Kimberlee, 163–171
knowledge management solutions, 105–111
Koop, C.Everett, 174
Kramer, Joey, 60

L

language issues
  consistency of voice, 210–213, 211
  conversational speech, 56
  English as a second language, 148, 212
  global content and, 226–227
  industry-specific jargon, 110

international organizations and, 142
multinational companies and, 87–88
plain English, 51, 133
taxonomy, 224
languages
on global sites, 118
Spanish language content, 179, 180
lead flow, tracking, 111
length issues
interest levels and, 68
literary content, 168
repurposed content, 168
visit times, 175
leverage, membership communities, 47
lexicon, up-to-date vocabulary, 24–25
links
browser-friendly sites, 215
to outside sites, 187–188
to shopping, 28
to unofficial sites, 195
user exploration and, 144
literary content, 167–169
localization, global sites, 117–118
logos, 7
Looks We Love section, 222
Lowery, Kevin, 81–88
loyalty building, 8, 43, 59, 60, 173
Lundgren, Michael, 59–68, 81

M

Mallaney, Alicia, 123–130
Mall.com, 27–28
management philosophy, 133
maps, interactive, 160
market research
on catalog content, 14
customer feedback and, 20
reports online, 119
target demographics, 75–76

marketing
budgets, 6, 47–48, 236
fees, 158
interest-based targeting, 72
to new patients, 177
subscription-based, 63
McNutt, Andy, 105–111
media
high-value content and, 70
mediabistro.com, 39–48
SARS epidemic and, 157–159
Media & Marketing Edition, WSJ, 76
media community, 43–46
mediabistro.com, 39–48
alternate content delivery, 220
consistency of voice, 211
multiple URLs, 219
needs analysis by, 209
Meetup, 200
membership communities
exclusivity and, 61–63, 61–65
fan-to-fan reviews, 66
fees for, 62
levels of membership, 62–63
mediabistro.com as, 41
registered users, 46–47
seniority value, 63
menus, 83, 175. *see also* navigation
message boards, 23, 227
metrics
appointments online, 180
measuring success with, 161
on site usage, 96
Modern Healthcare, 173
Mount St. Helens, 94
mStoner, 165
multinational companies, 81–88
multiplatform components, 144
multiversion testing, 20

N

navigation. *see also* menus
Alloy.com, 29
bite-size sections, 25–26

navigation (*cont.*)
  browser-friendly sites, 215
  consistency, 95, 114, 237
  Design Within Reach site, 31
  diverse audiences in, 153
  drop-down menus, 175
  levels of, 153
  map of cross linking, 134–135
  self-select paths, 124, 153,
      215–217
  testing, 20
  use of metrics in design, 96
needs analysis, comprehensive,
    209–210
Nelson, George, 37
networking parties, 40–48
Newman, Paul, 221
news reports, 69–77
newsletters
  advertising via, 108
  content delivery, 219–221
  cross-selling content, 45
  e-mail, 117
  members only, 63
  viral marketing through, 177
newspapers, tracking lead flow, 111
Nixon, Richard M., 194
nonprofit organizations
  donations to, 141–151
  on the Web, 8–9
nonsubscribers, free content for,
    71–75
Norton, Paula, 131–138

O

Office of the Registrar site, 167
offline business, 200–201, 212
offline content, 62
OpinionJournal.com, 74
organization
  of global sites, 117
  as information portal, 187
  site redesign, 165
organizations
  core values, 127
  partnerships, 47
  publishing by, 7–9

P

PARTNERS+simons, 116
Partridge, Robert, 183–191
pass-along value, 35
PDF content, 93
Perry, Joe, 60
personality, Web site, 210–213
personals, inclusion of, 45
Pets for Dean, 198–199, 211
pharmaceutical companies
    marketing, 191
  regulation of marketing by, 189
  on the Web, 8
philanthropy, 90, 93. *see also* dona-
    tions; donors
photographs
  Baby Gallery, 177–178
  close-up, 31
  as content, 221–223
  in Design Within Reach, 31
  educational use, 146
  library maintenance, 148
  online catalogs, 15
  Pets for Dean, 198–199
  political sites, 194
  premium listings and, 103
  stock supplied, 222
  wide-angle, 31
physician referrals, 175
Plute, Jason, 89–96
podiatric community, 190–191
policy makers, 90
political campaigns, 193–203
Political Diary, 75
polls, 23
Pop culture, 25
premium listings, 103
press information, 194
print media, 99
printer-friendly formats, 31, 55
prizes, 25, 26
product databases, 99
professional associations, 41
profiles, 31, 34, 127–129, 168, 178
property listings, 120
proposals, requests for, 85, 116, 160

proprietary information, 85, 119, 223–225
public companies, transition to, 31, 37, 132
public relations. *see also* reputations
   commitment to sustainability, 86–87, 133
   crisis recovery, 153–161
   environmental messaging, 95, 136–138
   environmental records, 86–87, 89–90
   investor relations and, 135
   mobilization of, 146–148
   philanthropy and, 90
   trust building, 134
   writing white papers, 109–111
publishing
   content and, 235–236
   Web style, 8–9

Q

questions, anticipation of, 18
quizzes
   on Alloy.com, 25, 26
   interactive, 179, 227

R

rationing of information, 68
real estate services, 113–121
recruitment, 123–130
   corporate culture and, 211
   events, 125
   Kenyon College, 163–171
   user profiles, 127–129
recycling projects, 95–96
redesign processes, 164, 165, 209
registrations, 46–47, 109
relationship management systems, 221
relationships
   consistency in voice and, 213

offline contact, 200–201
   personal, 40
Remeikis, Lois, 123–130
repurposed content, 186, 214, 236
reputations. *see* public relations
Request for Proposal (RFP) forms, 160
research
   of cities, 154
   needs analysis and, 209
   preparing content, 56
   by site visitors, 98
response mechanisms, 20. *see also* feedback
resume services, 73–74, 124
retail outlets, 33
return visitors, 84
review processes, 188–189, 212
reviews, by fans, 227
rock music, 59–68
Roosevelt, Franklin D., 194
Rosenthal, Marc C., 165
Rouda, Mitch, 97–104
RSS feeds, 219–221

S

salary information, 73
sales cycle, content links to, 231–233
SARS epidemic, 153, 157–159
search engines
   content optimized for, 51–52
   navigation and, 237
   optimization for, 237
search functions, 116
secrecy, corporate, 84–85
self-publishing, 8–9
self-select paths, 153, 215–217
seniority, in membership communities, 63
serendipity, 5, 212, 239
ServiceWare Technologies, 105–111, 216, 232
Sharp HealthCare, 173–181
   alternate content delivery, 220

Sharp HealthCare (*cont.*)
 interactive tools, 227
 photo content, 222
 viral marketing and, 230
shopping-cart abandonment, 16. *see also* bailouts
"show, don't tell" approach, 91, 147–148, 238
simplification, 175
sister sites, 46, 48
site visitors
 conversion to buyers, 233–234
 diversity of needs, 85–86
 facilitating exploration by, 144–145
 goals, 1
 levels of expertise, 18
 profile information, 127–129
 relationships with, 170–171
sites, rating of, 189
Skin Health Solutions site, 3, 183–191, 214, 228
skincare products, 183–191
slide shows, 160
Smith, Toby, 141–151
Snow, John, 165
software companies, 105–111
special offers, 102, 104
specifications
 in Design Within Reach, 31
 online catalogs, 15, *16*
 PDF format, 103
specificity, of content, 69
speed
 of access, 33, 223
 of quotes, 55
sponsorships, 23, 72, 102, 104
staleness, risk of, 129, 167
strategy consulting, 123–130
style, 25, 56
subscriptions
 automatic e-mail content and, 117
 to e-mail newsletters, 35
 free content introductions to, 71–75

marketing and, 63
from network sites, 74
paid memberships and, 67–68
The Wall Street Journal Online, 69–77
success, definition of, 22
surveys, 23
sustainability statements, 136–137
syndication, 111

T

tabs, homepage organization, 83
tagging, use of, 101–102
target audiences
 building professionals, 97–104
 content specificity, 45–46
 decision makers, 106
 demographics, 75
 direct mail approaches, 150, 151
 diverse, 159–160, 166–167
 educators as, 90
 employees as, 137–137
 environmental messaging, 95
 expertise levels of, 189–190
 fan clubs, 59–68
 healthcare, 179–180
 interest-based, 72
 international relief organizations, 145–146
 language of, 24–25
 managing diversity in, 153–154
 needs analysis and, 209–210
 online approaches, 150
 policy makers as, 90
 self-select paths, 215–217
 site redesign, 165
 teenage girls, 24
 tourists, 156—158
 The Wall Street Journal Online, 69
 Web familiarity and, 50
tax returns, online, 149
taxonomies, 100, 224
teamwork, site redesign and, 164
teaser content, 84

technical support, 8
technology
    consulting, 123–130
    news, 69–77
    speed of access and, 223
    support by, 237
teenage girls, 23–30
teenagers, 23–30, 24, 179–180
telephone call centers, 106
television, 5–6, 189
Time Magazine Online, 21
The Toronto Convention and
        Visitors Association, 153–161,
        231–232
Touby, Laurel, 39–48, 209, 210
tourism industry, 153–161
Tourism Toronto, 153–161
    interactive tools, 227
    photo content, 222
    sales cycle, 231–232
    self-select paths, 216
traffic volumes, 88, 186
transactions, 54–56, 84
Trippi, Joe, 195, 196
trust
    building of, 134
    consistency in voice and, 213
    content resources and, 126
    site organization and, 187–188
tsunami relief, 150
Tyler, Steven, 60, 64

U

updates
    contact management systems
        and, 167
    continuous, 193, 194, 221
    decisions about, 130
    sources of, 88, 197, 225, 226
    timing of, 56, 62, 67, 87, 150
UPS, 131–138, 210, 218
URLs
    multiple, 217–219
    subbrands and, 46

viral marketing and, 230
U.S. News & World Report, 164
usability testing, 20–21, 21–22, 128
user-generated content, 48
users. *see* site visitors

V

value-added content, 16, 47,
        107–109
value retention, 70
Velvet Rope Experience, 63
vertical market portals, 111
viral marketing
    Alloy success and, 27–28
    content as trigger for, 229–231
    in healthcare, 173, 176–179
    pass-along value and, 35
    recruitment services, 125
    for service businesses, 130
Virtual Field Trips, 145–146
vocabulary, 24–25, 211

W

The Wall Street Journal Online,
        69–77
    alternate content delivery, 220
    global content for, 226
    multiple URLs, 217
    proprietary information, 224
    self-select paths, 216
    voice, 212
"We also suggest" feature, 34
Web Browsers, 4
Web logs, 193–203
WebTrends data, 169
Weyerhaeuser, 89–96, 223, 227
White Mountains Insurance Group,
        50
white papers, 107–109
Whitford, Brad, 60
word-of-mouth marketing, 130
workflow, definition of, 118

writers
  in-house, 23
  internal creative services, 56
  mediabistro.com, 39–48, 40
  selection of, 19–20
  user-generated content, 48
writing. *see also* language; lexicon
  editorial voice, 23
  in-house staff, 95, 138
  industry-specific jargon, 110
  in plain English, 51
  resource allocation, 147–148
  target audience and, 26
  white papers, 109–111

More Great Books from Information Today, Inc.

Yahoo! to the Max
An Extreme Searcher Guide

By Randolph Hock

"We review many new publications, good or not so good, but we know straight away that if it's a Ran Hock title then it's going to be great." —William Hann, FreePint

With its many and diverse features, it's not easy for any individual to keep up with all that Yahoo! has to offer. Fortunately, Randolph (Ran) Hock—"The Extreme Searcher"—has created a reader-friendly guide to his favorite Yahoo! tools for research, communication, investment, e-commerce, and a range of other useful activities. In *Yahoo! to the Max*, Ran provides background, techniques, and tips designed to help Web users take advantage of many of Yahoo!'s most valuable offerings—from its portal features, to Yahoo! Groups, to unique tools some users have yet to discover. The author's regularly updated Web page helps readers stay current on the new and improved Yahoo! features he recommends.

256 pp/softbound/ISBN 0-910965-69-2 • $24.95

Internet Prophets
Enlightened E-Business Strategies for Every Budget

By Mary Diffley

"I get asked all the time 'How can I take my business online?' Now I can tell people to check out Internet Prophets. *This book with its supporting Web site is an excellent resource for businesses of all sizes."*

—Omar Wasow, internet analyst, MSNBC, and executive director, BlackPlanet.com

This readable, easy-to-use handbook is the first to provide the costs of proven e-commerce strategies, matching successful techniques with the budgetary needs of companies of all types and sizes. At the heart of the book are the Internet Prophets themselves—four helpful guides created by author Diffley. Each prophet speaks to a specific budget, showcasing strategies that really work while getting down to the nitty-gritty that every businessperson wants to know: "What's it going to cost?"

342 pp/softbound/ISBN 0-910965-55-2 • $29.95

The Skeptical Business Searcher
The Information Advisor's Guide to Evaluating Web Data, Sites, and Sources

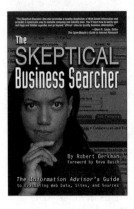

By Robert Berkman
Foreword by Reva Basch

This is the experts' guide to finding dependable, high-quality company and industry data on the free Web. Information guru, author, and editor Robert Berkman offers business Internet users effective strategies for identifying and evaluating no-cost online information sources, emphasizing easy-to-use techniques for recognizing bias and misinformation. You'll learn where to go for company backgrounds, sales and earnings data, SEC filings and stockholder reports, public records, market research, competitive intelligence, staff directories, executive biographies, survey/poll data, news stories, hard-to-find information about small businesses and niche markets, and more. The author's list of top starting points is a lifeline for business searchers under pressure, while his unique table of "Internet Information Credibility Indicators" allows readers to systematically evaluate Web site reliability. Supported by a Web page.

312 pp/softbound/ISBN 0-910965-66-8 • $29.95

Smart Services
Competitive Information Strategies, Solutions and Success Stories for Service Businesses

By Deborah C. Sawyer

"Finally, a book that nails down what every service business needs to know about competition and competitive intelligence. Smart Services offers competitive information strategies that firms can put to immediate use."

—Andrew Garvin
CEO, FIND/SVP

Here is the first book to focus specifically on the competitive information needs of service-oriented firms. Author, entrepreneur, and business consultant Deborah C. Sawyer illuminates the many forms of competition in service businesses, identifies the most effective information resources for competitive intelligence (CI), and provides a practical framework for identifying and studying competitors in order to gain a competitive advantage. *Smart Services* is a roadmap for every service company owner, manager, or executive who expects to compete effectively in the Information Age.

2002/256 pp/softbound/ISBN 0-910965-56-0 • $29.95

Super Searchers on Madison Avenue
Top Advertising and Marketing Professionals Share Their Online Research Strategies

By Grace Avellana Villamora
Edited by Reva Basch

Research professionals in the advertising and marketing game are a rare breed. Working in one of the business world's true pressure cookers, these super searchers find and analyze the information that fuels today's most successful product launches and advertising campaigns. Their market research expertise provides critical strategic support to new business teams, account managers and planners, copywriters, and sales promotion specialists at every major international ad agency. Here, Grace A. Villamora—director of knowledge management at Euro RSCG Tatham Partners—gets 13 research pros from such firms as TBWA/Chiat/Day, Leo Burnett, and Interpublic to share the tips, techniques, and resources that have made them the best in the business.

244 pp/softbound/ISBN 0-910965-63-3 • $24.95

Web of Deception
Misinformation on the Internet

Edited by Anne P. Mintz
Foreword by Steve Forbes

"Experts here walk you through the risks and traps of the Web world and tell you how to avoid them or to fight back ... Anne Mintz and her collaborators have done us a genuine service."

—Steve Forbes, from the Foreword

Intentionally misleading or erroneous information on the Web can wreak havoc on your health, privacy, investments, business decisions, online purchases, legal affairs, and more. Until now, the breadth and significance of this growing problem for Internet users had yet to be fully explored. In *Web of Deception*, Anne P. Mintz (Director of Knowledge Management at Forbes, Inc.) brings together 10 information industry gurus to illuminate the issues and help you recognize and deal with the flood of deception and misinformation in a range of critical subject areas. A must-read for any Internet searcher who needs to evaluate online information sources and avoid Web traps.

278 pp/softbound/ISBN 0-910965-60-9 • $24.95

The Web Library
Building a World Class Personal Library with Free Web Resources

By Nicholas G. Tomaiuolo
Edited by Barbara Quint

With this remarkable, eye-opening book and its companion Web site, Nicholas G. (Nick) Tomaiuolo shows how anyone can create a comprehensive personal library using no-cost Web resources. And when Nick says "library," he's not talking about a dictionary and thesaurus on your desktop: He means a vast, rich collection of data, documents, and images that—if you follow his instructions to the letter—can rival the holdings of many traditional libraries. This easy-to-use guide provides a wealth of URLs and examples of free material you can start using right away, but best of all it offers techniques for finding and collecting new content as the Web evolves. Start building your personal Web library today!

440 pp/softbound/ISBN 0-910965-67-6 • $29.95

Business Statistics on the Web
Find Them Fast—At Little or No Cost

By Paula Berinstein

This practical book shows readers how to use the Internet to find statistics about companies, markets, and industries, how to organize and present statistics, and how to evaluate them for reliability. Organized by topic, both general and specific, and by country/region, this helpful reference features easy-to-use tips and techniques for finding and using statistics when the pressure is on. In addition, dozens of extended and short case studies demonstrate the ins and outs of searching for specific numbers and maneuvering around obstacles to find the data you need.

336 pp/softbound/ISBN 0-910965-65-X • $29.95